L8meng

$ 11.95

D0850388

PLAY THE EVANS GAMBIT
A Study in Depth

PLAY THE EVANS GAMBIT

A Study in Depth

Bernard Cafferty
& Tim Harding

ROBERT HALE & COMPANY
LONDON

©Bernard Cafferty & Tim Harding 1976
First published in Great Britain 1976

ISBN 0 7091 5522 0

Robert Hale & Company
Clerkenwell House
Clerkenwell Green
London EC1R 0HT

Typeset by
Newstead Publishing Limited, Nottingham,
and printed in Great Britain by
Redwood Burn Limited
Trowbridge and London

Contents

Acknowledgements

We should like to take this opportunity of thanking everyone who has helped us in the past three years during which this book has been in preparation. It is not possible to mention all those with whom we have analysed variations of the Evans, but we should like especially to thank M.W. Wills for his many interesting games and analyses, and R.G. Wade for the extensive use we made of his library. K.C. Messere and Professor J.V. Luce also lent us valuable nineteenth-century works of reference, and the librarians both of Oxford's Bodleian Library and of Trinity College, Dublin, helped us to find many ancient sources.

B.C.
T.H.

Bibliography

The reader will find a great number of books and journals cited in the text. It would be pointless to list them all here, but what follows should guide any reader who wishes to check our story or strike out on his own. We have tried to examine all the major sources but in a few cases (notably nineteenth-century volumes of the *Deutsche Schachzeitung*) this was not possible at first hand. However a good digest of nineteenth-century chess theory and practice, to which we did have access, was the eighth edition of the *Handbuch des Schachspiels*, edited by Schlechter (1913-16). Some wrongly refer to this book as 'Bilguer' after one of the editors of the first edition (1843).

Although we prefer to quote modern games where possible, we did consult a great number of nineteenth-century English books and magazines. The most important general openings works for the student of the Evans were Wormald's *Chess Openings* (second edition, 1875) and *Chess Openings, Ancient and Modern* by Freeborough and Ranken. The best edition of the latter is the third (1896), while the second is also very useful — and has now been made available in a photographic reprint. Most of the other books mentioned here are out of print and must therefore be sought in reference libraries.

One of our major types of source was the collection of games by individual masters. Many of the *Weltgeschichte des Schachs* volumes supplied games (notably those on Anderssen and Morphy), as did the numerous and excellent volumes in Russian on Chigorin and in German on Anderssen and Steinitz, and Jonasson's little book on Baron Kolisch. In English, there was Tartakower's collection of his best games and (with J. du Mont) *500 Master Games of Chess*, H.E. Bird's *Modern Chess*, Graham's *Mr. Blackburne's Games at Chess* and George Walker's *Selection of Games Played by Alexander McDonnell*. For the biographical information about Captain Evans we read widely, but found the most detailed and reliable account to be that by D.J. Morgan: *Evans of the Gambit,* in *Y Draig* (the Welsh Chess Federation magazine), Autumn 1971 issue.

Levenfish's *Sovremenny Debyut* (Moscow 1940) is a *sine qua non* for serious students of the open game; more recent sources, such as Euwe, Keres, Pachman and the *Encyclopaedia of Chess Openings* draw heavily upon it. We also consulted American sources: *M.C.O.*, Horowitz and Larry Evans's booklet on the gambit for *Chess Digest*. The most fruitful source for post-war games was, inevitably, *Shakhmatny Bulletin* while other journals in which new games with the Evans from time to time appear include *Chess Player, Fernschach* and *Informator*.

Notation and Symbols

The notation employed in this book is standard English descriptive notation for all moves. Very occasionally, to avoid ambiguity and cumbersome locutions like **Black's QB4,** we have in the notes referred to squares in the algebraic notation (e.g., in this case, **c5).**

The symbols and abbreviations which we use should be familiar to most readers of chess literature. This is the code:

!	Strong move
?	Error
!!	Brilliant move
??	Losing blunder
!?	Interesting move
?!	Dubious move
±	Clear advantage to White
∓	Clear advantage to Black
±/∓	Slight advantage to White/Black
±±/∓∓	Decisive advantage for White/Black
=	Position with balanced chances
1-0	Black Resigns
0-1	White Resigns
½-½	Draw Agreed
+	Check
Ch	Championship
corres	Correspondence game

Numbers in brackets after a move in the text refer to the diagram of that number. *W* or *B* in italics by a diagram indicates whether it is White or Black to move.

1 The "Queen of Chess Openings"

The Evans Gambit begins **1 P-K4 P-K4 2 N-KB3 N-QB3 3 B-B4 B-B4 4 P-QN4**(1). White's fourth move distinguishes the Gambit from the other forms of the ancient opening which is known as the Guioco Piano or, on the continent, the Italian Game. In return for the pawn sacrificed, White obtains a fierce attack which, after a century and a half, has still not been refuted.

1
W

Play, as a rule, continues (from the diagram) **4...BxNP 5 P-B3.** This move of the QBP prepares the central thrust P-Q4, and also creates chances to develop the queen at QN3 or QR4. In the older forms of the Italian Game, White has the same strategic ideas in mind, and so often plays 4 P-B3, but that move has no immediate threat and allows Black to counter-attack by 4...N-B3 or create a solid defence by 4...Q-K2 5 P-Q4 B-N3. In the Evans Gambit, however, this essential preparatory move is played with gain of time; moreover, Black is faced with a sudden dilemma — should he retreat the bishop to guard the king or put it in a more active, but also less secure, place at QR4? He is also subject to a familiar psychological 'fork' known to all gambiteers: should Black, as so many textbooks recommend, return the pawn to free his game, or should he seek to win on material to punish White's 'arrogance'?

In the subsequent, analytical, chapters we shall be looking at the variations of the Evans Gambit in detail, and we back up our assessments of the main lines with a number of practical examples from master play, as well as with original analysis and suggestions for experiment. In general, we consider the Evans to be well worth playing, especially by club and junior players for whom it provides an education in tactics, thanks to the sharp and exciting middle-games that almost invariably arise. We do not despise Black's chances — especially if he troubles to learn one of the lesser-known defences — but in practice Black tends to find his correct line only when it is too late, in the 'post-mortem'!

The rest of this chapter is devoted to an historical survey of the Evans Gambit. This falls into three parts, as follows:

a) From Evans to Morphy and Anderssen, 1827-1858 (by Tim Harding);
b) The Era of Steinitz and Chigorin, 1858-1907 (by Bernard Cafferty);
c) Modern Interpretations of the Evans, 1908-1975 (by Tim Harding).

From Captain Evans to Morphy and Anderssen (1827-1858)

The origins of the Evans Gambit lie in the chess cafe and club society of London in the 1820s, when the generation that succeeded Philidor and Ponziani was eagerly debating the respective merits of methodical pawn play, a la the former mentor, or vigorous piece play, as the Italians favoured. Philidor, whose influence had been strongest in England, had helped to raise the general standard of positional and technical understanding in the chess world, but a certain dryness seemed to characterize the play of his followers in the first post-Napoleonic decade. Of course there were at this time no tournaments and few international encounters of any kind, but still chess was a popular pursuit for gentlemen in most European cities. The King's Gambit, the Bishop's Opening and Philidor's Defence were becoming thoroughly well-known; surely some new marvel must soon be found?

Should one be surprised that the man who was to be responsible for bringing "the gift of the gods to a languishing chess world" was not a sophisticate, engaged in constant duels on London's chessboards, but rather a practical man, a sea-captain, moreover a Celt, who perhaps one stormy night on the bridge thought of the move that would make him immortal, P-QN4 in the Italian Game? Maybe others had the same idea, in London, Paris or Berlin, but casually mentioning it to a friend (of one of the dogmatic schools) received a scoffing reply and thought no more of it? Captain Evans, however, had (after 1824, the year in which, he said, he first thought of the gambit) hundreds of lonely hours off-watch in his cabin with his chess set, plenty of time in which to bring his revolutionary idea to maturity. Then in 1827 (or some say late in 1826) he took some leave and came to London, eager to try his new idea.

In William Lewis's Chess Rooms in St Martin's Lane, he found Alexander McDonnell, probably Ireland's greatest-ever player (albeit not yet in his prime) who agreed to defend against the new gambit. Even H.E. Bird, in his book *Modern Chess* (a hundred years nearer to the origins than we are) states that he was unable to ascertain beyond doubt the first-ever game with the Evans Gambit, but traditionally (and here Bird concurs) it was the following miniature.

White: Capt. W.D. Evans.   Black: A. McDonnell

1	P—K4	P—K4
2	N—KB3	N—QB3
3	B—B4	B—B4
4	0—0	

It was soon realized that the offer is stronger at move four, but Evans' original move-order is still occasionally seen.

4	...	P—Q3
5	P—QN4!	BxNP
6	P—B3	

A century later, Tartakower suggested 6 P-Q4 and if 6...PxP then 7 P-B3! However, Evans's move is more thematic and probably just as strong.

6	...	B—R4
7	P—Q4	B—KN5

7...B-N3 or 7...B-Q2 would be more in accord with modern ideas, whilst 7...PxP 8 PxP B-N3 would give rise to what soon became known as the 'Normal position' of the Evans Gambit.

8	Q—N3

White unpins and attacks KB7, which is the first target in most open games.

8	...	Q—Q2?

A natural reply, which also effectively rules out 9 QxNP which would lose the initiative now that Black has protected his QN. However, as can be seen from the game Santasiere-Marshall (on page 63), 8...BxN was stronger.

9	N—N5

9 BxP+ would also have been a legitimate continuation, e.g. 9...QxB 10 QxP threatening both rook and knight with check.

9	...	N—Q1
10	PxP	PxP

10...N-R3 might at least give Black hopes of castling.

11	B—R3	N—R3
12	P—B3	B—N3+
13	K—R1	B—KR4

13...B-K3 would also lose, after 14 R-Q1 BxB 15 RxQ BxQ 16

R-K7+ K-B1 17 RxKBP+ K-K1 18 R-K7+ K-B1 19 RxKP+ P-B4 20
PxB etc. — *British Chess Magazine,* 1947.

14   R—Q1   Q—B1

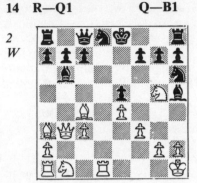

2
W

15   RxN+!?
It was also possible to force a win by 15 Q-N5+ N-B3 16 B-Q5.

15   ...   QxR
15...KxR would be met by 16 N-K6+! K-K1 (or 16...PxN 17 BxP
B-B2 18 Q-Q1+) 17 NxNP+ and 18 NxB.

16   NxBP!   Q—R5
16...NxN permits mate after 17 B-N5+ P-B3 18 Q-K6+.

17   Q—N5+
17 B-N5+ would be one move quicker.

17   ...   P—B3
18   QxKP+   K—Q2
19   Q—K6+   K—B2
20   B—Q6 mate

Who was this man, who thus launched a new romantic era in chess?
William Davies Evans was born on 27th January 1790, the son of a
Welsh farmer, in the parish of St Dogmell's. At the age of fourteen,
he went to sea and served until the end of the war in 1815, when he
transferred to the postal service. By 1819 he had reached the rank of
captain of a packet plying regularly between Milford Haven, in Wales,
and Waterford, in Ireland. He then was introduced to chess by a naval
lieutenant, Harry Wilson; and it was also on his boat that Capt.
Evans devised his gambit.

Evans remained with the postal service at Milford until his retirement, in about the year 1840, after which he travelled much abroad
and also frequented the London chess haunts; he died in Ostend on
3rd August 1872. After the invention of his gambit, Evans gradually
became a celebrated figure; in 1843, Staunton invited him to be his
second for the famous Paris match against Saint Amant, but other

duties prevented the captain from accepting. In 1845, he was one of the team which took part in the first game of chess ever played by the electric telegraph. Nor was his fame confined to the world of chess; he also had the distinction of being the inventor of the three-colour system of ships' lighting which was to become almost universal among European navies.

After his sensational London visit, Evans had to return to his ship, but he could not have left the fate of his gambit in safer hands. The loser of that first game, McDonnell, probably did more than any man to develop and publicize the new opening. Apparently, for a few years the Evans Gambit was known only in Britain, but this only made it the more ideal as a surprise weapon for use against the French champion Charles Mahe de La Bourdonnais, when the two men met in a series of matches, comprising over eighty games, in 1834 and 1835. In the first game of the second match (the twenty-sixth game in the sequence) the trap was sprung.

White: A. McDonnell   Black: C.M. de La Bourdonnais

1	P—K4	P—K4
2	N—KB3	N—QB3
3	B—B4	B—B4
4	P—QN4	BxNP

"La Bourdonnais's first time against the gambit" wrote Morphy, in his notes to the game in the New York *Ledger,* 3rd March 1860. Lewis's *First Series of Chess Lessons* (1831-2) had included analysis of the gambit, but the Frenchman did not know of this, it seems.

5	P—B3	B—R4!

Morphy thought this to be the strongest move, and it was the one usually played in the McDonnell-La Bourdonnais contest. However, in the 51st game, La Bourdonnais was successful with 5...B-K2 6 P-Q4 P-Q3?! and McDonnell more than once tried 5...B-Q3?!; both these ideas were revived later in the century.

6	0—0	

As Morphy wrote, this was believed best at the time, but the immediate 6 P-Q4 is stronger.

6	...	P—Q3

Morphy told his readers that the correct line was 6...N-B3 7 P-Q4 0-0 "and Black will preserve a safe and well-developed game". However, history absolves La Bourdonnais's sixth and seventh moves; he almost anticipated Lasker's Defence (chapter 4)!

7	P—Q4	B—N3
8	PxP	B—N5?

Correct is 8...PxP.

9 B—QN5

Possibly 9 Q-R4, as Kolisch later played, is stronger.

9	**...**	**BxN**
10	**QxB**	**PxP** *(3)*

3
W

For historical interest, here is the rest of the game: **11 Q-N3 Q-B3 12 B-N5 Q-K3 13 N-R3 N-B3 14 QBxN PxB** (Better is 14...QxB; Morphy gave the line 15 N-B4 0-0 16 BxN QxB 17 NxP Q-K3— but not 17...QxKP? as 18 N-Q7, threatening 19 N-B6+, would win the exchange.) **15 QR-Q1 B-B4 16 Q-N7 K-K2?** (16...R-KB1 — Morphy) **17 B-B4 QR-KN1 18 QxR RxQ 19 BxQ PxB 20 N-B2 R-N5 21 KR-K1** (A few technical difficultires remain.) **21...P-B4 22 PxP PxP 23 N—K3 BxN 24 RxB K-K3 25 R-R3 R-N2 26 R-R6+ K-K2 27 R-N1 N-Q1 28 P-B3 P-N3 29 R-Q1 N-B2** (29...N-K3 30 R-Q5 — Morphy) **30 R-QB6 R-N1 31 RxBP+ K-B3 32 RxP R-QB1 33 R1-Q7 N-N4 34 R/Q7-QB7 1-0.**

La Bourdonnais himself became enthusiastic about the gambit, and subsequently often employed it with the white pieces. McDonnell generally adopted the defence 5...B-R4 6 0-0 P-Q3 7 P-Q4 PxP!? 8 PxP B-N3 (the 'Normal Position' as it thereafter became known), with La Bourdonnais now trying 9 B-N2, 9 P-Q5 and 9 P-KR3. As the McDonnell-La Bourdonnais games were widely published, chiefly through the energies of George Walker, the whole world got to know of the exciting new gambit; Jaenisch's *New Analysis of the Chess Openings* (1842-3) gave the Evans a further boost. From the 1840s, nearly every leading player included the Gambit in his repertoire. Its themes of attack on the king — whether castled or stranded in the centre — in return for pawns or (still better) pieces appealed to the romantic imagination then prevalent in the chess world. Even Howard Staunton, whose positional bent made him rather an exception in those early days, admitted the soundness of the strategic basis of the gambit; he was often featured in the white team of consultation games, but for serious matches he tended to prefer closed openings.

The first chess tournament, organised by Staunton, was held in London in 1851, to coincide with the Great Exhibition; it resulted in a surprising, but well-deserved, victory for a German schoolmaster, Adolf Anderssen. Anderssen was a virtuoso of attack, and the Evans Gambit suited his style very well; he began to adopt it in 1851, and was still playing it fifteen years later in his match with Steinitz. His games, especially those played in the 1860s against his greatest pupil, Johannes Zukertort, laid the basis for much of the theory of the opening. Many of his ideas are revived in this book, after being overlooked for a century. Anderssen's concept of the opening in general was to sacrifice an insignificant pawn (the QNP or KBP usually) to gain a move or two, then offer a piece to expose the enemy king, and finally with a few carefully prepared tactical blows to force checkmate. These methods worked almost invariably against the inferior opposition which any chess master of that era encountered most of the time, and made him a very dangerous opponent for the best of his contemporaries almost to the end of his life.

Modern ideas of analytical soundness and economy of means as a prerequisite of beauty were not so prevalent then, and so Anderseen was not only very successful but also his style brought him the plaudits of the aesthetes. The two best-known chess brilliancies are both wins by Anderssen; the Immortal Game was a King's Gambit, played against Kieseritsky, and here is the other, the Evergreen Game, so-called since Steinitz designated it "an evergreen in the laurel-wreath of the greatest German chess-masters". It was played in July 1852 in Berlin, and the loser was one of Anderssen's regular sparring-partners.

White: A. Anderssen   Black: Dufresne

1	P—K4	P—K4
2	N—KB3	N—QB3
3	B—B4	B—B4
4	P—QN4	BxNP
5	P—B3	B—R4
6	P—Q4	

Anderssen almost invariably played this in preference to 6 0-0; the first great master to do so.

6	...	PxP
7	0—0	P—Q6?!

This experiment turned out badly, but others have repeated it from time to time. White is prevented from forming his centre, but attack by the pieces is hardly slowed up thereby.

8	Q—N3	Q—B3
9	P—K5	Q—N3

Not 9...NxP? 10 R-K1 P-Q3 11 Q-N5 + and wins a piece.

10 R—K1

10 R-Q1 has also been played successfully.

10	...	KN—K2

Bachmann, one of Anderssen's biographers, thought 10...B-N3 (with the idea of 11...N-R4) would be worth considering. 11 Q-Q1 might be necessary then.

11 B—R3

This gives White a strong attacking position, and is much better than the prosaic 11 Q-Q1 (to regain a pawn) which was played in a 1930s postal game.

11	...	P—N4?!

Black hopes to gain time to develop his Q-side and prepare a counter-attack, but Euwe's suggestion of preceding this advance by 11...P-QR3 is more embarrassing, and probably represents Black's last chance for a playable position.

12	QxP	R—QN1
13	Q—R4	B—N3

Castling was impossible on account of 14 BxN.

14	QN—Q2	B—N2

Dufresne envisages the eventual counter-attack against KN7. 14...0-0 must have looked too passive to him.

15	N—K4	Q—B4?

Now 15...0-0 would be met by 16 BxP threatening 17 N-B6 +, but it is just the same with the king of K1. Emanuel Lasker recommended 15...P-Q7! (gaining a tempo) 16 N4xP 0-0, but Black's game is still very difficult. The author won a postal game which continued 17 N-K4 KR-K1 (to free the QN) 18 QR-Q1! QR-Q1 19 N4-N5...

16	BxP	Q—R4 (4)

4
W

17   N—B6 + !?

Anderssen's lust to sacrifice could be contained no longer, although some commentators have suggested that 17 N-N3 Q-R3 18 B-QB1 would be a safer way of continuing the attack; 18 N-B5 is another idea.

17	...	**PxN**
18	PxP	**R—N1**

Dufresne is putting up quite a stiff resistance by the standards of his day, but it has not been noticed because of the brilliance of the refutation. Here he sets a superb trap: the plausible 19 BxN fails to 19...QxN because White has no effective discovered check. The best try, 20 B-Q6 + , fails to 20...N-K4! 21 RxN + K-Q1 22 B-K4 QxKBP + 23 K-R1 QxNP + ! 24 BxQ BxB mate.

19   QR—Q1

This much praised move was criticized by Emanuel Lasker. In his *Manual of Chess,* he wrote: "19 B-K4! gives an irresistible attack and frustrates the counter-attack". He offered these variations:

1) 19...P-Q4 20 BxQP QxB 21 QR-Q1
b) 19...Q-R6 20 P-N3 RxP + 21 PxR QxP + 22 K-R1 BxP 23 R-K2
c) 19...R-N5 20 Q-B2

**   19   ...   QxN?** *(5)*

Black is now two pieces up and threatens several mates, and yet is lost! In a long article entitled "A Glimpse into the Depths of Anderssen's Combination", P. Lipke examined no less than nine other moves for Black at this point, and showed that Black could have defended his position by 19...R-N5!, which avoids the mate that occurs in the game because there will be a flight square for the king at KN1! Lasker agreed with this conclusion.

We do not have the space to go into detail about Lipke's analysis and subsequent discussions thereof. The critical lines, however, after 19...R-N5 are 20 R-K4 RxR 21 QxR and 20 B-B4 Q-KB4 21 RxP!? What would Anderssen have played? That is a question to which there can be no answer.

5
W

20   RxN + !

Given this position, of course there could be no other move, but the genius of Anderssen lay in seeing, probably as early as move 17, that it led to a win.

20   ...   NxR?!

If 20...K-B1 21 R-K3 + , but Euwe suggested that 20...K-Q1 would put up a much tougher defence. There would follow 21 RxQP + ! K-B1! 22 R-Q8 + !: a) 22...NxR 23 Q-Q7 + ! KxQ 24 B-KB5 + and mate next move; b) 22...KxR! 23 B-KB5 + ! (23 B-K2 + N-Q5! 24 BxQ BxB with counter-chances) 23...QxR + 24 QxQ + N-Q5 and now after 25 P-N3! White would probably win eventually. "Black's rooks are disconnected, and it is hard to parry the attack of the queen combined with her two bishops" — Neistadt, *Shakhmaty do Steinitza*.

21	QxQP + !	KxQ
22	B—KB5 +	K—K1
23	B—Q7 +	K—B1
24	BxN mate	

Until the rise of Steinitz, the only challenge to Anderssen's European supremacy was made by the young American lawyer, Paul Morphy, who defeated him in a match in Paris in December 1858, in which, however, the Evans was only played once — perhaps just because it was such a favourite of both players, each may have feared the other's secrets. In the first match game, when Morphy was still recuperating from a serious illness, Anderssen defended the Evans in inferior fashion, but Morphy failed to find the refutation (which in a later game he demonstrated) and finally lost. After this, Morphy preferred the Ruy Lopez while Anderssen experimented with 1 P-QR3.

Morphy's career was, alas, all too short: only in the period 1857-9 did he really meet top-class opposition. A decade later he would have been confronted with a strong British school who had learned from his example, but in 1858 Staunton was in retirement and men like Bird, Blackburne, Fraser, Taylor and of course Steinitz were too young or not yet on the scene.

Morphy's secret was patience and a sense of positional balance that rarely failed him. Where others would rush to 'justify' their gambit play with impulsive sacrificing or threats too easily met, Morphy was always happy to complete his mobilization before seeking concrete advantages; having sacrificed a pawn, his main concern was to avoid blocking the position. Thus whereas, in the Normal Position (*see* Chapters 9 and 10) Anderssen would play 9 P-Q5, Morphy discovered 9 N-B3 which is not only a developing move but also preserves White's options with his central pawns and his QB. The following game will illustrate Morphy's treatment of the Evans Gambit; it was played in a match in New York, 1857.

White: P. Morphy   Black: C.H. Stanley

1 P-K4 P-K4 2 N-KB3 N-QB3 3 B-B4 B-B4 4 P-QN4 BxNP 5 P-B3 B-R4 6 P-Q4 PxP 7 0-0 P-Q3 8 PxP B-N3 9 N-B3 N-B3? 10 P-K5 PxP 11 B-R3! (Occupying the line which the previous move forced open.) 11...BxP 12 Q-N3 B-K3 13 BxB PxB 14 QxKP+ N-K2 15 NxB PxN 16 KR-K1 N3-N1 17 N-Q5 Q-Q2 18 BxN? (18 QxQ+ KxQ 19 NxN; now Morphy loses most of his advantage.) 18...QxQ 19 RxQ K-Q2! 20 R1-K1 R-K1! 21 R-K4 P-B3 22 RxP PxN 23 RxP+ K-B3 24 R-Q6+ K-B2 25 R-QB1+ K-N1 26 B-R4 N-R3 27 B-N3 K-R1 28 P-KR3 N-B4 29 R-Q7 P-KN3 30 R1-B7 NxB 31 PxN R-QN1 32 RxRP RxR 33 RxR P-R4 34 P-KR4 R-KN1 35 P-N4 P-QN4 36 P-R5 P-R5 37 P-R6 P-N5 38 R-KN7 R-R1 39 P-R7 P-N6 40 R-N8+ K-N2 41 RxR P-N7 42 R-QN8+ KxR 43 P-R8=Q+ 1-0.

The period 1827-1857, then, shows the rise of the Evans Gambit to a pre-eminent position — Bilguer's *Handbuch* called the Evans the "queen of chess openings" — at just the time when chess in general was developing into a major international sport, with regular matches and tournaments. Indeed the refinement of the theory of the Evans Gambit, with its alternate strengthenings of the attack and of the defence, almost parallels that of chess itself, at least until the end of the nineteenth century, when it began to slip into obscurity. But while the open game remained the *sine qua non* of chess at all levels, the Evans stayed the most popular opening of all.

The Evans Gambit in the Era of Steinitz and Chigorin (1858-1907)

The Evans Gambit received its most severe testing in the second half of the nineteenth century in the many games played between Anderssen and his pupil Zukertort, and in particular in the long creative controversy between World Champion Wilhelm Steinitz and his great rival Mikhail Ivanovich Chigorin. In fact the whole controversy over the worth of the gambit may be considered as a huge consultation game over the decades with the great masters of attack Morphy, Anderssen, Zukertort and Chigorin playing White against the great masters of defence Steinitz and Lasker.

We date the start of this epoch 1858, since it was in that year that Steinitz went as a student from his native city of Prague to Vienna. There he joined the main chess club, and like many a poacher turned gamekeeper before and after him, he started his chess career by playing gambits (and especially the Evans) which he was later to condemn as unsound!

When he came to London in 1862 he was called "The Austrian Morphy" because of his brilliant gambit play, but after a decade of such a traditional approach he gradually developed the principles of his 'New School' which laid down that the gambits were an unjustified attempt to disturb the initial balance of the position.

To the best of our knowledge, the last time Steinitz played the Evans in serious play was in his 1872 match with Zukertort. Thereafter, to his credit, he acted in accordance with his principles and only tried the Evans Gambit in simultaneous displays and off-hand games. It is a matter of some regret that his best period as a player only partly coincided with that of Chigorin (younger than him by fourteen years) so that when they clashed in Evans Gambit games the older man was able to explain his lack of success against the gambit by the difficulties of playing a tight defensive game against the twofold obstacles of a younger, stronger, attacking player and a time limit. (Steinitz's best years were 1866 — his victory over Anderssen — to 1889; Chigorin's were 1880 to 1896).

The earliest known Evans Gambit in which Chigorin was involved was Winawer-Chigorin, St Petersburg 1875, in which the young Chigorin adopted the Compromised Defence (which he always considered a feasible line for Black) but soon came a cropper. Unfortunately, records of the Russian's early games are very sparse, and he rarely played outside Russia until 1889. One of the earliest recorded games in which Chigorin was White in an Evans Gambit is his victory over Steinitz at Vienna 1882. The confidence of the young Russian civil servant in 'his' opening is shown by the speed of his play — Chigorin took 1 hour 30 minutes over the 39 move game, compared to the older man's 2 hours 15 minutes.

White: M.I. Chigorin   Black: W. Steinitz

1	P—K4	P—K4
2	N—KB3	N—QB3
3	B—B4	B—B4
4	P—QN4	BxNP
5	P—B3	B—B1!?
6	P—Q4	Q—K2
7	0—0	P—Q3
8	Q—N3	P—KN3
9	PxP	PxP
10	R—Q1!	B—R3

Not 10...N-B3? 11 N-N5 N-Q1 12 NxBP! NxN 13 BxN+ QxB 14 R-Q8+ K-K2 15 B-R3+ : a familiar sort of break-through in the Evans.

11	QN—Q2	Q—B3
12	B—R3	KN—K2
13	B—Q5	O—O
14	B5xN	PxB
15	Q—N4	P—B4

Returning the useless pawn to obtain some squares. Against 15...R-K1 Chigorin could choose between 16 Q-R5, 16 Q-B5 and 16 N-B4.

| 16 | QxP | N—B3 |
| 17 | N—B4 | R—K1 *(6)* |

17...B-N5 18 N4xP NxN 19 QxN QxQ 20 NxQ BxR 21 BxR loses a pawn, too.

Now Chigorin broke through by **18 N-Q6! PxN 19 QxN B-N5 20 RxP** and the remaining moves were **20...Q-N2 21 R1-Q1 B-N4 (21...QR-B1? 22 QxQR!) 22 N-N5 BxR 23 RxB QR-B1 24 Q-R4 Q-B3 25 N-B3 Q-K3 26 R-Q5 Q-N3 27 B-N4 R-K3 28 NxP R1-K1 29 R-Q6! Q-N1 30 N-Q7 Q-Q1 31 P-K5** (Chigorin later saw 31 N-B6+! QxN 32 QxR+ etc.) **31...P-QR4 32 B-R3 RxR 33 BxR R-K3 34 P-KR3 Q-N4 35 P-B4 Q-N6 36 N-B5 RxB 37 PxR Q-K6+ 38 K-R2 Q-B4 39 Q-K8+ 1-0.**

Chigorin also beat the uncrowned World Champion in an Evans Gambit the following year at the great London tournament, and in the same year he scored one of his finest wins in this opening when he beat Semyon Alapin (whose name will occur again in this chapter) at St Petersburg. Chigorin had the pleasure of sacrificing a great deal of material and finished the game off by announcing mate in ten on move 16!

One of the difficulties for Steinitz's few supporters was that over the years he proposed a variety of 'correct' defences to the Evans without ever having particularly good results with them. His ideas included Q-K2 or Q-KB3, to guard his threatened KP and KBP, while he often developed the KN at K2 or KR3 (allowing his K-side to be broken by QBxN), and he also sometimes went P-KR3 to prevent his queen from being harassed by B-KN5. His overriding aim in all this was to maintain Black's extra pawn. As a result he was often forced into conceding White the centre by KPxQP when White's two powerful pawns abreast at K4 and Q4 could be reinforced by N-QB3, the obstructing QBP having been removed, thus developing the knight on its most natural square.

On the other hand Tarrasch, who acted as a popularizer of Steinitz's ideas, had much less respect for a plus pawn obtained at the cost of a permanent cramp, and he always stressed the need to maintain Black's pawn at K4. This led naturally to easier defences such as the Sanders-Alapin Defence (suggested first by the Rev. T.C. Sanders in 1871) and then to the Lasker Defence itself. Chigorin was much less dogmatic in his attacking plans. Against Steinitz's hedgehog formations he had no scruples over closing the centre by P-Q5, blocking the main attacking diagonal of his QB, since N-QR3 (or N-Q2) and then N-QB4 soon renews the attack on K5 and prepares such strong attacking schemes as P-Q6 or Q-R4 followed by N-QN6 in view of the pin on Black's QRP.

In practice, then, the Russian had much the better of the argument, as we can see from the score for all the Evans Gambits played between the two men. This was: played 23, won 12, drawn 6, lost 5 from White's (i.e. Chigorin's) point of view. The greater part of these 23 games were played in the three matches between the two men in Havana 1889, by telegraph 1890-1 and again in Havana 1892. For the record, the overall score in these three matches, from Steinitz's point of view, were:-

first match: W 10, L 6, D 1;
telegraph match: W 0, L 2, D 0;
third match: W 10, L 8, D 5.

This last match was a Pyrrhic victory since Chigorin overlooked mate in two in the last game when in a winning position. After this close result there was little doubt that Steinitz would soon lose his title to a younger man.

In the first match Chigorin had nine whites, played the Lopez once and the Evans on every other occasion, scoring W 4, L 3, D 1. This comparatively narrow victory for White could be seen as a success for the defence, and after the match Steinitz claimed it as such. Naturally the claim had to be formulated in terms that pointed to Steinitz as the founder of the 'New Positional School', while the Russian was depicted as a late representative of the classical attacking school — a theoretical distinction Steinitz had been drawing for a number of years, and in particular since he wrote a number of critical comments in the 1886 number of his *International Chess Magazine* on the 1858 match between Morphy and Anderssen. This criticism had in its turn been a reaction to commentators who had made disparaging remarks about the Steinitz-Zukertort match of 1886, sighing for the return of 'the good old days'!

The following is quoted from Bachmann's *Schachmeister Steinitz:* "This was a match between an old master of a young school, and a young master of an old school. The young school won despite the age of its protagonist. The young master of the old school sacrificed pawns and pieces, the old master of the young school did more. He sacrificed a whole series of games." Steinitz then goes on to say that "in conditions of hard match play and time limitation" the defence he recommended to the Evans Gambit was a difficult line to play, but "I feel thoroughly convinced that the defence is right in principle and will be the best there is to be found once it has been analysed in depth".

This confident assertion and a further disagreement about the value of another controversial line, this time the Two Knights Defence with 9 N-KR3 (a move taken up by Fischer in modern times) led to the famous telegraph match which was a contest that is undeservedly forgotten in our days. Chess fans all over the world were able to follow the moves through the newspapers, and moreover were able to read Steinitz's comments as they changed from optimistic to gloomy as his positions grew worse and worse! Thus, before the match he wrote "You have to bear in mind that I have an extra pawn in each game, and therefore in theory I should win both. Naturally Chigorin has his own ideas about this and, one imagines, is hoping for some hidden attack on the K-side. Such an attack, according to the principles which I have followed in theory and practice for twenty years, leads to nothing special. In any event I am deeply convinced that I ought to win one game and draw the other. Hence I am fully convinced that I shall not disappoint my supporters and so I invite them to subscribe on my behalf." (Money stakes were being put up on both sides.)

The Evans game began **1 P-K4 P-K4 2 N-KB3 N-QB3 3 B-B4 B-B4 4 P-QN4 BxNP 5 P-B3 B-R4 6 0-0 Q-B3 7 P-Q4 N-R3** (Steinitz had always previously played 7...KN-K2 here.) **8 B-KN5 Q-Q3 9 P-Q5 N-Q1 10 Q-R4 B-N3 11 N-R3 P-QB3 12 B-K2 B-B2** *(7).*

7
W

At this point, Steinitz wrote: "My opponent is attacking in the style of our Havana games, that is as a representative of the old school. He is sure of the benefits of advancing his pawns or even of sacrificing one or several of them with the aim of embarrassing his opponent on the K-side, of or closing in his pieces. I, however, stress that the king is a strong piece which can defend itself in the majority of cases and that Chigorin, with his particular method of attack, has to bring his major pieces into play and thus cramp the action of his minor pieces. I, however, consider that my minor pieces will be well developed, and Chigorin's advanced pawns, not having the opportunity to retire, will become the object of my forthcoming counter-attack. I have an extra pawn. I shall probably lose it, as happened in my previous games, but on the other hand my position will get better."

There followed **13 N-B4 Q-B1 14 P-Q6! BxP** (14...P-N4 15 PxB N-N2 16 Q-N3 N-B4 17 Q-N4 PxN 18 Q-N8!) **15 N-N6 R-QN1 16 QxRP N-K3** (Steinitz lost with 16...N-N5 in a later game against Gunsberg!) **17 B-B1 N-N1 18 B-R3 P-QB4.** As late as the 17th move, Steinitz was claiming the better game and laying odds of 2-1 against a White victory, but after his 18th he was merely hoping to make a draw at least by a hard struggle. In fact White won without Black ever having much of a look in, and the same applies to the other game where he was White in the Two Knights. The remaining moves in the Evans game were: **19 QR-Q1! N-B3** (19...B-B2 20 B-N5 N-B3 21 N-Q5 B-Q3 22 N-R4!) **20 B-B4 B-B2 21 N-Q5! B-Q3 22 N-R4! NxN 23 N-B5! P-KN3 24 NxB+ QxN 25 BxN Q-B2 26 BxN BPxB 27 BxP R-R1 28 QxR QxB 29 Q-R4 K-Q1 30 R-Q2 K-B2 31 R-N1! R-Q1 32 R-N5! Q-B3 33 Q-N4 P-Q3 34 P-QR4 Q-K1 35 R-N6 Q-B1 36 Q-R5 P-Q4 37 PxP K-N1 38 P-Q6 1-0.**

The general reaction of good judges was that Steinitz had handicapped himself by adopting difficult defences, and was up against a real master of attack and analysis who had already shown his outstanding ability at telegraph and postal games. After the match,

Steinitz did give due praise to his opponent's play, but was reduced to claiming that Chigorin was showing signs of inclining more towards the methods of play in the New School! Modern Soviet writers tend to take the same view, but express it in different terms and the change is more apparent in some of the Russian's later opening ideas in the Ruy Lopez and Old Indian Defence than in the Evans Gambit!

In the return match of 1892, Chigorin played the Evans Gambit eight times in twelve games, and this time made a better showing: W 4, L 1, D 3. This was particularly creditable since Steinitz had received help from an unexpected quarter. Like many successful players, Chigorin had his prickly side, and even in Russia he had detractors as well as supporters. At the opening ceremony Chigorin was informed by his opponent (what close relations between the players, compared with many world title matches of the twentieth century!) that Steinitz had received letters from various parts of the world, including Russia, advising him not to play his favourite defence to the Evans Gambit. He had even received from St Petersburg a thick packet of analysis from Alapin who was now better known as an analyst than player (and a person not on good terms with Chigorin).

The analysis was a detailed survey of the Sanders-Alapin Defence: 5...B-R4 6 0-0 P-Q3 7 P-Q4 B-Q2. Steinitz said that he had examined a couple of lines suggested, but they didn't appeal to him. Chigorin's reply (quoted in *M.I. Chigorin* by Panov, Moscow 1963 — a purely prose work) was, that the man had not yet been born who could prove by analysis the soundness or unsoundness of the Evans Gambit.

Steinitz did in fact try the defence twice in the match, drawing one game and losing the other, but the sheer ill-will shown by the gesture must have been rather off-putting to the Russian far from home but still conscious of the hostility towards him in Russia. This is seen from the fact that he later characterized Alapin's conduct as "akin to an act of treachery in wartime". A cartoon in the Panov book shows in what light Alapin's act was viewed at the time. It is taken from a contemporary St Petersburg satirical magazine and shows Chigorin trying to climb a steep wall by means of a ladder. At ground level, there is a pig marked "a home-grown dirty trick" which is trying to upset the ladder.

Despite this outside help (admittedly not as powerful as chemical and electrical means, and swivel chairs!) Chigorin won convincingly in the Evans duel, and the figures quoted above were quite enough to persuade contemporaries where the truth of the matter lay. In his 1893 match with Chigorin in St Petersburg, Tarrasch (whom many good judges thought to be Steinitz's legitimate successor as champion) played 1...P-K4 only once — the 16th game of the drawn 22-game match — and Chigorin then opted for the King's Gambit. In the other ten games in which he had Black, the German grandmaster opted for the French Defence. He was honest enough to admit in his notes that he was concerned about his opponent's mastery in sharp openings. Many years later Tarrasch wrote generously, in his last great book *The Game of Chess* (1934), when analysing the Normal position of the Evans: "Chigorin nearly always carried this line of play to a successful conclusion for White."

However the turning of the tide was not far off. In the spring of 1895, young Emanuel Lasker, who had beaten Steinitz in a world championship match the previous year, gave a series of lectures on the game in London — which were subsequently published as the book *Common Sense in Chess*. He had been asked by his audience to deal with the Evans Gambit, and he suggested a simple defence based upon giving back the pawn, but retaining a sound pawn structure: 5...B-R4 6 0-0 P-Q3 7 P-Q4 B-N3 8 PxP PxP 9 QxQ+ NxQ. The defence had been mentioned many years before in an early edition of the *Handbuch*, but had never received much attention.

Although Chigorin refuted some minor details of the analysis Lasker gave, he avoided the crucial line when he next had the chance to play the Evans Gambit against Lasker. This was at the four-man tournament at St Petersburg (1895-6) and the game was an easy victory for the young title-holder. As a result, Chigorin finally seemed to lose his total love for the Evans Gambit, and in subsequent tournaments he preferred quieter openings for White such as the Guioco Piano in its slower forms, and the Ponziani. The next top-level game in which he tried the Evans also went against him (versus Pillsbury at London 1899) although not so disastrously.

However by this time the Russian was no longer the strong man of old; his health was badly undermined and he was not destined to live long in the new century. He died in January 1908 after several years of poor tournament results. He did have some success in gambit tournaments, of which there were quite a few in the first decade of the century, but in these events he always adopted the King's Gambit. His last tournament game with the Evans was White against Didier at Paris 1900, while his very latest idea against the Lasker Defence (8 B-K3!?) was demonstrated in a consultation game played in February 1907 at St Petersburg.

Having quoted from Steinitz, it is only fair to give Chigorin his say too. Generally speaking he was much less didactic and dogmatic than his great rival. In his game annotations he preferred to lay stress on the specific features of the position, and avoided generalizations which could not be rigorously proved. Every Soviet book on Chigorin has his dictum that the word 'theoretical' is often a synonym for 'stereotyped'. He held that one should try and think up moves of one's own, and they would often be no worse, and sometimes better than those currently approved by theory. The experience of the last few decades has been to prove him right.

Chigorin was once asked by a contemporary about his love of complications and gambit openings. Apparently at this point Chigorin lost his usual calm and said bitterly: "My critics seem to know more about me than I do myself. If I often play the King's Gambit or the Evans Gambit, it is not because I like losing a pawn at move two or move four, but because I have been able to convince myself by means of analysis of the genuine strength of these lines which offer the best chance of winning. What do they mean by love of complications ? What normal person would prefer the complex path to the simple one? The point is that I often foresee victory in the sort of position in which others can see only complications."

Few of Chigorin's successors followed his example when it came to choice of opening repertoire. The young Alekhine studied Chigorin's magazine *Shakhmatny Listok* and learned attacking technique from it, but there are no records of Alekhine playing the Evans in his youth. It was left to the New Romantics such as Tartakower to carry the Chigorin torch in the twentieth century.

Modern Interpretations of the Evans (1908-1975)

If Black could force Lasker's Defence, probably little would have been heard of the Evans Gambit in the twentieth century. In point of fact, Lasker played against Chigorin not 5...B-R4, as one would expect, but 5...B-B4 — so that it is all the more surprising that the Russian did not reply with 6 P-Q4, after which the Lasker Defence can be avoided (without even risking that Black might play the Compromised Defence). Twentieth-century masters invariably play 6 P-Q4 after 5...B-R4 or 5...B-B4 and are thus able to avoid the lines which frustrated Chigorin. For instance a popular line is 5...B-R4 6 P-Q4 P-Q3 P-Q3, when Tartakower popularized the key improvement 7 Q-N3!, which is discussed in chapter three. Black in turn can avoid this by playing one of the rare lines such as 6...Q-K2, 6...B-N3 or 6...P-QN4!?; comparatively little is known about these defences and they are probably worth investigating further.

Occasionally the well-analysed lines of the nineteenth century, such as the Compromised and the Normal, are seen again in contemporary master chess, but White tends to do even better in practice than 'theory' might predict. On the whole, if Black is the kind of player who wants such a keen struggle, he is more likely to play the Two Knights Defence — or the Sicilian. Modern masters defend the Evans conservatively as a rule, and if they do not like the aforementioned variations with 6...P-Q3 they will probably play 5...B-K2 or 4...B-N3. The former is the most common reply nowadays, while the Evans Gambit Declined had a vogue between the wars. These, like most of the other lines that appear from time to time, were known in the nineteenth century but not appreciated at their full value; nor did they suit the mood of the time. Black played more ambitiously in those days.

White, too, does not play the Evans in the twentieth century in the same spirit that he did in the nineteenth. Thus the Soviet master Kan wrote about the day he played 4 P-QN4 against none other than Botvinnik in the 6th USSR Championship (1929): "Obviously Black thought I had specially prepared the ancient gambit and so decided to be careful and decline it. In actual fact, this was an amusing misapprehension since I decided to play the Evans only just before the game on the advice of the old masters Duz-Hotimirski and Freyman. I thought about ten minutes before going 4 P-QN4 but the point of my long thought was a rather special form of preparation — I wanted to make sure that I kept a serious look on my face and didn't burst out laughing at my own boldness." Kan went on to win!

This is not an isolated example of the success of the Evans at high levels in the twentieth century. Grandmaster Gligoric was beaten by the Italian master (now grandmaster) Mariotti at the 1971 Venice tournament, and there have been several notable Evans games played by Soviet masters such as Ragozin, Romanovsky and Sokolsky, which will be found in the appropriate places in the following chapters. Other masters who have played the Evans in the post-war period include Alexander, Ciocaltea, Pfleger and Tal. World Champion Fischer has often employed the gambit in exhibition games, and indeed included two of his wins (one against grandmaster Fine) in his anthology *My Sixty Memorable Games*. His Two Knights' Defence against Bisguier, in the same book, suggests that he was prepared to play the Evans in a top-class game too; if only Bisguier had played 3...B-B4 instead of 3...N-B3...!

The acid test of postal play has also failed to reveal any flaw in White's best ideas; it will be recalled that many of Chigorin's wins with the Evans were by correspondence. It is arguable that the unlimited time and freedom to consult works of reference helps White at least as much as Black, and this tends to bear out Chigorin's claim that his play of the Evans Gambit was certainly not speculative. When White gets a good position, the freedom to analyse at length favours, if anything, the attacker. The Evans has been employed in correspondence tournaments by both its first and seventh World Champions (Purdy and Estrin); Purdy wrote, in *Chess World* that the Evans is "very lively and eminently suitable for correspondence play." Besides the authors, Felbecker (West Germany), Honfi (Hungary), Muir (U.S.A.) and many others have successfully employed the gambit in master-class postal events.

Of course one can never expect the Evans Gambit to regain its popularity of a hundred years ago, because chess is much broader now than it was then, and masters are eager to examine the new ideas in the half-open defences, Indian systems and flank openings. Nevertheless, a move towards re-interpreting many of the old openings is definitely under way, led by theoreticians like Estrin. It would be wrong, for example, to suppose that hypermodern positional theory has invalidated the concept of the strong pawn centre upon which much of White's play in the Evans must rest, although of course it has modified it; in the Evans Black is rarely able to challenge White's centre with the flanking blows ...P-QB4 and ...P-KB4, because his king is insecure.

Especially in postal play (because 1...P-K4 is a much more common reply to 1 P-K4 there, than in 'over-the-board' chess), we look forward to a resurgence of interest in the Evans. If a line was formerly rejected because of some incorrect analysis, or simply because of a change in fashion, it is quite likely to re-appear in the next few years. For we believe that the Evans Gambit is a fundamentally sound opening, offering equal chances at least — and in practice much more than that, especially at club and county match levels. The average defender of the Evans is not acquainted with 'theory' and will often fall into one of the many pitfalls and lose quickly. Even when the defence is good, the attack yields positional compensations that usually justify the pawn sacrifice, as in the main line following 5...B-K2 6 Q-N3 (see page 41). We do not entirely agree, therefore, with the old prognosis (quoted by Larry Evans in his recent booklet) that the Evans Gambit is "a yellow-fever attack"; even if the initial onslaught is lived through, the patient's condition may remain critical indefinitely. To think otherwise was part of Steinitz's mistake.

In the 1946 edition of *M.C.O.*, Fine wrote: "Despite a prodigious amount of analysis, this offshoot of the Guioco Piano still remains a problem child among the openings." We hope that our book will help to put these problems in a clearer light and encourage you to play the Evans Gambit.

2 Modern Main Line: 5...B—K2

As often as not nowadays, the Evans Gambit is met by the cautious positional defence (**1 P-K4 P-K4 2 N-KB3 N-QB3 3 B-B4 B-B4 4 P-QN4 BxNP 5 P-B3**)

    5 ...   **B—K2**(8)

This is not in itself a modern move: it was played successfully by La Bourdonnais against McDonnell in 1835! Thereafter it was slow to gain acceptance. Thus Zukertort wrote in 1874: "Theory and practice alike condemned 5...B-K2 because, by adopting it, Black's game becomes so cramped, that the pawn superiority does not atone for the difficulty of the position." Its present popularity dates from its adoption by Euwe (in 1946) and Bogoljubow (in 1949).

The modern interpretation of this move, seen in line A51 especially, is to allow White to regain the gambit pawn — but at the cost of time and the two bishops. If White prefers to continue in the gambit style, he has to move his bishop from its most effective QB4-KB7 diagonal, while Black feels that his own KB is better placed for defence than on QR4 or QN3. In particular, N-KN5 becomes impossible for White, while Black has the resource ...N-QR4. These points notwithstanding, we believe that White can keep the initiative against the Modern Main Line.

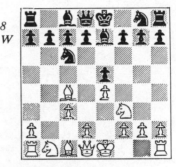

8
W

White can play:
A: 6 P-Q4
B: 6 Q-N3

A:
    6 P—Q4
By far the more popular of the two. Now:
A1: 6...PxP
A2: 6...P-Q3
A3: 6...N-B3
A4: 6...B-B3
A5: 6...N-R4!

A1:
    6 ...   **PxP**
Always a double-edged decision in the Evans!
    7 Q—N3
This is more direct than 7 0-0 when:
1) 7...PxP?! 8 Q-Q5 N-R3 9 BxN 0-0 10 B-K3 N-N5 11 Q-KR5! N-B7 12

NxP NxR (Pal-I. Bronstein, corres 1960) 13 RxN±

b) 7...N-R3 8 PxP 0-0 and now:

b1) 9 N-B3 or 9 B-N2 would give White play for his pawn.

b2) 9 P-Q5? B-B3 10 PxN BxR 11 BxN PxB∓ Bird-Steinitz, Vienna 1882

7 PxP!? is worth considering, as the reply 7...B-N5+ would merely transpose to line A in chapter 8.

7	...	N—R4
8	BxP+	K—B1
9	Q—R4	KxB
10	QxN	P—Q3

It has long been considered that 10...PxP 11 NxP would give White a good attacking position. In view of his exposed king, Black will experience difficulties in completing his development.

However after 10...P-Q3 White regains his pawn with the superior position: **11 PxP N-B3 12 N-B3 P-B3 13 N-N5+ K-B1 14 Q-R4 P-Q4** (Lehmann-Donner, Munich 1954). Now, besides the game continuation **15 P-K5 N-K1 16 P-B4,** a good attempt to carry on in attacking spirit would be 15 0-0 P-KR3 16 N-B3 NxP 17 NxN PxN 18 N-K5 B-KB4 19 Q-N3 (Cafferty).

A2:

6	...	P—Q3

This attempt to maintain the central strongpoint K4 also suffers from serious tactical drawbacks.

7 PxP!

Fischer's improvement upon the old 7 Q-N3 N-R4 etc.

7	...	NxP

In his book *My 60 Memorable Games,* Fischer analysed:

a) 7...N-R4? 8 BxP+! KxB 9 Q-Q5+ B-K3 10 QxN

b) 7...NxP 8 Q-N3 N-R4 9 BxP+ K-B1 10 Q-R4 with advantage, as Black's king is more exposed than if the pawn exchange had been omitted. If 8...N-B3 9 BxP+ K-B1 10 N-N5! N-R4! (Cafferty-Hewson, Birmingham 1975) White should play 11 Q-R4 P-B3 12 N-K6+ BxN 13 BxB through white-square control and the weak black KP — Cafferty).

8	NxN	PxN
9	Q—R5!	P—KN3
10	QxKP	N—B3

Or 10...P-KB3 11 Q-QN5+! and if 11...P-B3? 12 Q-N3 K-B1 13 BxN! and White wins — Fischer.

11 B—R3!*(9)*

White has the advantage, but must play accurately to keep it.

11	...	R—B1

At a Soviet seminar on Fischer's book, I. Zaitsev suggested an interesting defensive possibility 11...B-K3!? 12 KBxB 0-0, e.g.:

a) 13 B-N3 (13 B-B4 is still riskier.) 13...BxB 14 NxB R-K1 when '5 Q-QN5 P-B3 or 15 Q-KN5 Q-Q6 both give Black dangerous counterplay.

b) We think White should play simply 13 0-0!, when after 13...BxB 14 NxB R-K1 15 BxP+ KxB 16 Q-QN5 NxP 17 QR-Q1! his threats against Black's QNP, queen and king should soon yield concrete gains (17...N-Q3 18 Q-N3+ and 19 N-B4).

12	0—0	N—N5
13	Q—N3	BxB
14	NxB	Q—K2

15 B-N5+! P-B3 (15...B-Q2 16 QxP)

16 N-B4! Q-K3! 17 QR-Q1! PxB 18 Q-B7 and White has a winning attack; Fischer-Celle, from a simultaneous display with clocks, California 1964. This game may be found complete with the winner's deep notes, in Fischer, op.cit., pp. 306-310.

A3:

6	...	N—B3
7	PxP	

7 BxP+?! is best refuted by returning the piece, e.g. 7...KxB 8 NxP+ NxN 9 PxN P-Q4! 10 PxN BxP 11 PxP R-K1+ 12 B-K3 R-K4 — Müller.

7	...	N—KN5
8	Q—Q5	0—0
9	P—KR3	N—R3
10	0—0	

Best may be 10 B-B4, but not 10 BxN? PxB 11 0-0 P-Q3 12 PxP BxP∓ (Root-Olafsson, Students Olympiad, Lyons 1955).

10	...	P—Q3
11	PxP	PxP

11...BxP looks preferable, e.g. 12 BxN PxB 13 P-K5 B-K3!

12	Q—KR5	Q—R4
13	B—Q5	B—K3
14	R—Q1±	

Tal-Brakmanis, Latvian Olympiad 1959

A4:

6...B-B3 7 PxP NxP 8 NxN BxN 9 BxP+ KxB 10 Q-Q5+ K-B1 (10... K-B3 11 P-KB4) **11 QxB P-Q3** was played in Hall-Harris, Bognor Regis 1958. White should now keep queens on with a move like 12 Q-QN5 or 12 Q-N3!? .

A5:

6	...	N—R4! *(10)*

The most important continuation.

White now has to choose between:
A51: 7 NxP
A52: 7 B-Q3!?

7 B-K2 allows a variety of good replies, e.g. 7...N-KB3 8 PxP NxP 9 Q-Q5 N-B4 (Larry Evans) or 7...P-Q3 8 PxP PxP 9 Q-R4+ P-QB3 10 NxP B-B3.

7 BxP+? KxB 8 NxP+ K-B1! should win for Black.

A51:

7	NxP	NxB
8	NxN	P—Q4

Or 8...P-Q3 9 0-0 N-B3 when:
1) 10 P-K5 PxP 11 PxP (11 NxP 0-0 12 P-QB4 N-Q2) 11...QxQ 12 RxQ N-Q2 13 N1-R3 P-QR3 14 P-B4 P-QN4?! 15 N-R5 and White won in an 1862 game.
b) 10 R-K1 0-0 (10...NxP? 11 RxN P-Q4 12 R-K1 PxN 13 B-R3 B-K3 14 P-Q5) 11 B-N5 P-KR3 12 B-R4 P-B3 13 NxP!? comes into consideration.

9	PxP	QxP

Not 9...N-B3 10 Q-R4+ Q-Q2 (Or 10...B-Q2 11 Q-N3 — Euwe) 11 QxQ+ and 12 N-K3.

Now Black has tried:
A511: 10...Q-B3
A512: 10...Q-Q2
A513: 10...Q-QR4
A514: 10...Q-Q1

A511:

10	...	Q—B3

11 0-0 N-B3 12 P-QB4 0-0 13 P-Q5
Q-R3 14 N-B3 N-K1 15 Q-N3 Q-KN3
16 B-R3 BxB 17 QxB N-Q3 18 P-B5
N-K1 19 QR-Q1 B-Q2 20 R-Q4 N-B3
21 Q-N4 P-N3 22 P-B6 B-B1 23 P-Q6
PxP 24 RxP and White has a domi-
nating position (1-0, 34), J. Szabo-
Mititelu, Rumanian Ch 1958.

A512:
    10 ...   Q—Q2
11 0-0 N-B3 12 P-QB4 0-0 13 B-N2
(13 N-B3! or 13 Q-N3 look better.)
13...P-QN4!? 14 N-Q2 B-N2 15 Q-N3
P-QR3 16 P-QR4 QR-N1 17 RPxP
RPxP 18 PxP B-Q4 19 NxB NxN 20
N-B4 RxP= (½-½, 52) Skotorenko-
Krogius, USST 1962.

A513:
    10 ...   Q—QR4
    11 0—0   N—B3*(11)*

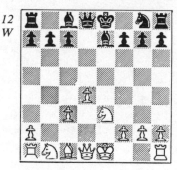

12 P—QB4!
Improving upon the Porreca-Euwe,
Berne 1957, game which went 12
R-K1 B-K3 13 P-QB4 P-QB3 14 B-N2
0-0-0 with an unclear position, but
Black winning in 48 moves.
    12 ...   P—B3
As Black cannot prevent P-Q5 in
the long run, he should seek some
other plan here.
    13 B—N2   B—K3
    14 N—B3   R—Q1

Also if 14...0-0-0!? White might
play 15 P-Q5!?
    15 P—Q5   PxP?
Black should avoid line-opening.
    16 N/B3xP   NxN
    17 PxN   0—0
18 Q-B3 BxP 19 Q-N3 P-B3 20
N-B5 (Decisive) 20...R-B2 21 NxB+
RxN 22 BxP R1-K1 23 BxR RxB 24
Q-N8+ K-B2 25 Q-B4+ K-N1 26
Q-B5 R-KB2 27 Q-K5 P-KN3 28
QR-B1 QxP 29 R-B8+ R-B1 30
RxR+ KxR 31 R-Q1 B-B3 32 R-Q8+
K-B2 33 Q-B4+ K-K2 34 Q-B8+ 1-0
Cafferty-van Geet, Amsterdam 1972.

A514:
    10 ...   Q—Q1*(12)*
The most conservative reply.

11 0—0
Also possible is 11 B-R3 N-B3 12
BxB QxB 13 0-0 0-0 14 R-K1 R-K1 15
N-Q2 B-K2, and now instead of
16 P-KB4? (of Pritchard-Veroeci,
Women's Olympiad, Skopje 1972)
Gipslis recommended 16 P-QB4.
    11 ...   N—B3
    12 P—QB4!
White must gain space. An alterna-
tive is 12 Q-B3 0-0 13 R-Q1 R-K1 14
N-Q2 P-B3 15 B-N2 Q-R4 16 P-B4

(Ivkovic-Sofrevsky, Yugoslav Ch. 1959).

12 ...   0—0
13 N—B3

13 B-N2 has also been played.

13 ...   P—B3
14 B—N2

Best may be 14 P-Q5 to creat a passed pawn and avoid the hemming-in of White's bishop; later N-B4 can help to break Black's blockade. 14 Q-N3, with the idea of continuing B-R3, is also worth considering.

14 ...   Q—R4

Possibly better is 14...P-QN4, e.g. 15 R-K1 PxP 16 NxP N-Q4 17 N-K5 B-N2 18 R-N1 B-N5 19 Q-B2 R-B1 20 P-QR3 P-QB4 21 PxP NxN 22 BxN Q-Q4 23 N-B3 BxB 24 QxB RxP 25 Q-N4 R-B2∓ Aijala-Strobel, Students Olympiad, Dresden 1969. Perhaps White could have made more of the weakness of Black's QBP.

15 P—Q5   B—QR6

If 15...R-Q1, then 16 Q-B3 is good.

16 BxB   QxB
17 Q—N3   QxQ?

As the resulting endgame is good for White, 17...Q-R4 is necessary here, with some drawing chances.

After **17...QxQ** the game Tartakower-Trifunovic, France v. Yugoslavia 1950, continued 18 PxQ PxP 19 N/B3xP NxN 20 NxN B-Q2 21 KR-Q1 KR-Q1 22 P-B3 (This threatens 23 N-N6!) 22...B-K1 23 N-B7 RxR 24 RxR R-B1 25 NxB RxN 26 R-Q7 R-N1 27 K-B2 K-B1 28 R-B7! (28 P-B5 P-QN3) 28...P-KN3 29 P-QN4 (29 P-B5 P-QR4!) and White won in 56 moves.

A52:

7   B—Q3!?*(13)*

This is a speculative move, retaining the bishop in preference to winning back the gambit pawn.

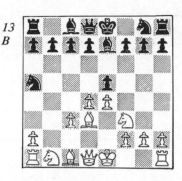

13
B

Black has now tried:
A521: 7...P-Q4!?
A522: 7...PxP!?
A523: 7...P-Q3

A521:

7 ...   P—Q4!?

An uncommon move. Play might go:

a) 8 KPxP PxP 9 Q-R4+ P-QB3 10 BPxP P-QN4 11 Q-B2 N-B3 12 PxP Q-N3 13 N-B3 P-N5 14 R-QN1 0-0 (Wills-J. Littlewood, corres. 1964) 15 N-K4±

b) 8 NxP PxP 9 BxP N-KB3 10 B-B2, intending B-N5 and Q-Q3, is another idea.

A522:

7 ...   PxP!?

This is risky, as it gives up the centre.

8 PxP   P—Q4

Poor moves are:

a) 8...N-KB3 9 B-Q2 N-B3 10 P-K5 N-Q4 11 B-K4 followed by P-Q5;

b) 8...P-Q3 9 Q-R4+ P-QB3 10 B-Q2 P-QN3 11 BxN PxN 12 QxBP+ B-Q2 13 Q-B2±

9 Q—R4+!*(14)*

Two games of interest for their middle-games.

a) Eisinger-Bogoljubow, Bad Pyrmont 1949, continued 9 N-B3?! PxP 10 NxP

N-KB3 11 NxN+ BxN 12 Q-R4+
N-B3 13 B-R3 B-Q2 14 0-0 B-K2 15
P-Q5 (The tournament book recom-
mended 15 KR-K1 0-0 16 BxB NxB
17 Q-N4). 15...N-K4 16 Q-Q4 BxB! 17
NxN 0-0 18 QR-N1 B-B1 19 KR-K1
B-Q3 20 R-K3 P-QN3 21 N-B6 Q-N4
22 P-KR4 Q-R3 23 R1-K1 B-QB4 24
R-K8 B-Q2 25 RxQR RxR 26 Q-K4
P-N3 27 P-Q6 Q-Q7! 28 N-K7+ K-N2
29 R-K2 Q-B8+ 30 R-K1 Q-N7 31
R-K2 Q-R8+ 32 R-K1 Q-B3! 33
N-Q5 QxBP+ 34 K-R1 BxP 35 R-K3
R-K1 36 Q-Q4+ B-K4! 37 Q-K4
B-KB3 38 R-B3 RxQ 39 RxQ RxP+
40 K-N1 B-Q5 0-1.
b) Wright-Schaufelberger, Basle
1968, went 9 P-K5?! P-QB4 10 PxP
N-QB3 11 0-0 B-KN5 12 B-KB4 BxP
13 QN-Q2 KN-K2 14 P-KR3 BxN 15
NxB P-KR3 16 R-N1 Q-Q2 17 R-K1
0-0-0? (Correct is 17...B-N3, intending
...Q-K3). 18 Q-B2 B-N3 19 P-K6 PxP
20 N-K5 Q-K1 21 KR-QB1 R-B1 22
B-N3 B-B2 23 Q-N3 B-N3 24 Q-R4
R-Q2? 25 RxB! 1-0. Even after the
correct 24...B-B2, White can very
likely win by 25 Q-R4! B-N3 26 RxB!
PxQ 27 BxP+ K-B2 28 R-N7+ etc.

10 PxP   QxP
11 N—B3

In two unconvincing games 11 0-0
was played, met by 11...B-Q2 and
11...N-B3.

11 ...   Q—QR4?

According to Keres, the equalizing
line is 11...B-QN5 12 B-Q2 BxN (or
12...Q-QR4!? — Larry Evans) 13 BxB
KN-K2.

12 QxQ   NxQ
13 N—QN5!

White has some advantage since,
despite the pawn minus, he has active
play with his minor pieces. The
continuation of the game Cafferty-
Clement, 5th Corres Olympiad
preliminaries (1962-3), was instruc-
tive: **13...B-Q1 14 B-KB4 P-QB3 15
N-Q6+! K-K2?** (15...K-B1 was
critical.) **16 0-0 B-K3 17 KR-K1 K-B1
18 B-B5! B-K2 19 BxB PxB 20 RxP
N-B3 21 N-B5 N-Q4? 22 RxB! NxR 23
B-Q6 K-B2 24 BxN K-K3? 25 P-N4
P-KN3 26 R-K1+ K-Q2 27 N-K5+
K-B2 28 B-Q6+ K-N3 29 N-Q7+
K-N4 30 R-N1+ K-B5 31 N-K3+
K-Q6 32 N-QB5+ 1-0.**

A523:
7 ...   P—Q3*(15)*

8 PxP!

For 8 0-0 N-KB3 9 PxP PxP 10 NxP
see below. Others are not so reliable,
e.g. 8 Q-R4+?! P-B3 (9 PxP PxP 10
NxP P-B3) 9...P-QN4 (9...N-B3 10

9 ...   N—B3

If 9...P-QB3 10 PxP followed by 11
B-Q2! The text move was recom-
mended by Konstantinopolsky in
Shakhmatny Bulletin 9/1959.

PxP PxP 11 BxB) 10 Q-B2 and now Fine recommended 10...P-B3, claiming an advantage for Black.

In the game Alexander-Euwe, Maastricht 1946, Black played instead 10...Q-B2 11 QN-Q2 N-B3 with a complicated game: 12 B-N4! N-N2 (Euwe later suggested 12...N-Q2!?) 13 P-B4 P-QR4 14 B-B3 P-N6 15 B-N2 PxP 16 BxP P-B4 17 B-N2 P-R5 18 R-QN1 and at this point White's chances are probably not worse, but Black won in 50 moves.

8 ...   PxP

Others include:

a) 8...N-QB3!? 9 PxP PxP 10 N-Q4 N-B3 11 0-0 0-0 12 N-Q2 (Intending N-B4) with an early draw in Adorjan-Portisch, Hungarian Team Ch 1969.

b) 8...B-KN5 when:

b1) 9 PxP PxP 10 0-0 N-KB3 11 P-KR3 BxN 12 QxB 0-0 13 N-Q2 N-Q2 13 B-R3 R-B1 15 QR-B1 B-N4 16 KR-Q1 N-K4 17 Q-K2 NxB 18 QxN BxN (Intending ...N-B5) 0-1 Klovan-Ravinsky, Moscow 1959

b2) 9 0-0 BxN 10 QxB PxP 11 R-Q1 B-Q3 12 B-QN5+ P-QB3 13 B-R3 Q-B3 (Wills-Gibbs, British Corres Ch 1969-70) 14 QxQ NxQ 15 BxB PxB 16 BxP± (16...NxP? 17 R-K1) — Wills

b3) Also worth considering is 9 Q-R4+ P-QB3 (9...N-QB3 10 QN-Q2 — Sokolsky) 10 QN-Q2 P-QN4 11 Q-B2.

9 NxP   N—KB3

This line seems to ensure Black an equal game, but usually the line recommended is 9...B-B3 e.g. 10 N-B3 N-B3 11 0-0 KN-K2. But in that case Black needs to find an improvement upon the following game:

Cafferty-Dobsa, Eberhardt Wilhelm Cup corres 1967-8: 9...B-B3 10 B-KB4! B-K3 11 0-0 P-KN4? 12 B-N3 P-R4 13 P-KR3 P-N5 14 PxP PxP 15 B-K2! QxQ 16 RxQ N-R3 17 N-R3

P-B3 18 N3-B4 NxN 19 NxN BxN? (Conceding the two bishops proves a bad idea.) 20 BxB BxP 21 QR-B1 B-B3 22 R-N1! P-N4 23 B-K2 R-Q1 24 RxR+ BxR 25 R-QB1! K-Q2 26 R-Q1+ K-K2 27 R-Q6 P-B3 28 RxQBP N-B2 29 BxKNP N-N4 30 B-B5 B-N3 31 B-Q6+ K-B2 32 B-B5 R-K1 33 BxB PxB 34 P-B3 K-N2 35 RxNP R-QR1 36 P-B4 N-B2 37 B-K6 1-0.

10 0—0   0—0
11 Q—B2

Heuer-Uusi, Estonian Ch 1962, went instead 11 P-KB4?! N-Q2 12 NxN BxN 13 B-K3 B-R5! and Black won in 47 moves.

11 ...   B—K3

Possibly not best, in view of:

a) 11...P-B4 12 B-N2 B-Q3 13 N-B3 P-B5! 14 B-K2 Q-B2 15 N-R3 P-QR3 16 QR-Q1 N-N5 17 P-R3 N-R7 18 R-K1 NxN+ 19 BxN and soon drawn, Hindle-Wade, British Ch 1965.

b) 11...P-QN3 12 N-Q2 B-N2 13 N-N3! NxN 14 PxN P-B4 15 P-B3 P-KR3 16 B-R6± Wills-Firth, corres 1967-8.

c) 11...N-Q2 12 NxN BxN (Gofman-Kropotin, Ukraine Corres. Ch 1961-5) also may be good.

12 R—Q1   Q—B1
13 N—Q2   R—Q1
14 N—B1   P—B4

The chances are roughly equal, although in the game Sokolsky-Shishov, ½-final USSR Ch 1959, Black weakened his Q-side pawns and lost in a queen ending. Meanwhile White's plan is to gain a space advantage by gradual advance of his K-side pawn majority.

B:

6 Q—N3 *(16)*

This, a totally different concept for White, stems from a game by La Bourdonnais. For a long time considered inadequate, it is in fact justifiable by a finesse at White's eighth move. One advantage of this line is that it is virtually unknown.

16
B

6 ...   N—R3
Black's fifth move has blocked in his queen, so he has little choice. **6...N-R4? 7 BxP+ K-B1 8 Q-R4 P-B3 (8...KxB 9 NxP+ and 10 QxN) 9 BxN KxB 10 NxP P-Q4 11 0-0 B-B3 12 P-KB4** leaves White a good pawn ahead; Wills-Wilkinson, London 1964.
7 P—Q4   N—R4
Now White can play:
B1: 8 Q-R4
B2: 8 Q-N5!

B1:

8 Q—R4   NxB
9 QxN   N—N5!
Thus White loses the opportunity to exchange Black's knight, whereas 9...PxP?! 10 BxN! (but not 10 PxP P-Q4!) would tranpose to B2, as in fact occurred in the earliest games with this variation.

In the game Ree-Bouwmeester, Hilversum 1967, Black experimented with 9...P-Q4!? but after 10 KPxP P-K5 11 N-K5 N-B4 12 Q-N5+ K-B1 13 0-0 we consider that the position is in White's favour; 13...P-KB3 would be met by 14 P-B3! Instead the game

continued 13...P-KN3 14 N-Q2 P-KB3 15 N-N4 (Not 15 P-B3 P-K6! but 15 NxKP!? PxN 16 PxP looks interesting.) 15...P-QR3 16 Q-N3 NxP 17 PxN BxN 18 NxP K-N2 19 QxP (19 N-B5!?) 19...B-K7 20 R-K1 (Possible is 20 B-B4 BxR 21 RxB R-QB1 22 R-B1 etc.) 20...B-N4? (Even 20... R-QN1 21 Q-B6 B-N4 22 Q-B2 is .) 21 B-B4 Q-Q2 22 QR-B1 KR-QB1 23 P-Q6! PxP 24 QxQ BxQ 25 N-B5! 1-0.
10 P—KR3
If 10 PxP then 10...P-Q3!
10 ...   N—B3
11 PxP
11 NxP 0-0 is possible but tame for White.
11 ...   P—Q4!
Black has the better game, in view of his two bishops and White's pawn weaknesses. That resource for Black was suggested first by Daniel Harrwitz but has apparently never occurred in a master game.
12 P4xP
If 12 P5xPep PxP, but possibly 12 Q-R4+ would be better.
12 ...   NxP
An interesting counter-gambit is 12...QxP!? when after 13 QxP Black has active compensation after any of:
a) 13...B-Q1 14 Q-Q6 Q-K5+ and 15...N-Q4, or
b) 13...N-K5 (Threatening ...B-Q1) 14 P-B4 Q-Q6! — analysis; or
c) 13...N-Q2 14 0-0 N-B4! — *Archives*, 1967.
13 0—0   0—0
14 Q—K2
Or 14 Q-K4, given by Collijn's *Larobok i Schack*. Black is cramped, but White must find tactical chances quickly.
14 ...   P—QB3
15 R—Q1   Q—K1!
Black stands well, and eventually will open the game with ...P-KB3 — *Archives*.

B2:

8 Q—N5!*(17)*

G. Popov's move, which enforces either the exchange of Black's KN or else favourable complications. In the main line, White plays positionally, his chief targets being Black's Q-side pawns. Black's doubled KRPs will mean that his material advantage is only nominal. It is worth noting that White's 8 Q-N5! does not appear in the *Encyclopaedia of Chess Openings, M.C.O.* or any of the other standard works of reference.

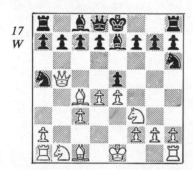

17
W

8 ...   NxB

8...P-QB3 9 QxKP seems good for White, albeit complicated:

a) 9...NxB 10 QxP R-KN1 11 QxN (11 QxRP!? RxP 12 BxN is also exciting.). 11...P-Q4 (11...RxP!?) 12 QxRP RxP 13 K-B1 R-N5 14 QN-Q2 intending an early QR-K1 or R-KN1 when he passed KRP is a trump — analysis.

b) 9...P-B3 10 Q-R5+ and now:

b1) 10...P-KN3 11 QxN B-B1! (11...NxB? 12 Q-N7 winning; Harding-Parker, corres. 1974) 12 B-B7+! KxB 13 Q-B4±

b2) Not altogether hopeless is 10...K-B1 11 B-Q3! N-B2 when White could try 12 0-0 followed by R-K1, or 12 B-R3 to take the sting out of a possible ...P-KN3; Q-R4 P-KB4 counter.

9 BxN!

Of course not 9 QxB returning to B1.

9 ...   PxB

9...N-Q3? 10 QxKP P-KB3 11 Q-KR5+ gives White a strong attack, e.g. 11...P-KN3 12 Q-R4 P-KB4 13 Q-R3 PxP 14 B-N7 R-KN1 15 QxRP RxB 16 QxR PxN 17 0-0 1-0 Popov-Nekson, corres 1963.

10 QxN   PxP

Others do not seem quite adequate:

1) 10...P-Q4?! 11 KPxP PxP 12 0-0 Q-Q3 13 QxQP R-KN1 14 K-R1 Q-KN3 15 R-N1 B-Q3?! 16 QN-Q2 B-KN5 17 QR-K1+ (but both sides' play might be improved here?) Harding-Turek, 3rd ICCF Cup corres 1974-5 (White won).

b) 10...P-Q3!? 11 PxP!? B-K3 12 Q-N5+ K-B1? (12...Q-Q2! and if 13 QxP 0-0∓, but 13 QxQ+ is feasible.) 13 QxP K-N2 14 0-0 Q-Q2 15 PxP BxQP 16 P-K5 KR-QN1 17 Q-K4 B-K2 18 QN-Q2 B-KB4 19 Q-Q4 Q-K3 20 N-N3 and White holds his extra pawn, Harding-Hodgson, corres 1974-5.

11 PxP*(18)*

18
B

An interesting position, which needs more practical tests; whether White will prefer this line to A51 or A52 is largely a matter of taste. The extra Black pawn is nothing to worry about, but his two bishops have to be kept under observation; still, "Chigorin often successfully carried on the struggle with the two knights." White has more space and development, and the chance of switching his attack between the black king and the exposed QNP and QBP. Also the half-open KN-file is a temptation to Black to leave his king in the centre.

11 ... P—Q3

Other possibilities are:

a) 11...R-KN1 12 0-0 P-Q3 see the note to Black's 12th move below.

b) 11...P-Q4 12 PxP 0-0 (12... B-KB4!? 13 Q-N5+ and 14 QxP) 13 0-0 B-Q2 (13...B-KB4 14 N-B3) 14 N-K5! (Intending N-B3-QN5 and QR-B1) with about equal chances — analysis.

c) 11...B-B3 12 N-B3 P-B3 13 0-0 0-0 14 P-K5 B-N2 15 N-K4 P-Q4 16 PxPep B-K3 17 Q-N4 B-Q4 18 KR-K1 R-K1 19 N4-Q2 R-K3 20 RxR PxR 21 R-K1 P-N4 22 N-K5 B-B1 23 R-K3 BxQP 24 R-KN3+ K-B1 25 Q-N1 Q-K2 26 N-K4 B3xN 27 PxB BxN 28 QxB R-B1 29 Q-KN4 K-K1 30 R-Q3 Q-KB2 31 R-Q6 R-B2 32 P-KR4 1-0 (On time!) Rozhlapa-Belova, USSR Olympiad 1972.

12 0—0 0—0

The sharp 12...R-KN1!? must be treated with respect:

a) 13 K-R1? can be met by:

a1) 13...B-N5 and if now 14 Q-N5+? (14 QN-Q2 is essential.) 14...Q-Q2! 15 QxP?? Black wins by 15...BxN 16 QxR+ B-Q1 17 PxB (17 R-N1 Q-R6) 17...Q-R6 18 Q-B6+ K-B1.

a2) 13...Q-Q2 when 14 QN-Q2 is once more necessary. In the game La Bourdonnais v. Boncourt and Mauret, Paris 1835, the continuation instead was 14 N-B3? P-QB3 (14...RxP 15

R-KN1 and N-Q5 is unclear.) 15 P-Q5 RxP 16 R-KN1 RxBP? (16...R-N3∓ 17 R-N3 P-QB4 18 P-K5 and White went on to win.

b) We recommend 13 R-B1! P-QB3 14 P-Q5 B-Q2 (Or 14...B-R6!? 15 P-N3 B-Q2) 15 QN-Q2 PxP (Or 15...P-B4 16 P-K5 P-N4 17 Q-K4) 16 QxP B-QB3 17 Q-KR5 R-N3 18 N-Q4 .

The position after the text move, 12...0-0, was given as better for Black in *Sovremenny Debyut,* following the original assessment in Schlechter's edition of the *Handbuch,* but we do not agree. There is no need for White to play dubiously for a quick mate, when he has targets elsewhere.

The only example so far available is a 1974-5 correspondence game Harding-Micklethwaite, which continued 13 N-B3 P-QB3 (Sensibly preventing N-Q5 and N-QN5) 14 QR-N1 K-R1 (14...R-N1!?) 15 K-R1 (Probably unnecessary) 15...R-QN1 16 P-Q5 P-QB4 17 P-K5 P-R3 18 P P-QR4 PxP (18...B-B4!?) 19 NxP B-B4 20 QR-K1 with plenty of active ideas for White. Black now blundered with 20...Q-B2? after which 21 Q-R4 (Threatening 22 N-N6+) regained the gambit pawn with a greatly superior position: the king at last comes under fire.

It is clearly too early for giving dogmatic assessments of the 6 Q-N3 line, but this preliminary enquiry suggests that White's chances may well be no worse than in the line 6 P-Q4 N-QR4 7 NxP and probably better than in the 7 B-Q3 variation. At any rate, we have made a case to be answered for 6 Q-N3.

3 Conservative Defence: Anti-Lasker Systems

In modern master play Black rarely takes the Evans Gambit pawn with a view to holding it for long. If the second player is not attracted to the charms of 5...B-K2, he is most likely to offer Lasker's Defence (see the next chapter); we recommend White to avoid this. Several ways have been tried, one or two of which are rather promising.

1	P—K4	P—K4
2	N—KB3	N—QB3
3	B—B4	B—B4
4	P—QN4	BxNP
5	P—B3	B—R4
6	P—Q4!	

After 6 0-0, as Chigorin used to play, White cannot prevent his opponent from setting up the Lasker formation of ...P-Q3 and ...B-N3, nor indeed from trying any of the other defences mentioned in Chapter 7. It is essential for White to commence active play forthwith, and to defer castling until there is time; in the final, and crucial, variation of this chapter it will be seen that White eventually castles Q-side!

| 6 | ... | P—Q3(19) |

The continuation recommended towards the end of the nineteenth century by Alapin and Lasker: Black offers to return the pawn at the cost of exchanges. Other moves will be discussed as follows:
a) 6...PxP in Chapters 5-10;
b) Rare 6th moves in Chapter 7.

19 W

White has tried here:
A: 7 Q-R4?!
B: 7 B-KN5?!
C: 7 PxP
D: 7 Q-N3!
    7 0-0 see Chapter 4;
    7 B-R3 B-N3 (7...N-B3?) 8 PxP PxP 9 Q-N3 Q-Q2 see D6312 below.
    7 N-N5 N-R3 8 0-0 B-Q2! — Maroczy

A:

| 7 | Q—R4?! | |

This dubious move was first analysed by Geza Maroczy in his book *Paul Morphy*. After one trial in a gambit tournament it has not been seen again.

7	...	PxP
8	B—KN5	N—K2
9	NxP	Q—Q2!
10	B—N5	

Maroczy's main line ran 10 BxN NxN 11 QxB N-B3! 12 Q-KN5 QxB

13 QxP QxP+ 14 B-K2 (Or 14 K-Q1 Q-N5+) 14...Q-K4 with advantage to Black.

10	...	P—QR3!
11	BxN/B6	NxB
12	N—B5	

Maroczy's analysis had ended 12 NxN B-N3!∓.

12	...	P—B3
13	B—K3	P—QN4
14	Q—Q1	Q—B2

15 0-0 BxN 16 PxB 0-0 17 Q-B2 Q-B5 18 P-QR3 N-K4 19 R-Q1 KR-K1 20 B-Q4 R-K2 21 BxN RxB 22 N-Q2 Q-KN5! (Not 22...QxP? 23 Q-R2+ K-R1 24 QR-B1 Q-Q6 25 N-B4±) 23 N-B3 R-QB4! (23...RxP? 24 P-R3) 24 R-Q3 QxBP 25 N-Q4 Q-K5 26 Q-Q2 R-N4 27 P-B3 Q-Q4 28 P-KB4 R-N3 29 P-B5 R-N5 30 K-R1 BxP! and Black soon won, Breyer-Reti, Baden 1914.

B:

7 B—KN5?! *(20)*

This move is usually credited to Sokolsky, or to a little-known pre-war Soviet player Steinsapir, but Alapin claimed to have discussed the variation as early as 1903. Unfortunately we have been unable to trace the source, a German magazine article. The move had a brief vogue in the 1950s but is no longer considered correct.

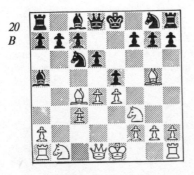

20
B

Black has tried:

B1: 7...Q-Q2?
B2: 7...N-B3
B3: 7...KN-K2
B4: 7...P-B3!

B1:

| 7 | ... | Q—Q2? |
| 8 | 0—0 | |

Now this quiet move leaves Black with severe development difficulties.

| 8 | ... | B—N3 |

Others:

a) 8...P-KR3 9 B-R4 KN-K2 (9... B-N3 10 B-N5) when:
a1) 10 BxN BxN 11 PxP (Steinsapir-Romanovsky, Leningrad 1937) 11... 0-0! 12 Q-N3 Q-N5 13 QN-Q2 N-N3∓ — *Sovremenny Debyut*
a2) 10 P-Q5 N-QN1 11 BxN forcing 11...KxB± — Romanovsky
b) 8...KN-K2 9 Q-R4 B-N3 10 B-N5 P-QR3 11 P-Q5 PxB 12 QxR N-R2 13 B-K3 and White's queen is safe — Cafferty.

9 PxP

Better is 9 B-N5! PxP 10 PxP P-Q4 11 PxP QxP 12 N-B3±

9	...	PxP
10	Q—R4	P—B3
11	R—Q1	Q—K2
12	B—QB1	B—Q2!

For the time being, Black has survived; Tal-Kampenus, Latvian Ch 1954.

B2:

| 7 | ... | N—B3 |
| 8 | Q—R4 | |

Not 8 BxN PxB! (8...QxB? 9 P-Q5 and 10 Q-R4+) 9 Q-R4 P-QR3 10 P-Q5 P-N4 11 BxNP PxB 12 QxP Q-Q2! 13 QxN (13 PxN Q-N5) 13... QxQ 14 PxQ B-R3∓ according to Sokolsky.

| 8 | ... | PxP *(21)* |

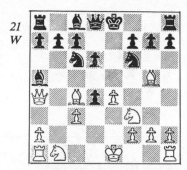

21
W

9 NxP?!

White has two possible improvements here:

a) 9 BxN PxB (9...QxB 10 B-Q5) 10 NxP B-N3 11 NxN PxN 12 QxBP+ B-Q2 13 Q-Q5 (Sokolsky) but we think 13...B-K3! equalizes, since after 14 Q-Q3 R-KN1 15 0-0 Q-Q2! the two bishops and open KN-file give Black a K-side attack.

b) 9 B-N5! when:

b1) 9...B-N3 10 PxP P-KR3 (10... B-Q2 11 P-K5 Q-K2 12 0-0!) 11 BxKN PxB (11...QxB 12 BxN+) 12 P-Q5 and wins.

b2) 9...BxP 10 NxB PxN 11 P-K5 and now:

b21) 11...PxP 12 R-Q1 B-Q2 13 BxQN PxB 14 NxP Q-K2 15 0-0 with a decisive build-up on the open central files.

b22) 11...P-KR3 12 PxN PxB 13 BxN+! PxB 14 QxBP+ B-Q2 15 Q-K4+ B-K3 16 PxP R-KN1:

b221) 17 NxP? QxN 18 QxR+ K-Q2 19 QxR Q-Q7+! 20 K-B1 B-B5+ 21 K-N1 P-B7 22 P-KR4 P-B8=Q+ and Black at least draws.

b222) 17 Q-B6+ B-Q2 18 QxP/B3 with advantage, thanks to the advanced passed pawn and exposed black king position — all analysis by Cafferty.

9 ...   B—N3!
10 B—N5

If 10 NxN PxB 11 QxBP+ B-Q2;

but Romanovsky, in *Shakhmaty v SSSR* 1966/3, suggested 10 BxN!?

10 ...   0—0
11 NxN?

White must try 11 BxN PxB 12 NxP or 12 QxBP

11 ...   PxN
12 BxP   BxP+!
13 K—K2   R—QN1
14 R—KB1   R—N7+
15 N—Q2?

According to Romanovsky, the best chance was 15 K-Q1. He then gives 15...B-N5+ 16 K-B1 R-K7 17 P-KR3 NxP (17...B-Q2!?) 18 BxQ B-K6+.

15 ...   NxP!

Since if 16 BxQ, Black wins by 16...B-N5+! 17 K-Q3 N-B4+ 18 K-B4 B-K7+ 19 K-Q5 RxN+.

16 QxN   QxB
17 KxB   B—B4!
18 Q—B3   B—N5
19 Q—K4   P—Q4!

White Resigned, since if 20 BxP RxN+ or 20 Q-K1 RxN+ 21 K-N1 B-Q2; Noakh-Kopylov, Leningrad gambit tournament 1937.

B3:

7 ...   KN—K2
8 P—Q5?!

Sokolsky gave just 8 BxN, forcing 8...KxB, and then 9 0-0 keeping the centre fluid. After 8 P-Q5 N-QN1 9 BxN KxB 10 Q-B1!? N-Q2! 11 0-0 (Or 11 Q-N5+ N-B3 12 QxNP R-KN1 etc.) 11...R-K1 12 N-K4 K-B1 13 N-B5 N-B4 14 N-N3 N-Q2 15 N-Q2 B-N3 16 N-B3 K-N1 Black had a good position with an extra pawn (0-1, 40), Klovan-Tal, Riga 1951.

B4:

7 ...   P—B3!
8 Q—N3   KN—K2!(22)

Others are less good:

a) 8...N-R3 9 BxN PxB 10 Q-R4 and Black is in minor piece trouble again.

b) 8...PxB 9 BxN Q-B3 10 PxP PxP 11 0-0 with complications; Black can try 11...B-Q2 12 NxP (12 QxP? R-N1) 12...0-0-0 or 11...B-N3 12 NxP N-R4.

22
W

9   B—B7+   K—B1
10 B—Q2

White has also tried:

a) 10 B-K3 PxP! 11 NxP (11 B-R5 P-Q4) 11...NxN 12 BxN N-B3 13 B-K3 Q-K2! 14 B-Q5 B-N3 15 N-Q2 N-K4 and Black has beaten off the pressure (But ½-½, 36), Cafferty-Napier, corres 1956-7.

b) 10 B-R5 when:

b1) 10...P-KN3 11 B-R6+ K-K1 12 B-N7 R-B1! — Panov in *Shakhmaty v SSSR* 1959/6

b2) 10...N-N3 11 B-K3 Q-K2 12 0-0 B-N3 13 QN-Q2 B-K3 14 P-Q5 N-R4 15 Q-N4 B-Q2 16 P-B4 N-B5 17 BxN PxB 18 N-R4 Q-K4 19 B-N6!? BxP+! 20 KxB Q-Q5+ 21 K-K2 B-N5+ 22 N4-B3 PxB 23 QxN RxP 24 R-KN1 P-KB4 25 QxBP Q-K6+ 26 K-B1 PxP 27 QxQP+ K-N1 28 NxP Q-Q6+ 0-1 Wolf-O'Kelly, Belgian Ch 1951

10   ...   B—N3
11   P—QR4

If 11 B-Q5 PxP.

11   ...   B—N5!
12   PxP   BxN
13   PxBP   BxKP
14   B—N5!

The end of Panov's analysis. There could follow 14...P-KR3 or 14...P-Q4, with Black emerging a pawn up but with some complications remaining.

C:

7   PxP*(23)*

23
B

7   ...   PxP

Not 7...NxP? 8 NxN PxN 9 BxP+ K-K2 10 Q-N3 (Threatening 11 BxN and 11 B-R3+) but 7...Q-K2!? 8 0-0 (8 P-QR4!?) as in a game Prince Dadian of Mingrelia v. Sizard, 1910, might be playable.

8   Q—N3

8 QxQ+ NxQ 9 NxP B-K3 should be compared with D53 in the next chapter.

8   ...   Q—B3

8...Q-Q2 transposes to D631 below.

8...Q-K2 is possible. Tartakower then suggested 9 P-QR4!? but 9 0-0 (9 B-R3?! Q-B3) may be better. Not then 9...N-B3 10 B-R3, but 9...B-Q2 (Chapter 4, C32) or 9...B-N3 (Chapter 4, D54) could favour Black.

9   B—KN5   Q—N3
10 QN—Q2   B—N3

Or 10...N-B3 11 P-KR4 P-R4 12 B-Q5 N-Q2 13 R-R3 B-N3 14 R-N3 N-B4 15 Q-B2 B-N5 16 B-K3 0-0-0∓ Muir-B. Andersson, ½-final 5 World Corres Ch 1962-5.

11 P—KR4!?

This plan was recommended by Tartakower and du Mont in their *500 Master Games of Chess*. It is not clear how effective it may be:

a) 11...P-KR3? 12 P-R5 and 13

BxBP+
b) 11...KN-K2 12 P-R5 etc
c) 11...P-KR4 12 R-Q1 or 12 B-N5
and 13 N-B4 (Or 13 Q-R4) also looks
nice for White. This might have been
tried, instead of 12 B-Q5, in the Muir
game.
d) 11...N-B3 when:
d1) Tartakower and du Mont say "12
B-Q5 and White will regain his pawn
with advantage". After 12...NxB 13
PxN N-R4 14 Q-R4+ (Or 14 Q-N4
Q-Q3) 14...B-Q2 15 QxB+ KxQ 16
NxP+ K-Q3 17 NxQ KR-K1+ (18
B-K7+? K-Q2!) the ending is possibly
in Black's favour — analysis.
d2) Also interesting is 12 B-N5 NxP
(12...0-0? 13 KBxN PxB 14 NxP Q-R4
15 P-B3 etc.) 13 P-R5! NxN
(13...Q-B4 14 Q-Q5) 14 PxQ NxQ 15
RxP 0-0 when Black emerges on top,
since after 16 PxN PxP 17 B-B4+? (17
R-KR4 B-K3) 17...KxR 18 0-0-0
B-N5! prevents the mate — analysis.

D:

    7 Q—N3*(24)*

The most reliable move, stemming
from an early game of Morphy's!

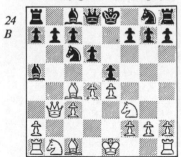

24
B

Now Black can try:
D1: 7...Q-B3??
D2: 7...PxP?
D3: 7...NxP!?
D4: 7...N-R3!?
D5: 7...Q-K2!?
D6: 7...Q-Q2

D1:

    7 ...   Q—B3??
    8 P—Q5   N3—K2
Or 8...N-Q5 9 Q-R4+ B-Q2 10
QxB P-QN3 11 Q-R6± — Keres.
    9 Q—R4+   P—B3
    10 QxB   Q—N3
11 QN-Q2 N-B3 12 PxP PxP 13 B-R3
NxP 14 NxP! PxN 15 QxKP 0-0 16
QxN/K4 B-B4 17 Q-B3 KR-K1 18 0-0
1-0 Cafferty-Kirkwald, corres 1969

D2:

    7 ...   PxP?
8 BxP+ K-K2 9 P-K5 PxP 10 0-0 with
a promising attack position for
White, e.g. 10...B-KN5 11 R-K1 BxN
12 B-R3+ B-QN5 13 PxB P-QN4 14
QxB Q-Q3 15 R-QB1 R-KB1 16 QxN
RxB 17 QxBP+ K-K3 18 Q-B8+
Q-Q2 19 N-Q2 R-K2 20 N-K4
winning, Alexander-Yates, England
1932.

D3:

    7 ...   NxP!?
A paradoxical move, which needs
careful handling. If now 8 Q-R4+
Black has a good reply in 8...Q-Q2!
    8 NxN   PxN
    9 BxP+
Here if 9 Q-R4+ the answer is
9...P-QB3 of course.
    9 ...   K—B1*(25)*

25
W

White has two moves here:
D31: 10 BxN?!
D32: 10 0-0

D31:

10	BxN?!	RxB
11	0—0	B—N3

The editor of the 1914 *Yearbook of Chess* preferred 11...Q-B3! 12 B-N2 Q-N3, and by analogy with the Scotch, Black has a satisfactory game.

12	B—N2	Q—B3
13	PxP	BxP
14	BxB	QxB
15	N—B3	P—B3

Half a century earlier, in Mlotkowski-Lovegrove, Los Angeles 1914 (Perhaps the first game with Black's 7th move?), 15...P-KN3?! was played. There followed 16 QR-Q1 Q-K4 (16...Q-N3!?) 17 R-Q3 K-N2 (17...R-N2!?) 18 P-B4 Q-QB4+ 19 K-R1 R-B1 20 N-Q5 R-B2 21 Q-N2+ K-N1 22 R-B1 QxR 22 QxQ B-K3 1-0.

16	KR—Q1	Q—N3
17	Q—B2	Q—B4
18	R—Q3	P—KN4

19 Q-Q2 R-N3 20 R-QB1 Q-K4 21 R-Q1 K-K2 22 R-K1 B-K3 23 N-Q5+ K-Q2 24 Q-R5 R-QB1 25 N-N6+ K-B2 26 QxQ (26 QxP!? and after 26...R-QN1 — 26...Q-QB4!? — 27 N-R8+ or 27 R-N1 QxKP 28 R3-Q1 come into consideration — Cafferty.) 26...PxQ 27 NxR but White's technique proved insufficient to win this difficult ending (½-½, 61), Sax-Tabor, Baja 1971.

D32:

10	0—0

Here we follow the much-quoted game A. R. B. Thomas-Unzicker, Hastings 1950-1.

10	...	Q—K2

Or 10...PxP?! 11 NxP BxN 12 BxN etc. If 10...N-B3? 11 P-K5.

11	B—QB4	N—B3
12	PxP	NxP
13	Q—KB3+	N—B3
14	N—B3	BxN

If 14...P-B3 15 B-R3 and QR-K1

(Tartakower), or 14...P-KR3 15 N-Q5 Q-Q1 16 N-B4 Q-K1 17 Q-Q3 (Wade in *Chess*).

15	QxB	B—B4
16	R—K1	Q—Q2
17	B—KN5	N—K5

Or 17...R-K1 18 BxN RxR+ 19 RxR PxB 20 Q-B3 P-B3 21 B-K6 BxB 22 QxP+ with a quick win for White — Tartakower.

18	RxN!	BxR
19	R—K1	P—Q4

Tartakower suggested 19...Q-N5, 'although 20 P-B3 QxB 21 PxB or 20 B-KB1 QxB 21 RxB would have set Black some difficult problems'.

20	RxB!	PxR(26)

26
W

21   Q—KN3?

Here White tragically missed the winning move 21 Q-N4+!:

a) 21...K-K1 22 QxP R-QB1 23 QxKP+ K-B1 24 Q-B4+ K-K1 25 Q-K5+ K-B1 26 B-K6 etc.

b) 21...Q-Q3 22 QxP R-K1 23 B-Q2! Q-Q1 24 B-N4+ R-K2 25 QxKP P-N3 26 Q-K6 K-K1 27 B-N5+ K-B1 28 Q-B6+ K-N1 29 B-B4+ mating.

21		Q—Q3
22	Q—N4	P—KN3
23	B—R6+	K—K1
24	QxKP+	K—Q2
25	Q—N4+	K—K1
26	Q—K4+	K—Q2
27	Q—N4+	K—K1

½—½

D4:

7 ... N—R3!?

Who but grandmaster Bronstein would play a move like this? Black gives back the pawn and allows his K-side to be shattered — in return for the two bishops and an active queen. If now 8 PxP, then 8...0-0.

8 BxN PxB
9 BxP+ K—B1
10 PxP

If 10 QN-Q2 PxP 11 PxP Q-B3, or 10 0-0 B-KN5 11 QN-Q2 PxP 12 PxP BxQN 13 NxB NxP — Ragozin.

10 ... Q—K2
11 B—Q5 NxP
12 NxN QxN *(27)*

27
W

13 Q—R3

White avoids any improvement for Black over the earlier, and unconvincing, game Sokolsky-Bronstein, Kiev 1944: 13 0-0 P-B3 14 Q-R4 B-Q1 15 B-N3 P-N4 16 Q-R3 B-N3 17 N-Q2 B-N5 18 K-R1 R-K1 19 P-KB4 Q-QB4 20 Q-N2 B-K7 21 KR-K1 B-Q6 22 P-K5 Q-B7 23 Q-R3 QxN? (23...B-B4) 24 QxP+ R-K2 25 Q-B6+ K-K1 26 QxR+ K-Q2 27 QR-Q1 1-0

13 ... B—N3
14 N—Q2 B—B4...

A major alternative, given by Ragozin, was 14...Q-B5 15 0-0-0! B-QB4 16 Q-N2 P-B3 17 B-N3 P-QR4 18 P-N3 and if 18...Q-B3 19 P-K5! Boleslavsky, *Shakhmaty v SSSR*, gave 14...P-B3 15 B-N3 (15 N-B4 B-QB4!)

15...Q-QB4 16 Q-N2!

15 Q—N2 P—B3
16 B—N3 P—QN4

If 16...P-Q4 17 0-0-0! P-Q5 18 N-B3 PxP 19 NxQ PxP+ 20 KxP is winning for White — Ragozin.

17 0—0 K—K2

Or 17...P-N5 18 QR-B1 B-R3 19 B-B4. Black hopes for play on the KB-file.

18 N—B3 Q—N2
19 K—R1 B—Q2
20 P—K5!+

20...QR-KB1 21 PxP KxP 22 N-Q4 K-B2 23 QR-Q1 B-Q3 24 KR-K1 Q-N4 25 B-K6! R-B3 26 BxB KxB 27 P-QR4 (Ragozin gave later 27 P-QB4! P-R3 28 N-B3 Q-KB4 29 RxB+ KxR 30 Q-Q4+.) 27...P-R3 28 PxP BPxP 29 Q-R2 R-R1 30 N-B3! Q-QB4 31 N-K5+ K-B2 32 Q-R5+ K-B1 33 N-Q3 Q-R4 34 P-R3 K-N2 35 P-QB4 R-B6! 36 N-B4!! RxN 37 RxB Q-B2 38 Q-N6+ 1-0 Ragozin-Bronstein, 14th USSR Ch 1945.

D5:

7 ... Q—K2!?

Because it appears to lose a piece, this move has been dismissed too lightly by some commentators. White must keep a clear head in the ensuing complications.

8 P—Q5 N—Q5! *(28)*

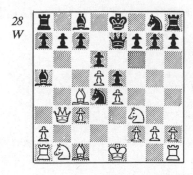

28
W

White now has:
D51: 9 B-QN5+
D52: 9 Q-R4+
D53: 9 NxN

D51:
9 B—QN5+
As played in an early Morphy game. However White denies himself all chance of winning Black's bishop by a fork, so the move has not been repeated. But there is a trap:
9 ...   P—B3?!
9...K-B1, 9...K-Q1 and 9...B-Q2 10 BxB+ QxB are all playable.
   10 NxN   PxN
   11 PxP!   QxP+
   12 K—Q1   B—KN5+
13 P-B3 BxKBP+ 14 PxB QxBP+ 15 K-B2 and Black is busted, (1-0, 26) Morphy-Ayers, Mobile 1855.

D52:
9 Q—R4+   B—Q2
The alternative is 9...Q-Q2 10 QxB P-QN3 11 NxN PxQ 12 B-QN5 PxN 13 BxQ+ BxB 14 PxP when the endgame may be tenable despite White's better pawns, Riello-del Pezzo, Venice 1950.
   10 QxB   N—B7+
It is probably better to slip in the zwischenzug 10...P-QN3 although White still stands better after 11 Q-R6 N-B7+ 12 K-Q1 NxR 13 B-N2 (13 N-R3!?) as in a pre-war Soviet postal game Yevgenev-Ratnikov.
   11 K—Q1   NxR
   12 N—-R3   N—B3
   13 R—K1   0—0
14 B-Q3 N-N5 15 R-K2 P-KB4 16 P-B4 PxP 17 BxP B-B4 18 BxB RxB 19 P-R3 (Intending N-Q4-K6) 19... NxBP+ 20 RxN P-K5 21 R-K2 QR-KB1 (21...PxN 22 RxQ P-B7 23 R-K1) 22 Q-B3 P-B3 23 B-N2 PxP 24 BxN P-Q5 25 QxP RxN 26 PxR RxP 27 RxP 1-0 A.R.B. Thomas-Schel-

fhout, Liverpool-Amsterdam Stock Exchanges match 1947.

D53:
9 NxN   PxN*(29)*
The opening of the king-file brings about an extremely tense situation. Its possibilities have hardly been explored as yet, but we think that the common assumption that White can without much risk win a piece is questionable.

29
W

10 Q—R4+!?
White's choice here is partly a matter of style. The offerer of a gambit hardly wants to be material up, and forced to defend! Other plans are therefore worth considering:
a) Keres recommends 10 0-0 B-N3 11 B-N2 with an attacking position for the pawn. A postal game Wills-Martin, 1974, continued 11...PxP 12 NxP N-B3 13 N-R4 0-0 14 NxB RPxN 15 QR-K1 N-Q2 16 P-B4 (Trying to force through P-K5) and White has, thanks to the doubled Black QNPs, an improved form of the Anderssen variation (chapter 10).
b) Cafferty suggests 10 B-N5+ and after the king moves (10...B-Q2 11 BxB+) then 11 0-0.
   10 ...   K—Q1
Black can also consider:
a) 10...B-Q2 11 QxB QxP+ 12 K-B1 (12 K-Q2!?) 12...P-Q6 13 N-Q2 (Keres) 13...Q-K7+ 14 K-N1 Q-K8+

15 N-B1 P-Q7 16 BxP QxR 17 QxBP
R-B1 — Larry Evans
b) 10...K-B1 11 QxB (11 0-0! —
Euwe) 11...QxP+ when:
b1) 12 K-Q2 (Or 12 K-Q1 P-Q6 —
Paoli) 12...B-B4 13 N-R3 QxNP 14
R-K1 QxBP+ and Black has a lot of
play for the piece; Wilkinson-Strauss,
corres 1952-3.
b2) 12 K-B1 "and White wins"
according to *M.C.O.* (11th ed.), but:
b21) 12...B-R6?! 13 R-N1 P-Q6 14
B-K3! QxB/B5 15 N-Q2! Q-KN5 16
PxB — *M.C.O.*
b22) 12...Q-B7! 13 B-Q2 Q-Q8+ 14
B-K1 P-Q6 — Euwe!

| 11 QxB | QxP+ |
| 12 K—Q2 | B—B4 |

Not 12...QxNP? 13 R-K1 N-B3 14
B-Q3 QxBP+ 15 R-K2 Q-N8 16 N-R3
B-N5 17 B-N2 and wins, Kislova-
Gresser, Subotica 1967.

| 13 N—R3 | QxNP!? |

In *Informator 4*, Maric suggested
13...N-B3 with an unclear game.

The text move was played in a 1952
postal game Puig-Escudero, which
continued 14 R-K1 QxBP+ 15 R-K2
Q-B5+ 16 K-Q1 Q-B8+ 17 K-Q2
when Black should have settled for
repetition of moves (17...Q-B5+), but
instead fell into a mating net after
17...P-QN3? 18 Q-N5 B-Q2? 19
QxB+!

D6:

| 7 ... | Q—Q2*(30)* |

This is Black's most popular
choice. He avoids immediate pitfalls,
but at the cost of bottling in his QB
and leaving his queen on an openable
file.

See diagram next column

Now White has:
D61: 8 P-QR4
D62: 8 0-0
D63: 8 PxP

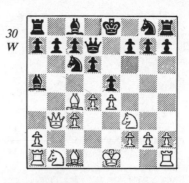

D61:

    8 P—QR4

Tartakower's continuation, which
we do not recommend.

    8 ...   PxP?!

This move allows White to carry
out his idea successfully. Others:
a) 8...P-QR3 9 PxP B-N3 10 P-R5!
NxRP 11 RxN BxR 12 PxP when:
a1) 12...P-QR4? 13 B-Q5 P-QB3 14
N-K5 1-0 Tartakower-Nyholm,
Vienna 1914
a2) 12...PxP! 13 0-0 P-QN4 14 B-Q5
B-N2 15 P-K5 e.g. 15...PxP 16 BxB
QxB 17 NxP N-B3 18 B-R3 ("With a
fine attack" — Tartakower) 18...
P-N5!?
b) 8...N-B3!? 9 0-0 0-0 10 PxP QNxP!
11 NxN PxN 12 B-R3 R-Q1 13 N-Q2
Q-K1 14 N-B3? (14 QR-Q1=)
14...NxP 15 KR-K1 NxN∓ Landau-
Takacs, Hungary 1930
c) 8...B-N3 9 P-R5 NxP 10 RxN BxR
11 PxP N-R3! and now:
c1) 12 P-K6?! PxP 13 N-N5 P-B3
(Jungwirth-Becker, corres 1932) is
usually reckoned better for Black,
although Tartakower suggested 14
0-0 (Not 14 NxKP P-QN4!) 14...Q-K2
15 BxP "and White has by no means
shot his bolt". However, after
15...P-N4 Black should be able to
gradually unravel his position.
c2) 12 BxN? PxB 13 PxP (nor 13 0-0

R-KN1+) 13...0-0 14 PxP BxP 15 0-0
Q-K2 etc. — Tartakower
c3) 12 0-0 ("Comparatively best," in
Keres' opinion) 12...0-0∓.

9	O—O	B—N3
10	P—R5!	NxP
11	RxN	BxR
12	P—K5	P—Q4

If 12...N-R3 White intended 13
R-K1 0-0 14 P-K6 Q-B3 15 BxN PxB
16 NxP Q-N3 17 P-K7 QxP 18
PxR=Q+.

13	BxP	P—QB3
14	B—QB4	Q-B2
15	P—K6	P—B3

16 NxP N-K2 17 B-R3 P-KN3 18
QN-Q2 0-0 19 N-K4 K-N2 (C.H.O'D.
Alexander-F. Alexander, British Ch
1932) and now instead of 20 R-Q1?
R-Q1 (But 1-0, 35 after further errors)
White could have played 20 B-Q6
Q-Q1 21 R-Q1 with a tremendous
bind on the position.

D62:

8   O—O*(31)*

Better now than at move 7, since
the Black queen has been denied
KB3. Nonetheless it is rather too slow
for White to gain an advantage.

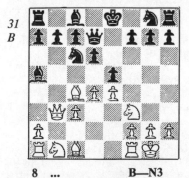

8   ...   B—N3
More consistent than:
a) 8...N-R3?! 9 BxN PxB 10 PxP PxP
11 R-Q1 Q-K2 12 B-N5 B-Q2 13
R-Q5! B-N3 14 QN-Q2 0-0-0 15 N-B4
B-K3 16 BxN PxB 17 RxP Q-B3 18
NxB+ BPxN 19 Q-R4 K-N2 20
R-QB5! B-Q2 21 N-K5 PxR 22
R-N1+ K-B2 23 N-B4 R-R1 24
Q-R5+ K-B1 25 P-K5! B-B4 26
Q-R6+ K-Q2 27 Q-N7+ K-Q1 28
PxQ 1-0 Vermeulen-Akohangas, 1948
(from *Schach-Echo* 1972).
b) 8...PxP transposing to Waller's
Attack (Chap. 6A) which is±.
c) 8...N-B3?! 9 PxP KNxP 10 R-K1
N-B4 11 PxP+ K-B1 12 Q-R3 QxP 13
QN-Q2 N-K3 14 Q-N3 N-B4 15 Q-B2
N-K3 16 N-K4± Thomas-Harris,
British Ch. 1950.

9   B—QN5?!

9 PxP PxP transposes to D6314. In
a 1963 USSR student game Litvinov-
Golenishev, there occurred instead
9...N-R4 10 Q-N5 NxB 11 QxN PxP
12 NxP (12 B-R3!? P-KB3) 12...Q-K3!
13 Q-R4+ P-B3 14 N-B3 N-K2 15
QN-Q2 0-0 16 B-R3 R-K1 17 P-K5
Q-N5 18 QxQ and the game was
drawn in 30 moves.

9   ...   P—QR3
10   B—R4

Or 10 BxN QxB 11 PxP when:
a) 11...PxP 12 NxP Q-K3 13 Q-R4+
P-B3 14 N-B4 B-B2 15 N-K3 N-B3?
16 B-R3! Wurtzburger-N.N., Germany 1934
b) 11...B-K3! 12 Q-B2 0-0-0∓ —
Sovremenny Debyut.

10   ...   B—R2
To meet 11 P-Q5 by 11...P-QN4 12
PxN QxP etc.

11	Q—Q1	P—QN4
12	B—N3	N—B3
13	P—QR4	B—N2

14 RPxP RPxP 15 B-R3 B-N3 16
QN-Q2 Q-N5 17 P-R3 Q-R4 18 Q-B2
PxP (Black's only problem is achiev-
ing castling) 19 P-K5 P-Q6! 20 QxP
PxP 21 KR-K1 P-N5! 22 PxP 0-0 23
P-N5 KR-Q1 24 Q-B1 N-Q5 (0-1, 31)
Spielmann-Salwe, Vienna 1908

D63:

8 PxP

Now Black has:

D631: 8...PxP

D632: 8...B-N3

8...NxP? 9 NxN PxN 10 BxP+ QxB 11 Q-N5+ B-Q2 when:

1) 12 QxKP+?! N-K2 13 QxB 0-0 14 0-0 (14 P-B3!?) is somewhat risky.

b) 12 QxB! Q-B3 (Or 12...Q-N3 13 QxKP+ N-K2 14 B-N5) 13 QxBP N-K2 14 0-0± — Cafferty.

D631:

8 ... PxP(32)

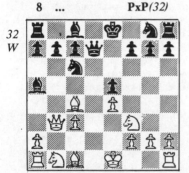

32
W

White can try here:

D6311: 9 P-QR4

D6312: 9 B-R3 B-N3 10 0-0

D6313: 9 B-R3 B-N3 10 QN-Q2

D6314: 9 0-0! B-N3 10 R-Q1!

D6311:

9 P-QR4

Little-explored but probably not strong. Black has:

a) 9...Q-K2 10 0-0 P-QR3 (10...B-Q2! — Morry) 11 R-Q1 B-N3 12 P-R5! BxP 13 RxB NxR 14 BxP+ QxB (14...K-B1 15 Q-R2!) 15 R-Q8+ K-K2 16 Q-Q1! (1-0, 49 after mutual errors), Morry-Wormald, corres 1942. This game is annotated in great depth in Morry's book *Chess — a Way to Learn*.

b) 9...B-N3 10 P-R5 B-B4 11 B-QN5 B-Q3 12 P-B4 Q-K2 13 Q-R4 B-Q2 14 P-R6 N-Q1 15 N-B3 PxP 16 QxP B-QN5 17 B-Q2 BxN 18 BxB P-KB3 19 BxB+ QxB 20 R-Q1 Q-K2 21 0-0 N-R3 22 Q-R4+ P-B3 23 B-N4 Q-K3 24 B-R3 N3-B2 25 N-R4 P-N3 26 P-B4 PxP 27 KR-K1 P-QR4 28 N-B5 R-KN1 29 N-Q6+ NxN 30 RxN Q-B2 31 P-K5 Q-R2+ 32 K-R1 PxP 33 RxP+ K-B2 34 P-B5 R-KB1 35 Q-Q4 K-N1 36 R-Q7 Q-R3 37 R-K1 N-B2 38 B-N2 1-0 Crown-Lipton (from *Chess*, 1947)

c) 9...N-B3! 10 B-R3 NxP 11 0-0 N-Q3 and 12...0-0 — Larry Evans

D6312:

9 B—R3 B—N3

10 0—0(33)

Also worth considering is 10 B-N5 (10 QN-Q2 see D6313) 10...P-B3 11 0-0 e.g. 11...N-R3 12 P-B4 B-Q5 13 N-B3 BxN 14 QxB Q-K3 15 N-Q2 B-Q2 16 N-N3 P-QN3 17 P-B5! with an excellent game for White, Kurkin-Korchaga, corres. 1964-5.

33
B

10 ... N—R4

10...N-R3!? has not yet been refuted. A game Hasek-E. Richter, Prague Teams Ch 1949, continued 11 R-Q1 Q-N5 12 B-N5 P-B3 13 P-R3?! (Better 13 BxN+ PxB 14 QN-Q2) 13...QxKP 14 B-Q3 Q-B5 15 Q-Q5 BxP 16 B-B5 Q-N6! and Black won quickly.

11 NxP!

An ingenious pseudo-sacrifice of

the queen, apparently first proposed by Levenfish.

| 11 | ... | NxQ |
| 12 | PxN | Q—K3 |

"12...N-B3 is also a thoroughly feasible move" — Keres, 1952.

13 BxQ   BxB

Keres said: "It is not at all clear why Black's position, with the two bishops and no pawn weaknesses, can be held to be bad". Yet when the line was tried in practice, White got the initiative; perhaps the disparity of strength between the players was the cause? We give the game complete so readers may judge for themselves:

Honfi-Czaszar, corres 1955-8:- 14 N-Q2 N-B3 (Euwe's 14...P-QR3 would be critical.) 15 KR-K1 N-Q2 (15...0-0-0 16 N2-B4 BxN would give up the advantages of which Keres boasted.) 16 NxN KxN 17 P-QB4 P-QB4 18 P-B4 K-B3 19 P-B5 B-Q2 20 B-N2 P-B3 21 P-KN4 B-B2 22 N-B3 KR-K1 23 QR-Q1 R-K2 24 R-Q5 QR-K1 (Better 24...P-QR4, although White retains his aggressive K-side pawn majority.) 25 P-N4! P-QN3 26 PxP (26 P-N5+ K-N2 27 P-N5 is also promising.) 26...PxP 27 P-K5 PxP 28 B-R3 K-N2 29 BxP B-B3 30 BxR BxR 31 PxB RxB 32 N-N5! P-KR3 33 N-K6 B-Q3 34 R-N1+ K-B1 35 R-QB1+ K-Q2 36 R-R1 K-K1 37 R-R6 R-Q2 38 P-R4! B-B2 (38...B-N1 39 R-B6) 39 K-N2 B-Q1 40 P-N5 PxP 41 PxP P-K5 (41...RxP!?) 42 P-N6! B-B3 43 P-Q6 B-K4 44 N-B7+ K-Q1 45 RxP K-B1 (45...RxP and 45...BxP also lose.) 46 R-R8+ K-N2 47 R-K8 B-Q3 48 N-K6 B-N5 49 P-B6! R-Q7+ 50 K-R3 PxP 51 P-N7 B-Q3 52 P-N8=Q R-KR7+ 53 K-N4 1-0.

D6313:

| 9 | B—R3 | B—N3 |
| 10 | QN—Q2 | N—R4*(34)* |

34
W

11 Q—N4

Also possible is 11 NxP!? NxQ 12 PxN as in the previous section. Not then 12...BxP+!? since after 13 K-K2 B-R5 14 N2-B3 B-B3 15 NxQ BxN 16 P-K5 B-K2 17 N-Q4 White had good play for the pawn, and went on to win in 46 moves; Estrin-Skrovina, USSR v. Czechoslovakia corres 1959-60.

11 ...   P—QB4!?

Black can get equality with 11...Q-K2!, e.g. 12 NxP (12 Q-N2 Q-B3! or 12 QxQ+) 12...NxB 13 N5xN QxQ 14 PxQ B-Q5 15 B-N2!? BxB 16 NxB B-K3 17 0-0 0-0-0 18 KR-Q1 R-Q5 19 P-QR3 N-K2 with the better ending for Black; Krimer-Vistanetzkis, Lithuanian Ch 1956.

| 12 | Q—N2 | NxB |
| 13 | NxN | Q—Q6? |

Possibly Black can do a little better with:

a) 13...P-B3 14 R-Q1 Q-B3 15 N-Q6+± Sokolsky-Shumakher, 2 USSR Corres. Ch 1954

b) 13...B-B2 14 N4xP Q-R5 15 BxP — Clarke

c) 13...Q-K3!?

| 14 | N3xP | QxKP+ |
| 15 | K—B1! | |

White's threats of N-Q6+, or R-K1 or Q-N5+ give him a decisive advantage. The game Hachaturov-Bykhovsky, Moscow 1955, ended: 15...Q-Q4 16 Q-N3! Q-K3 17 R-K1 N-K2 18 NxP KxN 19 N-Q6+ K-B3

20 RxQ+ BxR.21 N-K4+ K-K4 22
P-KB4+ K-B4 23 P-N4+ KxN 24
Q-K6+ K-B6 25 Q-K2 mate.

D6314:

9	0—0!	B—N3
10	R—Q1!*(35)*	

This is better than 10 B-R3 of
D6312, or 10 B-QN5 Q-K3 11 QxQ+
BxQ 12 BxN+ PxB 13 NxP N-K2 of
a postal game Duhrssen-Keres, 1935.

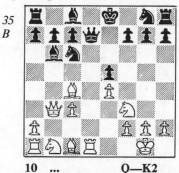

35
B

10 ... Q—K2

As so often, 10...N-R4 is met by 11
BxP+! and after 11...K-B1! (11...
QxB? 12 R-Q8+ K-K2 13 B-N5+) 12
Q-B2! Black can only try 12...Q-K2,
in view of the mating net after
12...QxB? 13 R-Q8+ K-K2 14 B-N5+
K-K3 (14...N-B3 15 RxR) 15 Q-Q2.
Note, however, that 12 RxQ NxQ 13
R-Q8+ is not convincing, in view of
13...KxB! 14 PxN P-B3! driving the
rook from the back rank — analysis.

11 P—QR4

Also interesting are:
a) 11 R-Q5!? P-QR3 12 QN-Q2 Q-B3
13 N-B1 B-K3 (Lisitsin-Rabinovich,
Leningrad 1940) 14 N-N3! KN-K2 15
B-KN5 Q-N3 16 BxN! and Black still
has troubles — Fine.
b) 11 B-R3 Q-B3 12 B-N5 (12 QN-Q2
KN-K2 and ...B-K3 — Keres) 12...
KN-K2 13 QN-Q2 B-N5 14 P-R3
P-KR4 15 P-B4 0-0-0 is unclear;
Contedini-Durao, Leipzig 1960.

11 ... P—QR3

Also critical:
1) 11...N-R3 (11...N-B3 12 B-R3) 12
P-R5! BxRP (12...B-QB4 13 P-R6!)
13 B-R3 Q-B3 14 B-N5 B-Q2 15 P-B4
with excellent attacking chances —
Keres.
b) 11...N-R4? again fails to 12 BxP+:
b1) 12...QxB 13 R-Q8+ K-K2 14
B-N5+ N-B3 15 QxQ+ etc.
b2) 12...K-B1 13 Q-R2 N-B3 14 B-R3
P-B4 15 B-Q5 B-N5 16 QN-Q2± —
Shaposnikov in *Shakhmaty v SSSR*
1959/2.
c) 11...B-K3 12 P-R5 BxB (12...NxP
13 RxN) 13 QxB Q-B4 (13...B-B4 14
R-Q5 B-Q3 15 P-R6) 14 Q-B1! NxP
15 R-Q5 e.g.:
c1) 15...QxP+ 16 QxQ BxQ+ 17
KxB N-N6 18 R-R3 — Aronin
c2) 15...Q-B5 16 RxP+ (16 QRxN —
Aronin) 16...N-K2 17 QRxN± Shapos-
nikov-Mezhgailis, USSR 1958
d) 11...P-QR4 12 B-Q5 B-N5? (12...
B-QB4 — Shaposnikov — 13 Q-B4!)
13 R-Q3 B-K3 (Or 13...0-0-0 14
QN-Q2 N-B3 15 N-B4 B-B4 16 R-N1!
— Evans) 14 B-R3 Q-B3 15 QN-Q2
KN-K2 16 N-B4 e.g. 16...R-R3 17
Q-N5 B-B1 18 N3xP 0-0 19 R-B3 QxN
20 BxP+ RxB 21 NxQ 1-0 Shapos-
nikov-Veltmander, RSFSR Ch 1958.
3) 11...B-B4 12 B-KN5?! (But 12
B-R3! — or perhaps 12 P-R5)
12...N-B3 13 B-Q5 0-0 14 P-R5
P-QR3 15 QN-Q2 N-Q1 and White
has failed to force concessions upon
his opponent; (0-1, 45) Yurkov-
Bykhovsky, Moscow Ch 1963.

12 P—R5 B—QB4

Not 12...BxRP 13 RxB NxR 14
BxP+ K-B1 15 Q-R2! etc.

13	B—R3	BxB
14	NxB	N—B3
15	B—Q5	N—Q1?

According to Euwe, Black can
defend by 15...0-0 e.g. 16 N-B4 (16
BxN!?) 16...B-Q2 17 N-K3 N-Q1 or 17
QxP? KR-N1 18 QxBP N-K1.

16	N—B4	0—0
17	N4xP	N—K3
18	QR—N1	N—B4

19 Q-R3 R-N1 20 N-N5 QxN 21 QxN NxB 22 RxN Q-B3? (22...Q-K1±) 23 NxRP 1-0 Sokolov-Sepp, USSR-Switzerland corres 1959-60.

These complicated analyses show that, although an advantage for White cannot be guaranteed, he has various ways of obtaining a promising game after 8...PxP. Consequently Black often makes no attempt to hold his pawn, preferring to obtain the two bishops.

D632:

| 8 | ... | B—N3*(36)* |

The continuation recommended by Euwe. 9...N-R4 is immediately threatened, and cannot be circumvented by a queen sacrifice here.

36
W

White can try:
D6321: 9 B-QN5!?
D6322: 9 B-Q5?!
D6323: 9 Q-B2?!
D6324: 9 PxP
D6325: 9 QN-Q2!

The 'also-rans' in brief:
1) 9 B-R3 N-R4 etc.

b) 9 0-0 N-R4 (9...PxP D6314) 10 Q-N4 NxB 11 QxN PxP 12 NxP Q-K3 with good play for Black — Keres.

D6321:

| 9 | B—QN5!? |

Recommended by Levenfish in *Sovremenny Debyut*

| 9 | ... | KN—K2 |

Or 9...P-QR3 when:
a) 10 Q-R4 KN-K2 (10...R-N1!) 11 PxP PxP 12 0-0 R-QN1 13 B-K2 0-0 14 Q-N3± Wade-Woolverton, Southend 1958
b) 10 B-R4 and now:
b1) 10...B-B4 11 P-B4 KN-K2 12 0-0 0-0 13 N-B3 Q-Q1 14 PxP PxP 15 N-Q5 NxN 16 KPxN N-Q5 (16...N-R4 17 Q-B3 and 18 B-N2) 17 NxN BxN 18 B-N2± — a 1902 Russian analysis quoted by Levenfish.
b2) 10...Q-K3 (Keres) 11 BxN+! PxP 12 0-0 R-N1! (Chandon-Moet v. Bottlik, corres 1974) 13 QxQ+! PxQ (13...BxQ 14 B-R3!±) 14 PxP PxP 15 B-R3± — Bottlik

| 10 | 0—0 |

Others:
a) 10 B-R3? Q-N5 11 0-0 N-N3 12 P-R3 Q-R4 13 N-Q4 BxP! 0-1 Renaud-G. Wood, ½-final 1 World Corres Ch 1947-8
b) 10 PxP PxP 11 0-0 0-0 12 R-Q1 Q-N5 13 B-R3 B-K3 = Wade-G. Wood, Nottingham 1946

10	...	Q—N5!
11	PxP	PxP
12	B—R3	B—K3

13 Q-R4 0-0-0 14 QN-Q2 Q-N3 15 KR-N1∓ Cafferty-Marriott, corres 1956-7.

D6322:

| 9 | B—Q5?! |

This is rare. Ciocaltea-Pogats, Debreczen 1961, continued 9...N-R4 10 Q-B2 P-B3 11 B-N3 NxB 12 PxN PxP 13 NxP Q-K3 14 N-B4 B-B2 15 0-0 N-K2 16 P-B4 Q-R3 17 Q-KB2 0-0 18 B-K3 B-K3 and Black won.

D6323:

9	Q—B2?!	PxP
10	B—R3	KN—K2
11	QN—Q2	0—0
12	B—N3	K—R1
13	0—0	P—B3
14	QR—Q1	Q—K1

Ragozin-Mikenas, ½-final 23 USSR Ch 1956. Black has an impregnable position, which can be freed gradually by exchanges and careful manoeuvring to exploit the material advantage.

D6324:

9	PxP	N—R4
10	Q—N4	NxB
11	QxN	QxP*(37)*

37
W

12 B—R3

Or 12 P-QR4 B-K3 13 Q-K2 0-0-0 14 P-R5 B-QB4 15 N-Q4 P-QR3 16 B-K3 N-K2 17 N-Q2 B-Q2 18 N2-N3 B-R2 19 0-0 P-QB4, eventually drawn in Levin-Zamikhovsky, Ukraine Ch 1959. This may be White's best idea, to keep the queens on.

12 ... B—K3

Better than 12...Q-N3 13 Q-N4! P-QB4 14 Q-R4+ B-Q2 15 QxB+ KxQ 16 N-K5+.

13 Q—K2

Improving upon 13 Q-N5+ Q-Q2 14 Q-N4 P-QB4 15 Q-N2 Q-Q6 16 QN-Q2 0-0-0 of Mnatsakanyan-Korelov, USSR Ch 1962.

13 ... Q—B3

According to Unsicker, 13...Q-Q2! is correct.

14	N—Q4!	Q—B5
15	NxB	QxQ+
16	KxQ	PxN=

(½-½, 31) Pfleger-Unzicker, 1st match game, 1963.

D6325:

9 QN—Q2!

Now if Black carries out his main idea of eliminating White's two bishops, he is subjected to an embarassing attack from the knights instead.

9 ... N—R4*(38)*

Black has also tried:

a) 9...PxP 10 B-R3 when:

a1) 10...N-R4 see D6312, note to White's 10th move.

a2) 10...N-R3?! 11 0-0 P-B3 12 QR-Q1 N-R4 13 Q-N4 NxB 14 NxN Q-K3 15 R-Q5 B-Q1 16 N-N5! P-R4 17 NxQ PxQ 18 NxNP+ K-Q1 19 BxP K-B1 20 KR-Q1 B-B3 21 R5-Q2 BxKP 22 B-K7± and White won, Agrinsky-Veltmander, Rostov 1961.

b) 9...N-R3 10 0-0 0-0 11 PxP (11 B-R3!) 11...QxP 12 B-Q5 N-R4 13 Q-N4 Q-N3 14 N-K5 Q-R4 15 N2-B3 P-B3 16 B-R3?! (Better simply 16 B-N3) 16...R-K1 17 B-N3 P-QB4 (17...NxB!? first) 18 Q-N5 RxN 19 NxR QxN 20 B-Q5 (Or 20 QR-Q1!? threatening 21 QxB) 20...P-B5? (20...Q-K2 was essential.) 21 B-N4! B-K3 22 BxN N-N5 23 P-N3 B/K3xB 24 PxB BxP+ 25 RxB NxR 26 KxN Q-B4+ 27 K-N1 1-0 Alexander-Tylor, Hastings 1935-6.

See diagram next page

10 Q—B2!

Others:

a) 10 Q-R3 NxB 11 NxN when Black is all right after either:

a1) 11...B-B4 12 Q-N3 N-K2 13 0-0 0-0 14 PxP PxP (Cafferty-Hoogendoorn, Hastings Challengers 1966-7);

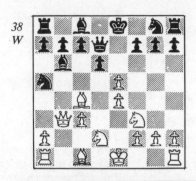

Best now would be 15 B-R3!
a2) 11...PxP 12 N3xP Q-K3 13
Q-R4+ B-Q2 14 N5xB QxN 16 NxB
BPxN 16 Q-N4 N-K2∓ see the note to
White's 13th move, below.
b) 10 Q-N4 N-K2 11 PxP N2-B3 12
Q-R4 0-0 13 B-R3 PxP 14 0-0 B-B4 15
QR-Q1 P-QR3 16 BxB PxB 17 Q-B2
NxB (½-½, 30) Maeder-Zuidema,
Amsterdam 1969

10 ...   NxB
Others:
a) 10...N-K2? 11 BxP+! KxB 12
P-K6+ KxP 13 N-N5+ K-B3 14
P-K5+! PxP (14...KxN 15 N-B3 K-R4
16 P-R3!) 15 N2-K4+ K-N3 16 N-B3
N4-B3 (Or 16...Q-Q4 17 P-B4! NxP 18
N-B3+ B-KB4 19 N-KR4+ etc.) 17
N-B5+ Q-B4 18 N-KR4+ 1-0 Barker-
Marshall, English qualifying tournament, World Junior Ch 1951.
b) 10...N-R3!? was a contemporary
suggestion, as yet untested. White
could try 11 0-0 (11 B-Q3 N-N5!)
11...0-0 12 B-Q3 — Cafferty.

11 NxN   PxP
An untried line here is 11...Q-K3 12
Q-N3 when there could follow,
according to our analysis:
1) 12...PxP 13 N-N5 Q-KB3 14
NxKP!
b) 12...N-K2 13 N-N5 Q-Q2 14 PxP
PxP 15 NxQP+! QxN 16 QxP+ followed by 17 B-B4 and 18 R-Q1 with a
promising attack for the piece.

Or 11...Q-B3!? 12 NxB RPxN 13
0-0 with a slight lead in development
for White.

12 N3xP   Q—K3
13 B—R3!
A significant improvement upon
the course of the game Sokolsky-
Korelov, Sverdlovsk 1943, which went
13 Q-R4+ B-Q2 14 N5xB QxN 15
NxB BPxN 16 Q-N4 N-K2 17 B-R3
N-B3 18 Q-B4 0-0-0 19 0-0 KR-K1∓
and was won by Black in 58 moves.
One of the main ideas of the new
move is to prepare Q-side castling;
the queen check is held in reserve
while the central tension can be built
up. The whole variation needs more
practical tests, but we believe White's
chances to be excellent.

13 ...   N—B3!?
Possibly stronger are:
a) 13...B-Q2 14 Q-N3 N-K2 (14...
0-0-0? 15 NxP!) 15 N5xB QxN 16
N-K5 Q-K3 17 QxQ PxQ 18 0-0-0
threatening 19 R-Q7
b) 13...N-K2 14 Q-R4+ B-Q2 15
N5xB QxN 16 NxB BPxN 17 QxQ+
KxQ 18 0-0-0+ K-K1 19 BxN KxB 20
R-Q3 with an endgame strategy
similar to that in the Exchange
Variation of the Ruy Lopez!

14 0—0—0!
In the game Cafferty-Clarke,
British Ch 1970, the less convincing
move 14 P-B4!? was played. There
followed 14...N-Q2! 15 R-Q1 NxN 16
NxN P-QB3 17 R-Q6 Q-K2 18 N-B4
Q-R5+ 19 P-N3 Q-R6 20 R-Q2 B-B2
21 Q-Q3 B-Q2 22 B-Q6 0-0-0 23 BxB
KxB 24 Q-Q6+ ½-½, though White's
position is still slightly better.

14 ...   B—Q2
If 14...N-Q2 15 R-Q5! meeting
15...P-QB3 by 16 N-Q6+, or
15...K-Q1 by 16 KR-Q1, or 15...
P-KB3 by 16 N-Q3 and 17 N-B4 —
analysis.

15 Q—N3!

Ruling out castling, while a threat is P-B4-5 netting the queen. After this Anderssen-style preparatory move, Black has no constructive plan.

15 ... R—Q1

To be free to move the knight in reply to 16 P-B4. Not 15...0-0-0? 16 NxP!, nor 15...BxP 16 QxP R-Q1 17 QxBP.

16 R—Q6!! *(39)*

39
B

16 ... PxR
17 NxQP+ K—B1
Of course not 17...K-K2? 18 N-B5+ K-K1 19 NxNP mate.

18 N6xBP+!

Black is lost, whichever way he goes:

a) 18...K-N1 19 NxQR BxN (Or first 19...QxQ 20 PxQ) 20 R-Q1 QxQ 21 PxQ:

a1) 21...NxP? 22 RxB B-N4+ 23 P-KB4! BxP+ 24 K-B2 P-KR3 25 N-N6 and White wins.

a2) 21...B-N3 22 NxB NxP? 23 NxB and 24 R-Q8+

a3) 21...B-B2 22 NxB NxP 23 R-K1 B-Q3 24 BxB NxB 25 R-K6!

b) 18...K-K1 19 N-Q6+ K-B1 20 NxB+! when:

b1) 20...QxN 21 N-B5+ K-K1 22 NxP+ QxN 23 Q-K6+ and mates.

b2) 20...K-K2 21 NxP+ KxN (21...K-B2 22 N-K5+ wins the Black queen!) 22 R-Q1+ K-B2 (22...N-Q4 23 QxN+ with three pawns up in an ending!) 23 QxQ RxR+ 24 KxR KxN 25 Q-K7+ and White must win.

This elegant line, from White's sixteenth move onward, is an original analysis by Bernard Cafferty, first published in *The Guardian* in November 1970.

4 Lasker's Defence and Allied Lines

In this chapter we look at more lines in which Black attempts a positional refutation of the Evans. They have it in common with the Conservative Defence of the previous chapter, that Black does not capture White's QP. Although White can avoid the lines of this chapter by 6 P-Q4, they have great historical significance, and their possibility (especially that of the Lasker Defence) plays an important role in determining White's early choices.

After **1 P-K4 P-K4 2 N-KB3 N-QB3 3 B-B4 B-B4 4 P-QN4 BxNP 5 P-B3 B-R4,** Chigorin used always to play:

6 0—0

His object in employing this order was to avoid the Compromised Defence. However that defence is too risky for the taste of most masters (it was even in the nineteenth century!) and is certainly less to be feared than Lasker's Defence.

6 ... P—Q3

For 6...B-N3 7 P-Q4 P-Q3 see D below.

Other replies are discussed in Chapter 7, B.

7 P—Q4 *(40)*

40
B

Now Black can play:

A: 7...N-B3
B: 7...B-KN5
C: 7...B-Q2
D: 7...B-N3!

7...PxP 8 PxP B-N3 see chapters 8-10.

A:

7 ... N—B3
8 Q—R4 PxP

This is risky, but if 8...P-QR3:

a) 9 B-Q5! B-N3 10 PxP N-KN5 (Or 10...PxP 11 R-Q1 B-Q2 12 BxN PxB 13 NxP — *Handbuch*) 11 PxP B-Q2 12 B-R3 N3-K4 13 Q-Q1 Q-B3 14 P-R3 P-KR4 15 Q-K2 and White emerges from the complications after 15...NxN+ 16 QxN QxQ 17 PxQ N-K4 with advantage (Unzicker), e.g. 18 P-KB4 retaining the extra pawn.

b) 9 P-Q5 is not so clear, as 9...P-QN4 10 BxNP PxB 11 QxP 0-0 (Better than the *Handbuch* line '11...R-QN1 12 QxN+ B-Q2 13 Q-R6 B-N3 14 Q-K2±.) 12 QxN B-R3 13 R-K1 B-Q6 may favour Black; Blackburne-Bloch, blindfold simul., 1878.

9 P—K5! N—Q2
10 BxP+!?

Richter and Teschner's openings book gives the simpler line, 10 B-KN5 P-B3 11 PxBP NxP 12 NxP!

10 ... KxB
11 N—N5+ K—K1
12 PxP PxP

13 R-K1+ N2-K4 14 P-KB4 PxP with an unclear position; Nielsen-Jensen, Copenhagen 1947.

B:

7 ... B—KN5 *(41)*

McDonnell's original defence, which has had very bad results in practice.

41
W

White has employed:
B1: 8 Q-N3
B2: 8 B-QN5
B3: 8 Q-R4!

B1:

8 Q—N3 BxN!

This is a major improvement upon the 8...Q-Q2 of Evans-McDonnell, for which see Chapter 1. 8...Q-B3 might be playable.

9 PxP!

Avoiding the blind alleys:
a) 9 QxP? BxKP 10 P-Q5 QN-K2 11 Q-N5+ P-QB3∓∓ — Marshall
b) 9 BxP+ K-B1 10 PxB B-N3 11 BxN RxB 12 P-Q5 N-R4 13 Q-B2 P-N4∓ — Levenfish

9	...	PxP
10	QxP	N—K4
11	K—R1	R—N1

12 Q-R6 NxB 13 QxN PxP 14 NxP BxN 15 QxB Q-B3 16 P-K5! PxP 17 R-K1 N-K2 18 RxP R-N4! 19 RxN+! KxR! 20 QxP+ K-K1 21 Q-B8+ Q-Q1 22 Q-B6+ Q-Q2 23 Q-R8+ ½-½ Santasiere-Marshall, New York 1926. This game is annotated in Marshall's book *My Fifty Years of Chess* (re-issued under the title *Marshall's Best Games of Chess*).

B2:

8	B—QN5	PxP
9	PxP	B—Q2
10	B—N2	

Later, in an 1899 Moscow simul. game, Chigorin tried 10 P-QR4 against one Isakov and the continuation was 10...N-B3? (Better 10... KN-K2) 11 P-K5 N-K5 12 Q-B2 P-Q4 13 B-R3 N-K2 14 B-Q3 P-KB4 15 PxPep NxP/B3 16 QN-Q2 BxN 17 NxB K-B2!? 18 N-B3 N-B3 19 KR-K1 P-KN3 20 N-K5+ and White won in about 30 moves.

10 ... N—B3

Freeborough and Ranken suggested 10...N-R3!?

The first game of the 1892 Chigorin-Steinitz match went instead **10...QN-K2?!** (hoping to gain relief by simplification) **11 BxB+ QxB 12 N-R3! N-R3 13 N-B4 B-N3 14 P-QR4! P-QB3** (14...P-R3 15 Q-N3! or 14... P-R4 15 NxB PxN 16 Q-N3 N-B1 17 P-Q5) **15 P-K5** (According to Chigorin, 15 P-Q5 was also promising) **15...P-Q4** (15...PxP 16 PxP! QxQ 17 QRxQ 0-0 18 R-Q7 or 15...B-B2 16 PxP BxP 17 NxB+ QxN 18 B-R3 and 19 R-K1) **16 N-Q6+ K-B1 17 B-R3 K-N1 18 R-N1 N3-B4** (18...R-N1 might be playable; but if 18...N-B1 Chigorin intended 19 P-R5! e.g. 19...NxN 20 PxN! BxRP 21 N-K5 Q-B1 22 P-Q7 Q-B2 23 Q-R5 B-N3 24 B-K7 etc. — Vasyukov & Nikitin.)

42

Emanual Lasker, in his *Manual of Chess*, suggested 19 P-R5 as a simple winning line now. Instead Chigorin played 19 NxBP!?, of which Lasker commented that even the most sympathetic critic would have to say that Chigorin fought with a corpse, gave him new life and then killed him again! The Russians of course have done their best to rebuff this sarcasm, notably in Vasyukov, Narkevich and Nikitin's 1973 work *Mikhail Chigorin*. The game continued:

19 NxBP! KxN 20 P-K6+ KxP 21 N-K5 Q-B1?! 22 R-K1 K-B3 23 Q-R5! P-N3 (23...N-N3 24 P-N4) **24 BxN+ KxB** (24...NxB 25 Q-R4+ P-N4 26 N-N4+ K-B2 27 QxNP) **25 NxNP+ K-B3 26 NxR BxP** (26...QxN 27 R-K5 Q-QB1 28 P-N4) **27 R-N3 Q-Q2 28 R-KB3 RxN 29 P-N4 R-KN1 30 Q-R6+ R-N3 31 RxN+ 1-0.**

Lasker said Steinitz should have played 21...Q-K1! 22 R-K1 K-B3 and pointed out that 23 P-N4 fails to 23...P-KR4 24 BxN+ QxB 25 PxN QR-K1 26 N-N4+ PxN 27 RxQ RxR 28 QxP R-R3 etc. However, following a suggestion by Bogoljubow in his rare 1926 work *Chigorin's Best Games*, G. Serzhanov analysed (in *Shakhmaty v SSSR* 3/1948) the winning line 23 BxN+! NxB (23...QxB 24 N-N4) 24 Q-B3+ K-K3 25 N-B7+ K-Q2 26 Q-N4+ K-B2 27 Q-B4+ K-Q2 28 Q-Q6+ K-B1 29 RxN etc. A posthumous Evans Gambit victory for Chigorin against Lasker!

However Steinitz found an improvement, playing 10...N-B3 in the 3rd, 5th and 13th games of the match. The 13th serves as the model for **Black:**

11	**N—R3**	**NxKP!**

11...0-0 led to draws in the other games.

12	**P—Q5**	**N—K2**
13	**Q—R4**	**B—B6!**

14	**QR—N1**	**BxB (0-1, 48)**

B3:

8   Q—R4!*(43)*

Introduced by Chigorin in the 15th game!

43 B

Steinitz tried:
B31: 8...PxP
B32: 8...BxN

B31:

8	**...**	**PxP**
9	**PxP**	**P—QR3**

Others:
1; 9...B-Q2? 10 P-Q5 N-K4 11 QxB NxB 12 Q-B3 Q-B3 13 QxN QxR 14 N-B3 P-QN4 15 Q-N3± – Pollock
b) 9...BxN 10 PxB see B32

10	**B—Q5**	**B—N3**
11	**BxN+**	**PxB**
12	**QxBP+**	**B—Q2**

13 Q-B3 N-K2 14 N-R3 0-0 15 N-B4 White has regained his pawn with central control and better piece coordination; (1-0, 47) Chigorin-Steinitz, 15th game, 1892.

B32:

8	**...**	**BxN**
9	**PxB**	**PxP**
10	**PxP**	

Chigorin later pointed out the possibility 10 B-QN5!? BxP 11 NxB PxN 12 BxN+ PxB 13 QxBP+ K-B1

14 QxP/B3 and if 14...Q-B3 15 Q-N3
QxR?! 16 B-N2.

10   ...   P—QR3

The critical line is 10...Q-B3!
when:

1) 11 P-Q5 QxR 12 PxN P-QN3 13
BxP+ K-B1 — Freeborough and
Ranken.

b) 11 B-QN5 QxBP 12 BxN+ PxB 13
N-Q2! BxN 14 QxP+ K-K2 15
QxBP+ K-K1! drawing (but not
15...K-K3? 16 P-Q5+ K-K4 17
B-N2+) — Chigorin.

After the move played, Black gets
into difficulties on the Q-side.
However as Pachman says in his *Open
Games,* this variation needs more
practical tests.

11   B—Q5   KN—K2
12   BxN+   NxB
13   P—Q5   P—QN4
14   Q—R3   N—Q5
15   QxB   Q—B3
16   Q—R3!

Not 16 N-B3 NxP+ 17 K-N2
N-R5+ 18 K-R3 Q-B6+ 19 KxN
P-R3 following Chigorin's notes in
Grekov's *M.I. Chigorin* (1948).

16   ...   N—B7

Chigorin also considered:

a) 16...N-K7+ 17 K-R1 NxB 18 RxN
QxR 19 N-B3

b) 16...P-N5 17 Q-Q3!? (If 17 Q-N2
not 17...NxP+?! 18 K-N2! but 17...
QxP=) 17...NxP+ 18 K-N2 N-R5+
19 K-R3 QxR (If 19...N-N3 20 P-K5
or 20 Q-QN3 Q-R5+ 21 K-N2) 20
KxN QxP 21 N-Q2! 0-0 22 Q-Q4.

After 16...N-B7 the 17th game con-
tinued **17 Q-Q3 NxR 18 Q-K2 0-0 19
B-N2 Q-R3 20 BxN QR-K1 21 K-R1
P-KB4 22 R-N1 R-B2 23 N-Q2 Q-R4
24 Q-Q3 P-N5 25 R-N3 P-R4 26
K-N2! Q-R5 27 PxP P-R5 28 N-K4
R-N1 29 N-N5 R2-B1 30 Q-K3 RxP
31 Q-K6+ K-R1 32 BxP+! KxB 33
Q-K7+ K-N3 34 N-K6+** with a
winning attack.

C:
Sanders-Alapin Defence

7   ...   B—Q2*(44)*

This defence was suggested by the
Rev. T.C. Sanders and then analysed
deeply by Alapin, who recommended
it to Steinitz (see Chapter 1). It leads
to interesting play but is not as solid
as Lasker's Defence.

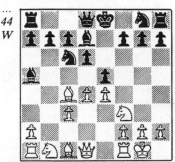

White now has a choice between:
C1: 8 N-N5
C2: 8 PxP
C3: 8 Q-N3

C1:
8   N—N5   N—R3
9   P—B4

Also playable is 9 P-Q5 N-K2 (—...
N-QN1 is also safe.) 10 N-K6! PxN 11
PxP B-B3 12 Q-R5+ N-N3 13 B-KN5
Q-B1 14 P-B4 (Fraser's 14 B-Q5
should be met by 14...BxB 15 PxB
N-B4, according to Ranken.) 14...PxP
and now:

a) 15 RxP when:

a1) A game Chigorin-N.N., St Petersburg 1892, continued 15...P-N4 16
BxN KNPxB 17 R-B6 B-N3+ 18
K-R1 PxB? 19 RxN PxR and White
announced mate in 5.

a2) Freeborough and Ranken recommend 15...B-N3+! 16 K-R1 B-K6,
which seems to be a defence.

b) 15 BxP P-N4 16 BxN (Ranken
refutes alternatives.) 16...KNPxB but

now instead of Ranken's 17 B-N3
Q-Q1 White plays 17 R-B6! reaching
a1. The critical question whether after
18...R-KN1 (Instead of 18...PxB)
White can find a way of continuing
the attack? For example, 19 P-K7!? is
not clear after 19...KxP 20 R-K6+
K-Q1 — analysis.

9	...	PxQP
10	P—K5?	0—0

10...PxP?! 11 B-R3 catches the
king in the centre.

11	P—K6	BxKP

Not 11...PxKP? 12 Q-Q3 P-KN3
(12...N-B4 13 NxKP) 13 Q-R3 K-N2
14 BxP± — Freeborough and
Ranken.

12	BxB	PxB
13	NxKP	Q—B3
14	NxR	RxN

Black has completed his mobili-
zation first and has two pawns for the
exchange. There could follow:
a) 15 PxP? NxP 16 B-N2 B-N3 17
K-R1 N3-B4 18 Q-Q3 N-K7!! 19 BxQ
N4-N6+ and Black won in a
Chigorin-Alapin game; after 20 PxN
RxB 21 P-N4 R-R3+ 22 Q-KR3
N-N6+ 23 K-R2 NxR+ 24 K-R1
RxQ+ 25 PxR B-Q5 Black emerges
two pawns up.
b) 15 Q-N3+ K-R1 16 QxP N-Q1 17
Q-N5 B-N3 18 Q-Q3 PxP+ 19 B-K3
P-B7 was a contemporary analysis in
The Field.
c) 15 B-N2 and if 15...PxP 16 Q-N3+
and 17 NxP seems more to the point.
The position then offers chances to
both sides.

C2:

8	PxP	PxP(45)

If 8...NxP, an old analysis runs 9
NxN PxN 10 Q-R5 Q-B3 (10...Q-K2 is
the same.) 11 BxP+ QxB 12 QxKP+
Q-K2 13 QxB QxP 14 N-Q2 Q-B3 15
N-B3±.

9	QN—Q2!

This was analysed by the Russian
master Hardin in 1893. For other
moves we follow Freeborough and
Ranken:
a) 9 Q-N3 Q-K2 see C32 below.
b) 9 Q-Q5 when:
b1) 9...Q-B3? 10 B-KN5 Q-K2 11
Q-N5 Q-Q3 12 Q-N3 (Or 12 B-Q5
B-Q2 13 R-Q1). 12...Q-N3 13 R-Q1
B-B1 (13...B-KN5 14 BxP+ QxB 15
QxP) 14 NxP QxB 15 NxP Q-K2 16
NxR±
b2) 9...Q-K2 10 B-R3 Q-B3 11 B-N5
B-N3 12 N-Q2 (12 BxN leads
nowhere.) 12...KN-K2 13 Q-N3 0-0-0
14 N-B4=.

9	...	Q—B3!

Hardin also considered:
a) 9...Q-K2 10 B-Q5 when:
a1) 10...N-B3 11 N-B4 B-N3 12 B-R3
B-QB4 13 BxB QxB 14 N4xP±.
a2) 10...BxP 11 R-N1 N-Q1 12 N-B4
P-KR3 13 B-R3 Q-B3 14 Q-N3 B-Q5
15 NxB PxN 16 P-K5 Q-N3 17 Q-N4±.
b) 9...BxP 10 BxP+ KxB 11 Q-N3+
B-K3 12 QxB/B3 Q-B3 13 N-B4 BxN
14 QxB+ K-B1 15 R-N1 P-QN3 16
B-N5 Q-N3 17 KR-B1 KN-K2 18
BxN+ NxB 19 NxP Q-R4 20 QxP±.

10	B—Q5	KN—K2

Or 10...BxP 11 R-N1 when:
a) 11...N-Q1 12 N-B4 P-QB3 (12...
N-K2 13 B-N5 Q-N3 14 Q-Q3 B-Q5
15 BxN KxB 16 BxNP) 13 B-R3 PxB
14 N-Q6+ K-B1 15 PxP N-K2 16

N-K4 Q-N3 17 NxB B-N5 18 NxP BxQ 19 NxQ RPxN 20 QR-Q1± — Hardin.

vb) 11...BxN 12 QxB (Hardin gave 12 NxB N-Q1 13 N-B4 P-QB3 14 B-R3!±) 12...R-N1 (12...N-Q1!?) 13 N-N5 N-R3 14 B-R3 Q-B5 15 QxQ PxQ 16 KR-B1 P-B3 17 RxN! PxN (17...BxR 18 BxB+ K-Q1 19 R-Q1+ K-B1 20 B-Q7+ K-Q1 21 N-K6 mate) 18 RxBP N-N5 19 R1xP RxR 20 RxR K-Q1 21 RxP and White won; Ljundqvist-Kjellander, 2 World Corres Ch 1956-59.

11 Q—N3   0—0
12 N—B4

Keres's 1955 German work on open games commented: "with a sharp and approximately equal game". Levenfish gave the continuation 12...P-KR3 13 P-QR4 B-N3 14 B-R3 (14 P-R5?! B-QB4 15 BxN NxB 16 QxP KR-B1!) 14...N-R4 15 NxN BxN 16 BxN QxB 17 QxP P-R3! 18 KR-K1! KR-N1 19 QxQR RxQ 20 BxR BxBP 21 QR-N1. Clearly, all these lines need further investigation, but are unlikely to receive it.

C3:
8 Q—N3*(46)*

The move most commonly employed at this point by Chigorin.

46
B

Black can try:
C31: 8...Q-B3
C32: 8...Q-K2

C31:
8 ...   Q—B3
9 PxP   PxP
10 R—Q1   P—KR3
11 B—R3

"With an attack for White" — Pachman. Regaining the pawn by 11 BxBP+ QxB 12 QxQ+ KxQ 13 RxB+ gives no advantage after 13...KN-K2:
a) Alapin recommended 14 R-Q1 QR-Q1 15 B-Q2 'with chances for White to draw'.
b) The ninth Chigorin-Steinitz match game, 1892, went 14 K-B1 K-K3 15 R-Q3 QR-Q1 16 N-K1 N-B1 17 K-K2 N-Q3 18 P-B3 P-QN4= (½-½, 34).

11 ...   R—Q1
12 QN—Q2   B—N3
13 B—Q5   N—R4?

Steinitz later pointed out, in *Deutsche Schachzeitung*, that he should have played 13...KN-K2. There could follow 14 N-B4 0-0 15 BxN/B6 BxB 16 N3xP and not now 16...BxKP? because of 17 N-Q7 Q-B3 18 N3-K5 etc — analysis. After the move played, White can regain his pawn without such a blunting of his initiative.

The seventh Chigorin-Steinitz 1892 game continued 14 Q-N4 P-B4 15 Q-N2 N-K2 16 N-N3 NxN (16...B-R5 17 NxN!) 17 QxN 0-0 18 BxNP N-N3 19 P-B4 N-N5 20 Q-K3 B-N5 21 B-Q5 KR-K1 (21...N-R6+ 22 K-B1 N-N4 23 NxN! BxR 24 NxP RxN 25 RxB K-R1 26 BxP may favour White; Steinitz probably should have played this nonetheless.) 22 B-N2 R-Q3 23 R-Q2! NxP?? (23...N-R6+ 24 PxN! BxN 25 R-Q3 B-KR4 is better, but does not shake White's central grip.) 24 KxN BxN+ 25 QxB Q-N4+ 26 K-R1 QxR 27 QxP+ K-R2 28 R-KN1 1-0. The tension of World Championship matches seems to breed such blunders.

C32:

8 ... Q—K2
9 PxP *(47)*

Others:

a) 9 QxP? R-N1 10 Q-R6 R-N3 winning the queen.

b) 9 B-R3 (suggested by Otto) when:

b1) In *Shakhmaty,* 1893, Chigorin gave a long analysis of which the main line ran 9...PxP 10 PxP QxP 11 BxP+ K-B1 12 BxN RxB 13 QN-Q2 BxN 14 QxP R-Q1 15 NxB QxQP 16 QxBP! QxN 17 QR-Q1 Q-R4 18 QxP+ K-B2 19 R-Q5 Q-R5 20 R-K1 P-KR3 21 R-K3 B-N5 22 R-KB3+ BxR 23 R-B5+ K-K1 24 R-K5+ NxR 25 Q-K6 mate. Further details can be found in Romanov's 'Tvorcheskoye Naslediye M.I. Chigorina' (*Creative Heritage of Chigorin,* 1956) p. 372.

b2) 9...N-R3! is better:

b21) 10 B-N5 0-0 11 Q-R4 B-N3 12 NxP NxN 13 PxN BxB 14 QxB N-N5! and if 15 PxP? Q-R5 16 P-R3 BxP+ 17 K-R1 Q-N6‡‡— Alapin, 1893

b22) 10 PxP NxP 11 NxN QxN 12 QxP? (12 P-B4 Q-R4) 12...N-N5! 13 P-B4 B-N3+ 14 K-R1 Q-KR4 15 P-R3 Q-R5!? 16 QxR+ K-K2 17 Q-Q5 Q-N6 18 Q-KN5+ P-B3 19 QxNP+ K-Q1 20 QxR+ B-K1 21 QxBP+ NxQ and Black won; Byelin-Alapin, St Petersburg 1898.

47
B

9 ... PxP

Or 9...B-N3 10 PxP PxP 11 Q-Q1 (Better 11 N-R3) 11...0-0-0 12 N-R3

(12 QN-Q2!?) 12...B-N5 13 Q-Q3 N-B3 (13...N-K4!?) 14 B-Q5 KR-K1 15 Q-B4 Q-Q2 16 N-Q4 B-QB4 17 NxN PxN 18 R-N1! K-B2 19 B-B4! BxN 20 Q-R6 R-QN1 21 QxRP+ K-Q1 22 RxR+ K-K2 23 R-N7 1-0 Krylenko-Lykum, USSR 1925.

10 R—Q1

Not 10 B-R3 Q-B3 11 QN-Q2 KN-K2 12 B-N5 0-0 13 N-B4 B-N3 14 BxN/B6 BxB 15 N4xP KR-K1 16 BxN RxB 17 NxB QxN 18 P-K5 Q-B4 19 QR-K1 R1-K1‡— Alapin, 1892.

10 ... R—Q1

Others:

a) 10...B-N3? 11 BxP+ (*Compare* C31, note to White's eleventh) 11...QxB 12 QxQ+ KxQ 13 RxB+ K-N3?! 14 QN-Q2 N-B3 15 N-R4+ K-R4 16 RxNP! QR-KN1 17 R-B7 N-KN5 18 R-B5+ R-N4 19 R-B3!! R-N2 20 P-N3 NxBP 21 RxN R-Q1 22 N2-B3 R2-Q2 23 P-KR3 1-0 Becker-Hoffmann, German Corres Ch 1966

b) 10...0-0-0 remains untested:

b1) 11 BxP?! B-N3 and now:

b11) 12 B-Q5 N-B3 13 P-KR3 N-QR4 14 Q-B2 Q-K1 15 P-QR4 Q-R4‡ — Schallopp

b12) 12 RxB RxR 13 BxN N-R4 14 Q-K6 RxB!‡ — *Sovremenny Debyut*

b2) 11 QN-Q2 N-R3 12 B-R3 Q-B3 is generally considered good for Black, although White gets some attacking chances in the *Sovremenny Debyut* line 13 B-Q5 B-N3 14 N-B4 N-R4 15 NxB+ RPxN 16 Q-N4.

11 R—Q5!

Not 11 B-R3? Q-B3 12 QN-Q2 KN-K2 13 B-N5 0-0 14 N-B4 B-N3 15 BxN/B6 BxB 16 N4xP BxKP — Alapin

11 ... B—N3
12 B—QN5 N—B3

Others:

1) 12...B-K3 13 P-B4± — Chigorin

b) 12...P-B3 13 B-R3 Q-K3 (13... Q-B2 14 BxN PxB 15 NxP! Q-R4 16

RxB) 14 B-B4 N3-K2 (14...Q-N5 15
RxP+! NxR 16 NxN) 15 RxP! PxR 16
BxQ BxB 17 Q-R4+ N-B3 18 QN-Q2
and wins — Chigorin.
c) 12...Q-K3 13 BxN QxB 14 NxP
Q-K3 15 RxB RxR 16 QxQ+ PxQ 17
NxR KxN (1-0, 60), St Petersburg-
Paris, cable match 1894-5. Chigorin,
who of course led the St Petersburg
team, gave as best now in his notes: 18
B-B4 N-B3 19 N-Q2 R-KB1 20 B-N3
N-R4 21 N-B3 with some edge to
White.

13	B—R3!	Q—K3
14	QN—Q2!	N—R4
15	Q—N4!	NxR

Chigorin thought 15...P-B4!? might
have been tried.

16	PxN	
16	PxN	Q—Q3
17	Q—N2	BxP+

Not 17...B-B4? 18 N-K4 or
17...QxP 18 P-B4 Q-K3 19 R-K1 P-B3
20 NxP (Chigorin) but anyway Black
has the worse of it. We are following a
game Chigorin and Saburov v. Alapin
and Schiffers, St Petersburg 1897: 18
KxB Q-QN3+ 19 N-Q4! BxB 20 QxB
P-QB3 21 Q-K2 RxP 22 R-QN1 Q-B2
23 N-B5 P-B3 (23...Q-Q2 no better) 24
N-K4 P-QN4 25 Q-N4 K-Q1 26
B-K7+ K-B1 27 QxP R-Q1 28 QxBP
(1-0, 43).

D: The Lasker Defence
7 ... B—N3*(48)*

The intention behind this move is
to keep as solid a position as possible,
while offering the immediate return of
the gambit pawn. When White wins
back his pawn, it is at the cost of an
ending where he has weakened pawns
and his opponent sometimes has the
two bishops. Although it had been
played occasionally before 1895, it
was only after its adoption and recom-
mendation by Emanuel Lasker, then
by Pillsbury and others, that it was

thought to present a decisive challenge to the Evans. This is not so, as
we have seen from the analysis of the
Anti-Lasker Systems in the previous
chapter that Black cannot force the
Lasker Defence. Furthermore,
White's ideas are not yet exhausted in
the diagram position, even if the
practical results with the defence have
been good for Black.

48
W

White has played:
D1: 8 B-KN5?
D2: 8 B-K3
D3: 8 B-R3
D4: 8 P-QR4
D5: 8 PxP

D1:

| 8 | B—KN5 | P—B3 |
| 9 | B—K3 | B—Q2 |

Black should not imitate Velt-
mander's play against Skotorenko in
the ½-final of the 1958 RSFSR
Championship: 9...B-N5 10 P-KR3
B-R4 11 P-QR4 K-B1? 12 P-N4 B-K1
13 QN-Q2 P-N4 14 B-Q5 N-R4 15
N-B4 P-KR4?! 16 NxB RPxN 17
Q-Q2 RPxP 18 NxNP! PxN 19
P-KB4! NPxP 20 BxBP K-N2 21 B-N5
Q-Q2 22 B-KB6+! NxB 23 Q-N5+
B-N3 24 RxN R-KR3 25 R1-KB1 1-0.

10	N—R4	P—N3
11	N—R3	Q—K2
12	N—B2	P—B4!

Not 12...Q-N2 13 P-Q5 N-Q1 14
P-B4± Herman-Lyut, Riga 1904.

13	P—N3	P—B5
14	B—B1	0—0—0
15	P—R4	P—N4∓

Analysis by Levenfish

D2:

8	B—K3	N—B3

Also possible 8...B-N5 (Levenfish) or 8...B-Q2 (Compare D1). If 8...PxP 9 PxP see Chapter 8 (Normal variation).

9	QN—Q2	0—0
10	Q—B2	PxP!?
11	PxP	P—Q4

12 PxP N-QN5 13 Q-N3 N5xQP 14 B-KN5 P-B3 (14...B-K3 15 N-K4 P-B3 16 NxN+ would lose the pawn back.) 15 N-K4 Q-B2 16 NxN+ NxN 17 BxN PxB 18 Q-K3 K-N2 19 Q-K4 and White has fair attacking chances.

This was Chigorin's final idea against the Lasker Defence. A game **Chigorin & Protoklitov v. Znosko-Borovsky & Levin**, St Petersburg 1907, continued 19...Q-Q3 20 QR-K1 P-KB4 21 Q-R3 B-Q1 22 Q-R3 B-B3 (22...P-B5 23 Q-R5 Q-N3 24 Q-K5+ Q-B3 and White can take a draw or risk 25 Q-QB5!?) 23 B-Q3 (Romanov's book suggests 23 N-K5 BxN 24 PxB Q-N3 25 P-B4 with the idea RK1-K3-KN3.) 23...Q-B5 24 N-K5 B-K3 25 R-K3 QR-Q1 26 R-N3+ K-R1 27 R-N4 Q-Q7 28 P-B4 BxN (28...R-KN1 29 BxP QxQP+ 30 K-R1 R-N2 31 BxB PxB 32 RxR KxR 33 Q-N4+ K-B1 34 QxP winning — Chigorin) 29 BPxB R-KN1 30 Q-R4 RxR 31 QxR+ R-N1 32 Q-B6+ R-N2 ½-½. Possibly 8 B-K3 merits further attention.

D3:

8	B—R3	PxP!

Also quite good is 8...Q-B3!? since the White QB no longer has the KN5 option. A game Nicholson-Harding, Charlton 1973, continued 9 B-N5 B-Q2 10 QN-Q2 KN-K2 11 N-B4 (11

N-N3!?) 11...PxP (11...N-N3!?; 11...0-0-0!?) 12 BxN (12 PxP BxP!) 12...NxB 13 P-K5! NxP 14 N4xN PxN 15 PxP!? PxP 16 R-K1+ B-K3 17 Q-R4+ P-B3 18 N-K5 (18 B-Q6!? Q-Q1! 19 Q-R3 P-QB4) 18...0-0-0! 19 NxQBP! B-Q2! 20 NxP+ K-N1 21 N-N5 P-Q6! and White is probably lost (0-1, 36); this is an example of returning material gains for a timely counter-attack.

The text move brings about a form of the Normal Variation in which White has put his bishop offside at QR3: see chapter 8, page 125.

D4:

8	P—QR4(49)	

This space-stealing idea should prove too slow.

49
B

Black has tried:
D41: 8...P-QR4
D42: 8...P-QR3
D43: 8...N-QR4
D44: 8...N-B3
D45: 8...PxP!
Gunsberg even played 8...B-N5!?

D41:

8	...	P—QR4
9	PxP	

a) 9...PxP when White should, however, stand rather better than in D52 below.

b) 9...B-N5? 10 Q-N3 Q-K2 11 PxP Q-Q2 12 P-K5 B-K3 13 N-R3 N-Q1

14 R-Q1±± Blackburne-N.N., blind-fold simul at London's Athenaeum Chess Club in 1875.

D42:
    8 ...   P—QR3
Another reaction that justifies White's 8th move.
    9 Q—N3
Or 9 PxP PxP 10 Q-N3 Q-K2 11 B-R3 Q-B3 12 R-Q1! KN-K2 13 P-R5 NxP? 14 BxP+ QxB 15 R-Q8+ KxR 16 QxQ and White won; Wiarda-Meyer, 1907.
    9 ...   Q—K2
   10 B—Q5   P—R3
   11 P—R5   B—R2
12 PxP PxP 13 QN-Q2 Q-B3 14 N-B4 KN-K2 15 B-R3 R-QN1 16 QR-Q1 B-N5 17 R-Q3 0-0 18 P-R3 B-R4 19 KBxN PxB 20 Q-R2 R-N4 21 Q-K2 R-K1 22 P-N4 (1-0, 37) Naglis-Grigoriev, Moscow 1934. White has good attacking chances and the pawn minus does not mean much. However, neither player's conduct of this game was particularly convincing.

D43:
    8 ...   N—QR4
    9 B—R2   PxP
   10 PxP   B—K3
10...B-N5 is probably stronger.
   11 N—B3
11 P-Q5!? is also interesting (11... Q-B3 12 P-K5).
   11 ...   BxB
   12 RxB   N—K2
   13 K—R1   0—0
14 P-N4!? N-N3? (Better 14...P-Q4 or 14...Q-Q2) 15 P-R4! R-K1 (15...NxP 16 B-N5) 16 P-R5 N-B1 17 B-N5 Q-Q2 18 N-R4 N-K3 (Better 18... P-KB3, intending ...P-Q4) 19 B-K3 N-QB5 20 N-B5 NxB 21 PxN P-QB3 22 P-N5! B-Q1? (22...NxNP was the last chance.) 23 Q-N4 P-Q4 24 P-N6 BPxP 25 RPxP P-KR3 26 NxNP!

B-N4 (26...QxN 27 R-B7 Q-R1 28 R2-KB2 R-KB1 29 P-N7!) 27 R-B7 Q-B1 28 N-B5 N-Q1 29 QxB! NxR 30 PxN+ 1-0 Charousek-Richter, Berlin 1897 (From *Charousek's Best Games*, ed. Sergeant).

D44:
    8 ...   N—B3
    9 B—QN5
Others:
a) 9 B-Q5?! NxB! 10 PxN N-R4 11 PxP 0-0 12 B-N5 Q-Q2 13 R-K1 PxP 14 NxP Q-B4 15 B-R4 P-KB3 16 N-B3 B-Q2 17 N-R3 QR-K1 18 P-B4 RxR+ 19 QxR N-N6∓ Chigorin-Lipke, Vienna 1898
b) 9 P-R5!? NxRP 10 PxP PxP 11 RxN BxR 12 Q-R4+ P-B3 13 B-R3 N-Q2∓ Meister-Soller, Swiss Corres Ch 1942
    9 ...   P—QR3
   10 BxN+   PxB
   11 P—R5   B—R2*(50)*

50
W

Here White tried:
D441: 12 PxP
D442: 12 Q-R4?!

D441:
   12 PxP   NxP
   13 Q—K2?!
Zak's 1963 book on Lasker comments: "The combination thought up by White is incorrect and brings him a lost game. He had to reconcile himself to the real state of

72   *Play the Evans Gambit*

affairs and play for a draw by:
a) 13 PxP 0-0! (13...PxP 14 Q-K2
P-Q4 15 N-Q4 BxN 16 PxB 0-0 17
N-Q2 is not dangerous to White.) 14
PxP PxP 15 Q-K2, or else
b) 13 Q-R4 N-B4 14 QxP+ B-Q2 15
Q-Q5 0-0 16 PxP B-N4 17 R-Q1 (17
P-B4 can be met by 17...P-QB3.)
17...QxP 18 QxQ PxQ 19 B-K3!''

13 ...   P—Q4
14 N—Q4?!   NxQBP
15 NxN   BxN

16 Q-Q3 P-QB4 17 Q-N3 B-K3 18
B-N5 (18 QxP K-Q2!) 18...Q-Q2 19
QR-B1 P-KB3 20 PxP PxP 21 B-B4
R-KN1 22 Q-B3 0-0-0 23 KR-K1
P-B5 24 Q-K2 B-KB4 25 Q-R2
RxP+! 26 K-R1 (26 KxR B-R6+ 27
K-R1 Q-N5 etc.) 26...RxBP 0-1
Chigorin-Lasker, St Petersburg
1895-6.

D442:
12 Q—R4?!
Chigorin's next idea, which had no
better result, when he tried it in a
consultation game.

12 ...   PxP

12...0-0 may be even better, e.g.:
a) 13 B-N5 Q-K1 14 PxP PxP 15 BxN
PxB 16 R-K1 P-QB4 17 Q-B2 P-B5!
18 QN-Q2 B-K3.
b) 13 PxP PxP 14 NxP (14 R-Q1
Q-K1 15 B-R3 P-B4 16 Q-B2 B-N2)
14...Q-K1 15 QxP? QxN 0-1 (N.
Urusov-Hardin, 1895) since only now
did White see 16 QxR N-N5 17 P-N3
loses to 17...NxRP! 18 QxKP N-B6+
19 K-N2 QxKP.

13 PxP
Nenarokov's *Course in Chess
Openings* (1928) gave 13 P-K5?! PxP
14 B-R3 (14 NxKP 0-0 15 QxP Q-Q4)
14...B-Q2 15 NxP P-B4 16 NxB QxN
17 R-K1+ K-B1! 18 Q-B2 R-K1 19
N-Q2 R-K3∓.

13 ...   B—Q2
14 P—K5

Or 14 Q-B2, when Black might
reply 14...P-R3, 14...N-N1 or 14...0-0
15 B-N5 P-R3 16 B-R4 P-N4 17 NxP
NxP!

14 ...   N—Q4
15 B—R3   0—0

16 Q-B4 (16 PxP!?) 16...N-B5! 17
K-R1?! (17 N-B3 — Levenfish; 17
PxP B-K3 18 QxBP B-Q4 19 QxBP
Q-B3!) 17...B-K3! 18 Q-B1 NxP! 19
KxN B-Q4 20 K-N3 P-KB4 21 QN-Q2
P-B5+ 22 K-N2 Q-N4+ 23 K-R1
Q-B4 24 Q-B3 BxP (0-1, 33) St
Petersburg-Vienna, cable match
1897-8.

D45:
8 ...   PxP!
9 PxP   B—N5*(51)*
This is generally reckoned to be a
clearer refutation of 8 P-QR4 than is
8...N-B3.

10 B—N2
An exhibition (or friendly?) game
Chigorin-Lasker, St Petersburg 1897,
went instead 10 B-QN5 P-QR3! 11
BxN PxB 12 P-R5 B-R2 13 B-K3
N-K2 14 N-B3 0-0 15 Q-B2 BxN 16
PxB P-KB4 and Black took the ini-
tiative (0-1, 56).

10 ...   Q—B3
11 B—N5   BxN
Tarrasch recommended deferring
this move in favour of 11...P-QR3.

12 PxB   P—QR3
13 BxN+   PxB

14 N—R3 N—K2

15 K-R1 0-0 16 N-B4 P-Q4 17 NxB PxN 18 Q-K2 N-N3 19 R-KN1 KR-K1 20 R-N3 Q-K3 21 R-K1. Now 21... P-KB4 favour Black, but in the game Charousek-Blackburne, Nuremberg 1896, there was played 21...P-N4? 22 P-R5! R-R2 23 Q-Q2 P-KB4 24 P-K5 R-KB2 25 P-B4 Q-Q2 26 B-R3 . Black is hamstrung; after further errors, White even won, by Q-side infiltration, in 46 moves.

D5:

8 PxP

Relatively the best chance for White

8 ... PxP (52)

8...B-N5?! is only of historical interest:

a) 9 B-QN5 see McDonnell- La Bourdonnais (Chapter 1).

b) 9 PxP BxN 10 QxB N-K4 11 B-QN5+ P-B3 12 Q-N3 QxP 13 B-K2 N-K2 14 K-R1 0-0 15 P-KB4 N4-N3 16 N-R3 B-B2 17 N-B2 P-KB4 18 B-B4+ K-R1 19 P-K5 Q-Q1 20 N-Q4 Q-B1 21 B-R3 P-N4 22 BxN NxB 23 N-K6 N-N3 24 B-N3 R-K1 25 NxB! QxN 26 QxN! 1-0 Kolisch-Loyd, Paris 1867.

52
W

White now has:
D51: 9 QN-Q2
D52: 9 BxP+?
D53: 9 QxQ+
D54: 9 Q-N3

9 Q-K2 B-N5! 10 B-R3 Q-B3 11 QN-Q2 KN-K2 12 P-R3 P-KR4! 13 B-N5 0-0-0∓ Grüntal-Zonn, Riga 1910

D51:

9 QN—Q2 Q—B3
10 B—Q5 KN—K2
11 P—KR3 P—KR3

12 N-B4 0-0 13 N-R2 R-Q1 14 N-K3 B-K3 and Black soon won in a game Marshall-Blackburne.

D52:

9 BxP+? KxB
10 NxP+

This sacrifice has been known to be unsound for decades, yet only a few years ago White won with it in 12 moves in a postal game. What is still more surprising, the game was published with completely misleading notes in that bastion of official chess theory, the *Informator!*

10 ... K—K1!
Others:

a) 10...K-B3?? 11 B-N5+! KxB 12 N-B7+ etc.

b) 10...K-B1?? 11 B-R3+ KN-K2 12 Q-B3+ 1-0 Ecke-Schönewald, corres 1967-8.

c) 10...K-K2? 11 NxN+ PxN 12 B-N5+ N-B3 13 P-K5 regaining the piece with a fair game.

d) 10...K-K3!? 11 Q-N4+ KxN when: d1) Not 12 B-B4+? ("White wins" — *Informator*) 12...K-B3 13 B-N5+ K-N3 and it is Black who wins — Estrin!

d2) 12 Q-B4+ is better, but after 12...K-K3 13 Q-B5+ K-K2 14 B-R3+ N-N5! (14...K-K1! 15 Q-B3+ K-Q2 16 R-Q1+) 15 BxN PxB4 16 BxP+ (16 Q-K5+ K-B2) 16...BxB 17 QxB+ Q-Q3 18 Q-KN5+ Q-B3 19 Q-QB5+ K-B2 White will run out of play — analysis.

11 Q—R5+
Again *Informator* claimed a win for

White! But not so...

11	...	P—N3
12	NxP	N—B3
13	Q—R6	R—KN1 *(53)*

53
W

14   N—R4

As proposed in *Chess Digest Magazine* 4/1969. The older move 14 N-B4 had been analysed to Black's advantage by S. Mlotkowski in *B.C.M.* 1917, e.g. 14...N-K4 15 N-Q5 R-N3 16 NxN+ QxN 17 QxP N-N5 18 B-R3 NxBP and Black soon won in a 1950 postal game Lane-Black.

14   ...   N—K4!

White is lost, according to an analysis by American amateur D. Forthoffer in *Chess Digest Magazine* 2/1970:

a) 15 B-N5 N4-N5 16 BxN QxB! and if 17 QxP then 17...BxP+ 18 K-R1 R-R1 19 Q-N6+ QxQ 20 NxQ RxP mate.

b) 15 Q-B4 N4-N5 16 P-K5 NxBP! 17 B-K3 N-R6+.

c) 15 N-B5 N4-N5 16 Q-B4 NxBP! 17 Q-K5+ K-R1! 18 B-R3+ (18 B-K3? N7-N5) 18...K-B2 19 N-R6+ K-N3 20 Q-N3+ KxN! 21 B-B1+ K-R4 22 Q-K5+ K-R5 23 P-N3+ K-R6 24 Q-QN5 (Intending RxN) 24...N2xP+ 25 K-R1 N-B7+ 26 K-N1 N-Q6+ 27 K-R1 B-Q2 and Black mates.

D53:

9	QxQ+	NxQ
10	NxP *(54)*	

White regains his pawn, but Black welcomes the resulting ending. Lasker gets the credit for understanding this because Staunton, for one, had dismissed the line as good for White.

54
B

Now:
D531: 10...B-K3
D532: 10...N-B3!

D531:

10   ...   B—K3

According to Lasker, in his *Chess Magazine* (1906, page 242), this line of defence, which is now universally attributed to him, had been given in an early edition of the *Handbuch*. But it was missed out from later editions until resurrected by him in *Common Sense in Chess* (1896). Lasker now considered 10...B-K3 to equalize, but his second thought, 10...N-B3! to do more.

Let us now turn to Romanovsky's article on the Evans, published in *Shakhmaty v SSSR* 9/1951. Romanovksy wrote:

"The books assess this position as advantageous to Black because his pawn formation is superior to White's. Normally reference is made to Chigorin-Pillsbury in which White lost in a bishop ending. Is it really possible, however, to make such a categorical middle-game judgement on the basis of such slight considerations?"

11 N—Q2

This is better than 11 B-R3 P-KB3! 12 BxB NxB 13 N-B4 B-B4!∓ Johner-Zauer, corres 1912.

11 ...   N—K2
12 B—R3

Levenfish suggested 12 P-QR4.

12 ...   P—KB3
13 N—Q3   N—N3

Romanovsky: "Why should Black's position be favoured here? After all, the main factor in assessing such positions with a lot of pieces left must be the worth of each player's development and the reality of their respective plans. White has these factors working for him, as his plan of making the opponent's development difficult is quite obvious. To reduce the assessment of the position to the single fact of the isolated QBP is sheer scholasticism, quite foreign to our native school of chess."

In the game Karaklajic-Longer, Yugoslav Ch 1951, Black played instead 13...BxB 14 NxB N-K3 15 KR-Q1 R-Q1. Now, as an improvement upon the game continuation 16 K-B1 K-B2 17 R-Q2 N-B3 (Black won in 45 moves), we suggest 17 NxB RPxN 18 P-K5 and White certainly stands no worse.

14 QR—N1   K—B2?!

Chigorin suggested 14...BxB 15 NxB N-K3, when one can envisage these continuations:
a) 16 P-K5 0-0-0 17 KR-K1 18 N3xP NxN 19 NxN RxR+ 20 RxR R-Q1 21 RxR+ KxR and the endgame may be good for Black.
b) 16 QR-Q1! 0-0-0 17 NxB+ RPxN 18 P-KB4 with good chances for White, as the position retains middle-game character — analysis.

15 B—Q5   R—K1
16 P—B4?

"Only this mistake gives the advantage to Black. After the obvious 16

N-B4 White keeps the better game as the development of the enemy Q-side is rendered difficult" — Romanovsky, following Chigorin.

16 ...   P—B3!
17 BxB+   NxB

In Chigorin-Pillsbury, London London 1899, Black won in 47 moves. Romanovsky remarked: "Only now did Chigorin see that 18 P-B5 is met by 18...R-Q1, while there is a threat of ...QR-Q1. Black now has the advantage...(but) from all that has been said it is clear that one should not fear Lasker's Defence." Unfortunately, Black has the last word...

D532:
10 ...   N—B3!

Lasker's suggested improvement, which remains untested since 9 QxQ+ is rarely played. Lasker's comment was: "Black's solid pawns and good, sound development will make it hard for White to keep up the equilibrium, as his QRP and, more so, the QBP, require constant care."

11 B—KN5

This was recommended by Chigorin. However, there could follow 11... B-K3 (11...N-K3!? but not 11...NxP? 12 BxN) 12 QN-Q2 BxB 13 N5xB N-Q2 14 N-N3 N-K3 (14...0-0? 15 KR-Q1) and Lasker's judgement begins to be borne out. Also if 11 N-Q2 0-0 or 11 B-R3 NxP the complications favour Black. Therefore the next variation is crucial.

D54:
9 Q—N3*(55)*

This is the beginning of a manoeuvre designed to regain the pawn without exchanging queens.

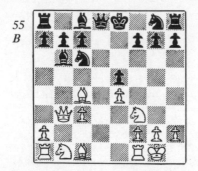

55
B

9 ...   Q—B3
9...Q-K2 may also be playable, hoping for 10 R-Q1? N-R4 11 BxP+? when 11...K-B1! wins a piece. White can improve upon this with, for example, 10 B-Q5, intending the familiar manoeuvre QN-Q2-B4, and holding back B-R3 as a reply to ...N-KB3. Or possibly 10 B-R3.
10   B—KN5
Other ideas:
a) 10 B-Q5 P-KR3 (10...KN-K2 11 B-N5 see below) when:
a1) 11 B-R3 KN-K2 12 QN-Q2 N-R4 13 Q-B2 0-0 14 N-N3 NxB 15 BxR NxN 16 QxN N-B5 17 B-R3 NxP 18 P-B4 (18 KxN? B-R6+ mates.) 18...N-B5 19 K-R1 B-R6 20 R-KN1 BxP 21 QxP R-QB1 22 B-N2 N-Q6 23 NxP BxR 24 Q-N3 Q-N4 0-1 Belov-Barsky, 'Trud' club ch, USSR 1959.
a2) White could try 11 BxN+ PxB 12 QN-Q2 N-K2 13 N-B4 N-N3 14 B-R3 P-B4 15 KR-Q1.
b) A game Morphy-Brien, New York 1859 (at knight odds), went 10 B-QN5 B-K3? (10...B-Q2!) 11 Q-R4 N-K2? 12 B-N5 Q-N3 13 BxKN KxN 14 BxN PxB 15 NxP Q-B3 16 NxP+ K-B1 17 P-K5 Q-N4 18 P-R4 Q-R4 19 Q-R3+ and smothered mate.
10   ...   Q—N3
11   B—Q5
11 QN-Q2 is less forcing:
1) 11...KN-K2 12 BxN KxB 13 B-Q5

N-R4 14 Q-N4+ Q-Q3 15 N-N5 P-KB3 16 N-B7 QxQ 17 PxQ R-B1 18 PxN BxRP 19 N-B4 B-N3 20 NxB RPxN 21 P-B4 P-B3 22 PxP PxB 23 N-Q6 QPxP 24 QR-B1 B-Q2 25 R-B7 PxP 26 R-Q1 K-K3 27 NxNP B-N4 28 R-Q6+ K-B4 29 RxKNP K-B5 30 RxNP B-Q6 31 R-N2 K-K6 and Black went on to win; Bampton-Shipley, corres 1906.
b) 11...N-B3 12 Q-R3 N-Q2 13 B-K3 Q-Q3 14 QxQ PxQ 15 BxB NxB 16 B-N3 N-R4 17 KR-Q1 K-K2 18 N-B1 B-K3∓∓ Ciocaltea-Alexandrescu, ½-final Romanian Ch 1954 (0-1, 49).
11   ...   KN—K2
Not 11...N-R4? 12 NxP when:
a) 12...QxB? 13 B-B6+! K-K2 14 QxP+ K-Q3 15 R-Q1+ 1-0 Hasek-Jereba, Prague 1929.
b) 12...NxQ 13 NxQ NxR 14 NxR B-K3 15 BxB PxB 16 N-R3 B-B4 17 N-N5±.
12   BxN/K7   KxB
13   BxN   QxB
14   NxP   Q—K3
15   Q—R3+ (56)
Keres (1955) preferred 15 N-B4 "with real chances of equalizing the position."

56
B

Another crucial Evans Gambit position. Black has:
D541: 15...K-B3
D542: 15...P-B4
D543: 15...Q-Q3!

It can be seen that at the 'cost' of giving up his two bishops for Black's knights, White has won back his pawn, more or less by force. Lasker thought this position was greatly in Black's favour, but Chigorin, who was often prepared to carry on the struggle with two knights versus two bishops, remained sceptical. We shall quote extensively from Chigorin's *Novoye Vremya* (*New Time,* the main Russian newspaper of that era), 30/1/1897, which is reprinted in Romanov's book. Finally we shall see that the diagram position probably does favour Black, although not after the moves which Lasker had recommended in *Common Sense in Chess.*

D541:

   15 ...   K—B3

After this move, and after 15...P-B4, Lasker claimed that Black has two bishops, excellent development and a sound position. Chigorin disagreed of course.

   16 N—B3

a) 16...P-N3 17 P-B4 "freeing QB3 for the knight and threatening both P-B5 and Q-N2+."

b) 16...R-Q1 can be met by 17 P-B4 with the same idea, or 17 QN-Q2 R-Q6 18 Q-N2 — Chigorin.

c) 16...B-Q2 17 QN-Q2 B-B3 18 N-Q4 when "Black loses the 'advantage of two bishops' and his king remains open to attack."

D542:

   15 ...   P—B4
   16 P—KB4!   R—Q1

Others:

a) 16...P-B3 17 N-B3 intending P-B5, P-B4, N-QB3-Q5.

b) 16...B-Q2 17 P-B4, N-QB3 etc.

c) 16...Q-Q3 17 N-B4 Q-QB3 18 NxB QxN 19 P-B4 Q-N5 (19...B-K3 20

Q-QB3 intending P-B5) 20 Q-KN3 QxP 21 N-B3 (Or 21 Q-N5+ K-K1 22 R-Q1) "should win for White".

   17 P—B4

"White could get an excellent position by 17 N-KB3 and then P-B5 or QN-Q2 etc, but I wish to give variations which clearly show the strength of the knight at Q5" — Chigorin.

   17 ...   P—B3
   18 N—QB3!   PxN
   19 N—Q5+   K—B1

Chigorin also analysed:

a) 19...RxN 20 KPxR then 21 PxP and 22 P-K6

b) 19...K-K1 20 QR-N1! B-Q2 (20... R-N1 21 RxB!) 21 Q-KN3 Q-N3 22 Q-R4 Q-B2 (Or 22...K-B1) 23 PxP±±.

   20 QR—N1!   B—Q2

The only alternative is 20...R-N1 21 P-B5 Q-R3 (21...Q-Q3 22 P-B6 P-N3 23 Q-K3) 22 P-B6 RxN 23 KPxR PxP 24 RxB PxR 25 Q-R7 winning, e.g. 25...Q-K6+ 26 K-R1 Q-K7 27 R-B1 Q-Q7 28 R-KN1 — Chigorin.

   21 P—B5   Q—R3
   22 R—N3

Chigorin gave now two variations that suggest Black has no defence:

a) 22...K-N1 23 R-R3 Q-N4 24 R-KN3 Q-R3 25 P-B6 P-N3 26 Q-QB3 Q-R4 (26...B-K3 27 P-B7+ BxP 28 N-K7+/B6+ K-B1 29 R3-B3/R3 etc.) 27 P-B7+ K-R1 (27...K-B1 28 N-B6 Q-R3 29 QxP B-B3 30 R-KR3) 28 N-B6 Q-R3 29 NxB RxN 30 QxP+ etc.

b) 22...Q-Q7 23 R-Q3 Q-K7 (23... Q-R4 24 Q-B1 intending P-B6 and R-QR3) 24 P-B6 P-N3 25 Q-B1 Q-R4 26 NxB PxN 27 Q-Q2 K-K1 28 R-Q1 etc.

Chigorin commented that in these lines the two bishops could not play an active role in defending the king which was menaced by just one knight! "These variations", he admitted, "do not exhaust the defensive possibilities. Black could put up better resistance by not going ...P-KB3, but then White's knights dominate on K5 and Q5; to play QBxN would give White a significant passed pawn on Q5. Hence the position depends not on the possession of bishops or knights as such, but the roles which the pieces actually occupy *vis-a-vis* the other pieces".

D543:
    15 ...   **Q—Q3!***(57)*
In view of Chigorin's analyses, this move, suggested by Levenfish, is undoubtedly Black's best. He thus forces the exchange of queens and, even with only one bishop against a knight, keeps good chances of exploiting White's weakened Q-side. In fact it would often be bad judgement for White to take on QN6, since that would give the Black QR strong pressure in many cases.

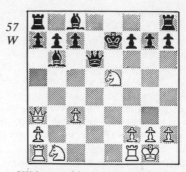

57
W

White could try:
a) 16 QxQ+ PxQ 17 N-B4 B-K3 when Black has the better ending, according to Levenfish. For example 18 NxB PxN 19 P-QR3 KR-QB1 20 R-B1 R-R5 21 N-Q2 P-Q4 22 PxP BxP and the question is whether White can hold on?
b) 16 R-Q1 QxQ 17 NxQ B-K3 18 N-N5 KR-Q1 19 N-Q4 when the knights' activity offers chances of maintaining equality. If this fails, White will have to try Keres' 15 N-B4 or abandon the whole variation.

5 Compromised Defence

This is the variation of the Evans where Black takes all the pawns he is offered and hopes to weather the storm. Theoretically the line is important, but the practical difficulties for Black are so great that few players wish to conduct the defence. Moreover it goes against modern positional ideas to swallow so much material at the cost of development and the safety of king and queen. Chigorin thought that Black's game was playable, and this belief of his probably accounts for his preference for 6 0-0 rather than 6 P-Q4. **Anderssen, Zukertort and Emanuel** Lasker (unfaithful to his own defence!) also tried it but, like Chigorin, had to concede defeat when their opponents' played accurately. White's attack really is very strong!

The Compromised Defence arises by the sequence 1 P-K4 P-K4 2 N-KB3 N-QB3 3 B-B4 B-B4 4 P-QN4 BxNP 5 P-B3 B-R4 6 P-Q4 PxP 7 0-0 PxP!? (58)

58
W

White has now tried:
A: 8 B-R3!?
B: 8 P-K5!?
C: 8 Q-N3!
  8 B-KN5 KN-K2 — Levenfish.

A:

  8 B—R3!?

This move seems premature, since it is important to attack the KBP and so force Black's queen into an exposed position. Nonetheless it deserves attention because it was once played by Paul Morphy, in a game that Reti annotated misleadingly in his *Masters of the Chess Board*.

  8 ...   P—Q3

8...KN-K2 was recommended by Levenfish. Then instead of 9 N-N5? N-K4, White could keep some pressure by 9 Q-N3 0-0 10 NxP B-N3 11 N-Q5 (11...NxN 12 BxN N-R4 13 Q-B3 Q-B3 14 P-K5 for example) — analysis.

  9   Q—N3   N—R3
  10 NxP   BxN?

Reti was right to criticize this move. Better is 10...0-0 when:
a) 11 QR-Q1 N-KN5 12 P-R3 N5-K4 13 NxN NxN 14 B-K2 B-K3! but not 14...BxN transposing, nor 14...B-N3 15 K-R1 and P-B4 — analysis.
b) 11 P-K5!, and if 11...B-N3 12 B-Q5 with still some attack for White, may have been Morphy's intention.

  11 QxB   0—0
  12 QR—Q1

It is evident that White must force

through P-K5, opening lines.

12	...	N—KN5
13	P—R3	N5—K4
14	NxN	NxN
15	B—K2!*(59)*	

15	...	P—KB3

As suggested by Reti; the game Morphy-N.N., from a New Orleans blindfold simul in 1858, continued instead 15...P-KB4?! 16 P-B4 N-B3 17 B-B4+ K-R1 18 B-N2 Q-K2 19 QR-K1 R-B3 20 PxP Q-B1 21 R-K8! QxR 22 QxR Q-K2 23 QxP+! QxQ 24 P-B6 QxP+ (24...Q-KB1 25 P-B7+ leads to mate.) 25 KxQ BxP+ **26 KxB P-KR4 27 R-KN1 1-0. Reti** commented: "Inasmuch as White has a strong advantage in development, Black should above all be bent on keeping the game closed, for instance by playing P-KB3 and N-KN3; in order to control the key-position, White's K5...In playing along these lines Black, considering his material superiority, very probably would be at an advantage".

This is sound general advice, but it neglects the concrete features of the position, in particular the double pin on Black's QP. After:

16	P—B4	N—N3
17	P—K5!	BPxP

If 17...P-Q4 18 RxP, before taking the exchange.

| 18 | PxP | |

Our analysis demonstrates that White has excellent winning chances, so that Reti was wrong in supposing that Black could prevent his opponent from opening up the game. There could now follow:

a) 18...NxP 19 RxR+ QxR! 20 QxN! PxQ 21 B-B4+ K-R1 (21...Q-B2?? 22 R-Q8 mate) 22 BxQ BxP!? 23 BxP+! and White ought to win the ending.

b) 18...RxR+ 19 BxR! B-B4 20 PxP PxP 21 RxP Q-N4 22 Q-N3+ K-R1 23 QxP and White has recouped his investments with a winning attack to boot!

B:

8 P—K5!?*(60)*

White threatens 9 Q-N3, meeting 9...N-R3 by 10 BxN and 9...Q-K2 by 10 B-R3, but the move loses time.

8	...	KN—K2

Others:

a) 8...B-N5? 9 Q-N3 Q-K2 10 B-KN5 Q-B1 11 NxP BxN 12 QxB P-KR3 13 B-R4 KN-K2 14 QR-Q1 P-KN4 15 B-N3 Q-N2 16 KR-K1 P-KR4 17 P-KR4! PxP 18 NxP R-KN1 19 Q-B3 N-R4 20 P-K6! (1-0, 34) Steinitz-Meitner, Vienna 1859

b) 8...P-Q4!? 9 PxPep (9 BxP B-K3!) 9...QxP 10 Q-N3 B-K3 11 BxB PxB 12 R-Q1 Q-N5 13 QxKP+ Q-K2 14 Q-N3 P-B7 15 QxBP R-Q1 16 QN-Q2 Q-B2 17 B-R3 BxN 18 RxB RxR 19 QxR KN-K2 20 R-K1 0-0∓ Black-burne-Mason, Hastings 1895.

9 B—R3

Or 9 Q-N3 (9 N-N5? NxP) 9...0-0 10 NxP N-N3 11 B-R3 KNxP 12 NxN NxN 13 BxR NxB 14 QxN QxB∓ — *Handbuch*

9 ...   0—0
10 Q—Q3!?   P—Q4
11 PxPep   PxP

12 NxP B-B4 13 Q-K3 R-K1 14 N-QN5 P-Q4 15 QR-Q1 B-QN5 16 BxB NxB 17 B-N3 P-QR3 and White has little for his two pawns, Marshall-Janowski, Monte Carlo 1901.

C:

8 Q—N3! *(61)*

61
B

C1: 8...P-Q4?
C2: 8...Q-K2
C3: 8...Q-B3

C1:

8 ...   P—Q4?

This is a clear abuse of the principle of returning sacrificed material; the Black king is rapidly stripped of all protection, e.g. 9 BxP B-K3 10 BxB PxB 11 QxKP+ KN-K2 (11... Q-K2!?) 12 N-N5 N-Q5 (12...R-KB1 13 NxRP) 13 Q-B7+ K-Q2 (Charousek-*K.V.*, Berlin 1897) and now instead of 14 R-Q1 K-B1! the most accurate continuation would have been 14 B-K3, according to Sergeant.

C2:

8 ...   Q—K2

An unpopular move, although no clear refutation has been shown. This was the choice of grandmaster Reuben Fine in his well-known game against Fischer, annotated in depth in the latter's *My 60 Memorable Games.*

9 NxP *(62)*

A game Steinitz-Strauss, Vienna 1860, went instead 9 B-R3 P-Q3 (9...Q-B3 would be a tempo lost on C3.) 10 NxP BxN (The threat of N-Q5 was unpleasant.) 11 QxB (Threatens P-K5) 11...N-K4 12 NxN QxN 13 Q-B2 (Not 13 Q-Q2 N-K2 threatening the KP) 13...N-B3 14 B-N2 Q-QB4 (14...Q-KR4 15 P-K5 PxP 16 P-B4) 15 P-K5 N-Q4 16 PxP PxP 17 Q-K4+ B-K3 18 QR-Q1 N-B2 19 BxB NxB 20 BxP R-KN1 21 QxRP K-K2 (21... K-Q2 22 B-Q4!) 22 KR-K1 Q-KN4 (22...QR-K1 23 QR-B1 Q-N3 24 RxN+ KxR 25 Q-K4+ K-Q2 26 Q-B5+) 23 RxN+! KxR 24 Q-K4+ K-Q2 25 QxP+ K-K3 26 R-K1+ K-B4 27 QxBP+ K-N5 28 Q-B3+ K-R5 29 Q-KR3 mate. Black's play might have been improved by 11...P-B3 followed by ...B-Q2, striving to prevent excessive line-opening.

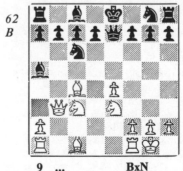

62
B

9 ...   BxN

Also important:
a) 9...N-B3? 10 N-Q5! NxN (10...QxP 11 N-KN5 was a little better — Fischer.) 11 PxN N-K4 (11...N-Q1 12

B-R3) 12 NxN QxN 13 B-N2 Q-N4 14 P-KR4! (1-0, 17) Fischer-Fine, New York 1963 (skittles game). For the finish, and the variations seen by **Fischer, see op.cit. p276-9.**

b) 9...Q-N5! 10 BxP+ K-Q1 is the best defence according to Fischer, e.g. 11 B-N5+ (11 BxN QxQ holds.) when:

b1) 11...N-B3 12 N-Q5 QxQ 13 PxQP-KR3 14 B-R4 R-B1 15 B-N5 P-Q3 16 P-K5 PxP 17 KR-Q1± — Freeborough and Ranken (3rd ed., 1896)

b2) 11...KN-K2 12 N-Q5 QxQ 13 PxQ and now:

b21) 13...B-N3 14 KR-B1 P-KR3 15 RxN PxB 16 NxB BPxN 17 RxNP — F&R

b22) 13...B-N5! (Fischer) leaves the position unclear, since 14 R-R4 is met by 14...P-QR4. We suggest instead 14 KR-Q1, bringing White's last piece into relevance. If 14...P-KR3?! there can come 15 N-B4!, threatening N-K6 mate, and after 15...P-Q3 there is the comical win of the exchange 16 N-N6 R-R2 17 B-N8!?. Or if 14...P-Q3? 15 N-Q4 K-Q2 16 BxN winning a piece.

10 QxB   P—B3

If 10...N-B3 11 B-R3 P-Q3 12 P-K5 N-K5 13 Q-N2 QNxP 14 NxN QxN 15 KR-K1! winning — *Handbuch.*

11 B—R3

Also interesting is 11 P-K5!? e.g. 11...PxP 12 NxP NxN 13 KR-K1 P-Q3 14 P-B4 B-K3 15 BxB (Better 15 RxN and 16 B-R3! — Backmann, *Schachmeister Steinitz)* 15...QxB 16 PxN P-Q4 17 QxP Q-N3+ (½-½, 25) Fraser-Steinitz, third game of second match, Dundee 1867.

Not so clear is 11 B-Q5 Q-N5 12 Q-B2 KN-K2 13 R-N1 N-Q5 as in a game Hirschfield-Zukertort.

11 ...   P—Q3
12 B—Q5!   B—Q2
13 KR—K1

Fischer suggests 13 QR-N1 which

may be more precise; then if 13... 0-0-0. 14 N-Q4 "is crushing".

13 ...   0—0—0
14 QR—N1   B—K3?

Necessary is 14...Q-K1, followed by ...KN-K2 or ...P-QN3, as suggested in *Sahs,* 1970.

After the move played, White wins by 15 RxP! KxR (Or 15...BxB 16 PxB QxR+ 17 NxQKxR 18 PxN+) 16 QxN+ K-B1 17 Q-R6+ K-Q2 18 B-B6 mate, Steinitz-Grand, London 1872.

C3:

8 ...   Q—B3*(63)*

63
W

9 P—K5

This is better than 9 B-KN5!? Q-N3 when:

a) 10 P-K5 P-N4? (10...KN-K2 — Bachmann) 11 B-Q5 P-N5? (11... R-QN1) 12 R-K1 P-KR3 13 P-K6 BPxP 14 B-R4 R-QN1 15 BxN PxB 16 NxP B-N3 17 QR-Q1 N-B3 18 RxP+! (1-0, 31) Grand-Steinitz, London 1872

b) 10 NxP BxN 11 QxB and now:

b1) 11...N-B3 12 B-Q3 (12 P-K5 N-K5 13 Q-K3 — Freeborough and Ranken.) 12...0-0 13 QR-K1 P-N4?! 14 P-K5 N-Q4 15 Q-B2 Q-R4 16 P-QR3 P-KR3 17 B-Q2 N4-K2? (Better 17...N3-K2) 18 R-K4 N-N3 19 R1-K1 B-N2 20 P-N4 Q-R6 21 R1-K3 and won, Steinitz-Zukertort, second match game 1872

b2) 11...P-Q3 12 B-Q5 KN-K2 13

BxN NxB 14 QxBP NxB 15 PxN 0-0 16 KR-K1 B-R6 17 N-R4 Q-N5 18 Q-K7 P-B4 19 K-R1 R-B3 20 QxQNP R1-KB1 21 PxB QxN (0-1, 42) Janowski-Lasker, Manchester 1901 b3) 11...P-B3 12 B-B4 P-Q3 — Freeborough and Ranken

9 ...   Q—N3

Not 9...NxP? 10 R-K1 P-Q3 11 Q-N5+ winning the bishop.

10 NxP(64)

10 B-R3 should transpose to C335.

Now:

C31: 10...P-N4
C32: 10...BxN
C33: 10...KN-K2

10...N-R3? 11 N-Q5 0-0 12 B-Q3 Q-K3 (12...Q-R4 13 N-B4 Q-N5 14 P-KR3) 13 N-KN5 QxP 14 B-B4 Q-K1 15 NxRP± Allies-Blackburne, 1906

C31:

10 ...   P—N4
11 NxP   R—N1

Black's idea, as in C334 and C3353 below, is to return some of his material in order to mobilize his Q-side pieces.

12 Q—K3!

Also interesting is 12 N-KN5!? e.g. **12...N-R3 13 P-B4** (13 Q-K3! *MCO*, 1946) 13...0-0 (13...P-QR3! — *MCO*, 1946) 14 Q-Q1 P-QR3 15 B-Q3 P-B4 16 PxPep QxBP∓ Alexander-Spencer, Worcester 1931.

12 ...   KN—K2

If 12...P-QR3 13 N-Q6+! — F&R

13 Q—K2!   Q—R4

White was threatening to net the queen by N-R4.

14 B—R3   B—N2

14...0-0 would be preferable, according to Grunfeld in the *Deutsche Schachblatter* 1929, although Black's position remains difficult after 15 QR-Q1 — Alexander in *B.C.M.* 1947.

15 QR—Q1!   N—B4?

Grunfeld recommended 15...R-Q1.

16 RxP!   KxR
17 P—K6+   K—B1
18 PxP   B—R1

19 NxRP+! NxN (19...K-N2 20 NxN KxN 21 N-K5+!) 20 Q-K6+ K-Q1 21 R-Q1+ N-Q3 (Kolisch-Anderssen, London 1861) and now the simplest finish would have been by 22 BxN. Kolisch played 22 RxN+?! and won in 34 moves.

C32:

10 ...   BxN
11 QxB(65)

Here Black has tried:

C321: 11...N-Q1?
C322: 11...P-N3?
C323: 11...KN-K2

11...P-Q3?! 12 PxP PxP 13 B-KN5! B-B4 14 KR-K1+ KN-K2 15 BxN NxB 16 B-N5+ B-Q2 17 Q-B7± Campbell-Loman, England 1929

C321:

    11 ...   **N—Q1?**

    12 B—R3

Or 12 R-K1 P-KR3 13 B-R3 N-K2 14 N-Q2 Q-QB3 15 N-K4 N-K3 16 Q-N4 N-N3 17 K-R1 P-QR4 18 Q-N3 NxP 19 B-Q5 N-Q5 20 Q-N3 QxB 21 QxP and White won, Hirschfield-Mayet, Berlin 1861.

    12 ...   **N—R3**

    13 KR—K1   **P—N3**

    14 B—Q5   **B—N2?**

14...P-QB3 was the only chance. — Neistadt, *Shakhmaty do Steinitza.*

    15 P—K6!!   **1-0**

Neumann-Anderssen, Berlin 1864. Black resigned in view of:

a) 15...BxB 16 PxQP+ KxP 17 R-K7+ and 18 QxBP mate

b) 15...QPxP 16 BxB NxB 17 Q-B6+

c) 15...BPxP 16 BxB NxB 17 QxBP N-B4 18 BxN PxB 19 N-K5

C322:

    11 ...   **P—N3?***(66)*

    12 N—N5!?

Others:

a) 12 P-K6!± — *MCO*, 1939

b) 12 B-R3 N-R3 13 B-Q3 (13 KR-K1 — Bachmann) 13...Q-R4 14 N-Q4 B-N2 15 P-K6 BPxP 16 NxP PxN 17 B-R6? (17 B-K4) 17...Q-R4 18 QxP 0-0-0 Taylor-Steinitz, London 1865.

c) 12 N-R4 Q-R4 13 P-K6! BPxP 14 Q-KN3 — a 1929 analysis quoted in *Sovremenny Debyut.*

    12 ...   **N—R3**

    13 R—K1   **0—0**

    14 B—Q3   **Q—R4**

15 BxP+ and White appears to have a good attack (½-½, 27) Taylor-Steinitz, London 1865. The Steinitz who played the Compromised Defence was only in embryo the future World Champion.

C323:

    11 ...   **KN—K2***(67)*

    12 B—R3

Others:

a) 12 N-N5?! N-Q1 (12...0-0 13 B-Q3) and now:

a1) 13 P-B4 P-KR3 14 N-B3 0-0 15 N-Q4 N-B3 16 NxN (16 B-Q3 NxN) 16...QxN (½-½, 38) Blackburne-Marriott, blindfold simul 1873.

a2) 13 R-K1 P-N3 (13...P-KR3 14 N-K4 0-0 15 B-R3 R-K1 16 N-B6+ with an attack — Levenfish) 14 P-B4?! B-N2 15 B-R3 P-QB4 16 QR-Q1 B-B3 (0-1, 53) Schallopp-Anderssen, Berlin 1864.

b) 12 R-K1 0-0 13 B-Q3 R-KB4 (13...Q-R4 14 R-K4 N-N3 15 P-N4) 14 B-QB4+ K-R1 15 B-N2 P-Q4 16 PxPep PxP 17 QR-Q1 P-Q4 18 BxP NxB 19 RxN R-KN1 20 R-Q6! etc. — Rosenthal.

    12 ...   **0—0**

12...P-N3 has also been deeply analysed:

a) 13 KR-K1 B-N2 14 QR-B1 and not

now 14...0-0-0? 15 BxN NxB 16 BxP Q-QB3 17 Q-R3 with a strong attack — Nenarokov. Keres (1955) concurs.
b) 13 B-Q3 Q-R3 (13...Q-R4? 14 BxN KxB 15 P-K6) 14 KR-Q1 B-N2 "and it is difficult to see how White will make good his minus of two pawns." Lasker, *Common Sense in Chess*. But in a later work...
c) 13 KR-K1 B-N2 14 QR-B1 "...but all of this is rather unsatisfactory, undefined, aimless, as dancing upon a tightrope from which the dancer may easily fall; for instance 14...N-R4 15 B-Q3 Q-R4 16 QxP BxN 17 B-K2 wins" — Lasker, *Manual of Chess*.

13	QR—Q1!	R—K1
14	KR—K1	QR—N1
15	B—Q3	P—B4

Or 15...Q-R3 16 B-QB1 Q-R4 17 R-K4 N-N3 18 P-N4 Q-R6 19 B-B1 — Nenarokov.

16	PxPep	QxBP
17	Q—N3+	K—R1

Or 17...P-Q4 18 QxQP+! NxQ 19 RxR+ K-B2 20 R-B8+ K-K3 21 B-B4! N3-K2 22 R-K1+ K-Q2 23 N-K5+ — *Handbuch*.

18	B—N2	Q—B1
19	N—N5	P—Q4
20	R—K6!	BxR

21 NxB Q-B2 22 BxNP+ K-N1 23 BxP+ KxB 24 Q-KR3+ K-N3 25 Q-R6+ K-B4 26 P-N4+ K-K5 27 Q-K3 mate, Martin-Hart, English corres 1908.

C33:

10	...	KN—K2 *(68)*

See diagram next column

White now can try:
C331: 11 N-Q5
C332: 11 N-KN5
C333: 11 R-K1
C334: 11 R-Q1
C335: 11 B-R3!
C336: 11 N-K2!?

68
W

C331:

11	N—Q5?!	NxN
12	BxN	0—0
13	N—N5	

Black now has two good continuations:
1) 13...P-Q3 14 P-K6 PxP 15 BxP BxB 16 NxB Q-B2! (0-1, 41) Asharin-Chigorin, Riga 1892.
b) 13...P-KR3 14 B-K4 Q-R4 15 N-R7 NxP 16 NxR KxN — Chigorin.

C332:

11	N—KN5	NxP

Sokolsky recommended 11...0-0 e.g. 12 P-B4 B-N3+ 13 K-R1 N-Q5 14 Q-Q1 P-Q3!

12	R—K1	NxB
13	QxN	BxN
14	QxB	P—KR3?

15 RxN+! KxR 16 QxBP Q-Q6 (But 16...PxN 17 B-R3+ K-B3! leads to a draw.) 17 B-R3+! QxB 18 R-K1+ K-B3 19 Q-KB4+ K-N3 20 QxP+ with a winning attack, Scott-Dake, USA 1934. However, 14...Q-KB3!(and if 15 Q-R3 P-Q3) could be good for Black.

C333:

11	R—K1	P—N4!?

Chigorin suggested in 1904 the line 11...R-QN1 12 N-R4 Q-R4 13 R-K4 BxN!14 B-K2 QxB 15 RxQ N-Q5!∓.

12	NxP	R—QN1

13   N—R4   Q—R4

Freeborough & Ranken suggested
13...Q-N5 14 Q-R4 K-Q1 15 N-KB3
BxR 16 NxB P-QR3∓.

14   R—K4!   P—N4
15   B—K2   Q—R3

16 Q-QR3 P-R3 17 N-Q4 B-N5 18
Q-Q3 NxN 19 RxN Q-N2 20 N-B5
(Not Freeborough and Ranken's 20
N-B3 P-R3) 20...NxN 21 QxN B-K2
22 R-N1! and Black still has many
problems to solve — *Handbuch*.

C334:
11   R—Q1*(69)*

This was investigated by the
English player V. Potter.

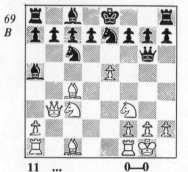

69
B

11   ...   0—0

Others:

a) 11...B-N3 12 Q-R3 0-0 13 N-K2 13
B-KB4 or 13 B-Q3.

b) 11...P-N4 12 NxP R-QN1 13 B-Q3
Q-K3 (Or 13...Q-N5 14 B-K2 P-QR3
15 N-N5 Q-B4 16 P-N4) 14 Q-N2
P-QR3 15 N5-Q4.

12   B—R3   P—N4

White gets a plus after 12...P-QR3
13 B-Q3 Q-K3 14 N-Q5.

13   B—Q3   Q—R4
14   N—K4   B—N3

Potter also considered:

a) 14...P-N5 15 N-N3 Q-N5 16 P-KR3
(16 B-N2! ?) 16...Q-K3 17 B-B4 Q-N3
18 B-QB1=

b) 14...B-N2 15 BxN NxB 16 QxNP.

c) 14...R-N1 15 P-KR3 threatening

16 N4-N5 ± .

15   BxP   R—N1
16   Q—Q3   R—K1

Potter thought 16...R-Q1 better; he
gave the unclear continuation 17
N-B6+!? PxN 18 PxP BxP+ 19 KxB
QxB 20 QxQ RxQ 21 PxN R-K1 22
QR-B1 etc. After 16...R-K1 the line
17 B3xN NxB 18 BxP R-Q1 19 B-N4
RxQ 20 BxQ= was given also, in the
journal *Land and Water*.

C335:
11   B—R3!*(70)*

This move of Wilfred Paulsen's has
been primarily responsible for the dis-
appearance of the Compromised
Defence. There are still one or two
unanswered questions but it probably
ensures White an advantage.

70
B

Black has:

C3351: 11...P-QR3
C3352: 11...R-QN1
C3353: 11...P-QN4
C3354: 11...0-0!

  11...BxN 12 QxB see C323
  11...P-Q3 12 PxP PxP 13
QR-Q1 0-0 probably favours White
— Lasker.

C3351:
11   ...   P—QR3
12   N—Q5

12 QR-Q1 is also possible. The text
move was analysed by J. Malkin in
Schachwelt, 1913. Black's best

defence, Malkin said, only offers him drawing chances. One practical example is available:

12	...	NxN
13	BxN	P—N4
14	P—K6!	BPxP

15 BxN PxB 16 N-K5 Q-K5 17 Q-N3 P-N3 18 QR-Q1 P-N5 19 KR-K1 Q-B4 20 NxBP PxB 21 QxRP! 1-0 Roikov-Orlov, ½-final Leningrad Ch 1968.

C3352:

| 11 | ... | R—QN1 |
| 12 | N—Q5! | NxN |

Or 12...P-N4 13 NxN! NxN (13... PxB 14 QxR NxQ 15 NxQ) 14 BxN KxB 15 Q-R3+ and now:

a1) 15...K-K1 16 QxB PxB 17 QxBP **Q-N3 18 Q-Q6! QxQ 19 PxQ B-R3 20** KR-K1+ K-B1 21 R-K7 with a fine attack — Zukertort.

a2) 15...K-Q1 16 B-Q3 Q-N3 17 N-N5 (Zukertort) or 16 BxBP QxB 17 QxB (Brodsky in *Deutsche Schachzeitung*, 1889.)

13 BxN*(71)*

71
B

| 13 | ... | P—N4 |

Or 13...N-Q1 14 QR-Q1 P-N4 15 R-Q4 P-N5 16 N-R4 Q-N3 17 B-N2 N-K3 18 N-B5! P-N3 19 BxN BPxB 20 N-N7+ K-Q1 21 NxP+ K-K2 when:

a) 22 N-B4+!? (0-1, 42 after further errors) Zukertort-Mortimer, London 1883

b) 22 N-N5! R-B1 23 NxP R-B2 24 Q-KR3 (Or 24 N-N5 and 25 R-R4) wins — Zukertort.

14 P—K6!

Proposed by Dufresne. Others:

a) 14 B-B5 (Freeborough and Ranken): they thought the column move premature.

b) 14 QR-Q1 P-N5 15 P-K6?! BPxP? 16 BxN QPxB 17 N-K5 Q-B4 18 NxP 0-0? 19 N-K7+ 1-0 Chigorin-Mortimer, London 1883. Wayte wrote in the tournament book: "Chigorin's combination was pronounced unsound, as we are informed by several leading players who analysed it, but we have not seen the result of their lucubrations". Presumably 15...PxB should have been tried.

14	...	BPxP
15	BxN	PxB
16	N—K5	Q—K5
17	Q—N3	P—N3
18	Q—N5!?	

Presumably 18 QR-Q1, as Roikov played in the analogous position, would be at least as good.

| 18 | ... | P—N5 |
| 19 | QR—Q1! | |

Dufresne analysed 19 Q-B6 R-B1 20 Q-N7 PxB 21 QR-Q1! Q-KR5 22 NxBP, while Freeborough and Ranken gave the variation 20...R-N4 21 QR-Q1 R-Q4/Q-R5 22 NxBP.

19	...	0—0
20	B—N2	R—N4
21	N—B7!	P—K4

Ending:

a) 22 N-R6+ K-R1 (22...K-N2 23 Q-K7+) 23 R-Q8 K-N2 24 RxR KxR 25 Q-B6+ K-K1 26 N-N8 1-0 Tarrasch-Kelz, Nuremberg 1890.

b) 22 Q-B6! (Forcing P-KR3/4 when N-R6+ wins the rook) Sandford-Brancon, English corres 1898.

C3353:

| 11 | ... | P—N4 |
| 12 | NxP | R—QN1 *(72)* |

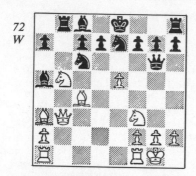

72
W

13   Q—R4!?
Also to be considered:
a) 13 Q-K3!? e.g. 13...B-N3 14 Q-KB4 0-0 15 QR-Q1 P-KR3 16 N-B3 B-N2 — *Handbuch*.
b) 13 BxN KxB (Wormald's 13... P-QR3 is met by 14 Q-R4!) and now:
b1) 14 Q-R3+ B-N5 15 Q-K3 K-Q1 16 N-N5 R-B1 17 QR-Q1 P-QR3 18 P-K6 with a fierce attack — *Deutsche Schachzeitung*.
b2) 14 Q-K3!? when:
b21(14...B-N2 15 QR-Q1 B-N3 16 Q-R3+ K-Q1 17 KR-K1 R-K1 18 B-Q5 P-QR3 19 N-B3 K-B1 20 P-N3 N-R2 Tippin-Fink, California Ch 1930.
b22) 14...B-N3 15 Q-R3+ K-Q1 16 KR-K1 B-N2 17 QR-Q1 Q-B7 18 P-K6! with a winning attack, e.g. 18...N-K4 (18...QxB 19 N-N5!) 19 N3-Q4 (Romanov's book gives 19 RxN! QxR+ 20 R-K1 Q-B7 21 P-K7+ K-K1 22 Q-B5!!) 19...NxB 20 NxQ NxQ 21 RxP+ K-B1 22 N2xN PxP 23 RxNP P-QR3 24 NxP R-B1 25 R-QB1! BxBP+ 26 K-R1 B-K6 27 NxKP+! BxR 28 R-QB7 mate, Winawer-Chigorin, Petersburg 1875.
13   ...   P—QR3!?
Zukertort's suggestion. Others:
a) 13...0-0? 14 BxN and White wins a piece.
b) 13...B-N3 14 KR-K1 0-0 15 QR-Q1 R-K1 16 B-Q3 Q-R4 17 R-K4 N-N3 18 B-N2 — Blackburne's analysis?
c) 13...B-N2 14 QR-Q1 and now:

c1) 14...B-N3 15 B-Q3 P-B4 16 PxPep QxP 17 KR-K1 K-Q1? (17...0-0!) 18 NxRP?! (18 B-K4 wins.) 18...N-Q5 19 Q-KN4 N-Q5 20 B-N2 NxN+? (20... BxN) 21 PxN QxB 22 QxP+ KxQ 23 B-N5 mate, Blackburne-Martin, blindfold simul. 1876.
c2) 14...NxP!? 15 N-R4 N-B6+ 16 NxN BxN 17 NxBP+! K-B1 18 BxN+ K-N1 19 P-N3 BxN 20 RxP B-B3 21 QxP Q-K5 22 QxR+! BxQ 23 R-Q8+ mating, Orchard-Burille, 1893.
14   N—Q6+!   PxN
15   PxP   N—B4
16   KR—K1+   BxR
17   RxB+
This line is given by most books as the refutation of Black's eleventh move, yet Blackburne himself came to believe that the rook sacrifice is not completely sound. There can follow:
a) 17...K-B1 18 QxN! PxQ 19 P-Q7+ and mates next move; Blackburne-N.N., blindfold simul., Manchester 1875.
b) 17...K-Q1 would have been met by 18 N-K5 NxN 19 Q-R5+ K-K1 20 QxN winning — Blackburne.
c) "...But in a later simul., a Glasgow player found 17...N4-K2! and it is difficult to see how White can do more than draw." This position deserves further examination; Ranken, for example, gave 18 B-Q5!? but Black might then castle. 18 PxN seems critical, to refute 18...R-N8? (18...B-N2!?) by 19 BxP+! KxB (19...QxB 20 RxR) 20 Q-KB4+! Q-B3 (20...K-K1 21 Q-B8+) 21 Q-B4+! etc. But one can certainly not say dogmatically that White has a forced win at move 17. This is an example of the perpetuation of error in modern books about old openings; all East European books take *Sovremenny Debyut* (itself heavily reliant on the *Handbuch*) as their main source, so what Levenfish's team missed, so do they all.

C3354:

11	...	0—0!
12	QR—Q1*(73)*	

Others:

a) 12 N-Q5 NxN 13 BxN (13 BxR? N-B5!) when:

a1) 13...R-K1? 14 N-N5! NxP 15 P-B4 P-QB3 16 B-K4 Q-R4 17 PxN P-Q4 18 PxPep 1-0 Judge Labatt-Em. Lasker, simul., USA 1907 (or 1908).

a2) 13...P-Q3 14 PxP (If 14 QR-Q1 R-Q1, and not *Handbuch's* suggestion 14...B-K3 because of 15 QxP winning a second pawn or keeping the attack — Chigorin.) 14...PxP 15 QR-Q1 B-B2 16 KR-K1 R-N1 17 B-K4 B-B4! 18 N-R4 B-K3 and Black won; Allies-Chigorin, Moscow 1901.

b) Another Chigorin friendly went 12 N-K2 P-Q3 13 B-Q3 B-B4 14 N-R4 Q-K3 15 NxB NxB 16 Q-B2 N3-Q5! 17 NxN NxN 18 BxRP+ K-R1 19 Q-Q3 QxKP 20 Q-R3 N-K7+ 21 K-R1 N-B5 22 Q-R4 and now after 22...Q-R4 Black should win.

73
B

12	...	P—QN4

Also to be considered:

a) Chigorin recommended 12...R-Q1 but there are no examples of this. We suggest 13 BxN! (13 B-Q3 Q-R4 14 N-K4 P-Q4!) 13...NxB 14 Q-R3 e.g.:

a1) 14...BxN 15 QxN R-B1 16 N-N5 P-Q4 17 PxPep B-K3 (17...B-KN5 18 P-Q7! or 17...B-QN5 18 NxBP!) 18 BxB and 19 PxP.

a2) 14...N-B3 15 N-Q5 with strong threats:

a21) 15...R-N1 (15...P-Q3 16 B-N5!

or 15...P-N4 16 BxP) 16 B-N5 Q-K3 17 BxN NPxB 18 N-K7+ K-R1 19 N-N5 Q-B5 20 Q-Q3! forces mate.

a22) 15...R-K1 (15...B-N3 16 NxB BPxN 17 R-Q6) 16 B-N5 B-N3 17 NxB BPxN 18 R-Q6 R-K3 19 KR-Q1 and 20 B-B4, and Black is tied up.

b) 12...R-K1 when:

b1) 13 N-K4!? QxN? (13...P-KR3! — Keres) 14 BxP+ K-B1 15 B-N8! P-Q4 16 PxPep NxB 17 N-N5 Q-B4 18 Q-B7+ QxQ 19 N-R7 mate — Lasker.

b2) 13 B-Q3 Q-R4 14 N-K4 NxP 15 NxN QxN and now:

b21) 16 B-N2 Q-K3 17 Q-N5 Q-N3 18 Q-R5 QxB 19 N-N5± was a game Lasker-Marshall, quoted in a late edition of the *Handbuch*.

b22) 16 P-B4 Q-K3 17 Q-R4 N-B3 18 N-N5 Q-K6+ 19 K-R1 P-KR3 20 R-B3± Hart-allies, corres. 1934 *(BCM)*.

c) 12...P-QR3 when:

c1) 13 N-Q5 NxN 14 BxN R-K1 15 N-N5 N-Q1 16 P-B4 Q-N3+ 17 QxQ BxQ+ 18 K-R1 P-R3? (18...R-N1 — Bachmann, *Schachmeister Anderssen*) 19 N-K4 R-N1 20 P-N4 B-R2 21 P-N5 PxP 22 PxP N-K3 23 R-Q3 P-N4 24 N-B6+ PxN 25 NPxP K-R2 26 R-R3+ K-N1 27 R-KN3+ K-R2 28 R-B5 1-0 Riemann-Anderssen, Breslau 1874.

c2) 13 B-Q3 Q-K3? (13...Q-R4 and if 14 N-K4 NxP is necessary.) 14 BxKRP+ K-R1 15 N-Q5 NxN (Bokhtor-Meszaros, Budapest 1964) and now best would be 16 RxN e.g. 16...R-K1 17 B-N1 Q-R3 18 B-B1 — *Chess.*

13 B—Q3

Or 13 NxP R-N1 when:

a) 14 BxN NxB 15 Q-R3 N-B3 16 NxRP (16 N3-Q4? B-N5∓ W. Paulsen-Zukertort, Leipzig 1877) 16...B-N5 17 Q-R4 NxN 18 QxN B-N2 19 N-R4 and 20 Q-Q4 — Schallopp in the tournament book.

b) 14 N3-Q4 P-QR3 (14...NxN 15

RxN B-N2 16 Q-R3) 15 NxN NxN 16 BxR KxB 17 B-Q3 Q-R4 18 R-B1 P-N4 19 RxN PxR 20 Q-R3+ K-N1 21 QxB — Schallopp.

13 ... Q—R4

Or 13...Q-N5 14 P-R3 Q-K3 15 N-Q5 P-N5 16 BxP+ K-R1 17 N-N5 (17 B-B1 NxN 18 RxN N-K2 19 B-K4 B-N2! *Chess Monthly*) 17...NxN 18 NxQ BPxN 19 B-N1 PxB 20 Q-B2 R-B4 21 RxN N-N5 22 Q-B5 NxR 23 BxR 1-0 Young-Zukertort, from the former's *Field Book of Chess Generalship*.

14 N—Q5 NxN
15 QxN P—N5
16 B—N2 R—N1

17 KR-K1 B-N3 18 R-K4 N-K2 19 Q-N3 N-N3 20 P-N4 Q-R6 21 B-KB1 Q-R3 22 B-B1 (Of course the win should just be technique now.) 22... N-B5 23 RxN Q-QB3 24 B-B4 B-N2 25 B-Q5 Q-B6 26 BxP+ K-R1 27 B-N2 QxQ 28 PxQ B-B3 29 N-R4 QR-K1 30 P-N5 R-K3 31 R-Q3 P-N34 32 R-B6 RxR 33 NPxR 1-0 Taylor-Zukertort, from the former's *Chess Skirmishes*.

C336:
11 N—K2!?*(74)*

The beginning of a relatively forgotten plan for White.

74
B

11 ... P—N4!

11...0-0 is generally considered to be an error: 12 B-Q3:
a) 12...Q-R4 13 N-B4 Q-N5 14 P-KR3.

b) 12 Q-N5 13 N-B4 P-Q4 14 P-KR3 Q-Q2 15 P-K6 PxP 16 N-N5 N-Q5 17 BxP+ K-R1 18 Q-Q1 — *Deutsche Schachzeitung,* 1876.
c) 12...Q-K3 13 BxP+ K-R1 14 Q-R4 P-Q3 15 N-B4 (15 Q-R4 Q-N5) 15... Q-Q2 16 P-K6 PxP 17 N-N5 P-K4 18 N4-K6 R-B3 19 Q-R4 R-B3 but now instead of 20 N-B7+ (F&R), White has an annihilating blow in 20 N-B8!

12 B—Q3!

Not 12 BxNP R-QN1 13 Q-R4 P-QR3 14 BxN NxB∓ — *Handbuch.*

12 ... Q—K3
13 Q—N2

Another Anderssen idea was 13 Q-N1!? e.g. 13...N-N3 14 B-N2 B-N2 15 P-QR4 P-N5 16 N-N3 0-0-0 17 R-K1 N-B5 18 B-K4, but this looks artificial.

13 ... N—N3
14 N—B4

Blackburne-Steinitz, London 1872, went 14 B-KB4!? 0-0 15 QR-B1 P-QR3 16 KR-Q1 B-N2 17 B-N3 B-N3 and Black had a solid position (0-1, 55).

14 ... NxN!

Not 14...Q-K2 15 N-Q5 Q-K3 16 B-K4 0-0 17 B-Q2± — Anderssen, 1872.

15 BxN*(75)*

The critical position of Anderssen's variation.

75
B

Black can try:
C361: 15...P-KR3
C362: 15...P-QR3
15...Q-N5 16 Q-B1! B-N2 17

P-KR3 Q-K3 18 BxP± — Anderssen in *Deutsche Schachzeitung* 1873

C361:

15 ...	P—KR3
16 N—R4	

Others:

a) 16 BxP R-QN1 17 Q-K2 — Monck — 17...0-0 18 B-B4 P-Q4!∓.

b) 16 QR-B1 P-R3 17 KR-Q1 0-0 (Or 17...B-N2 18 Q-N1 QR-Q1∓ — Wormald) may be good for Black, according to Ranken. Salvioli's *Il Gambitto Evans* (1875) gave 16... R-QN1 B-N1 0-0 18 N-R4 Q-N5 19 P-N3 etc. or 17...B-N2 18 KR-Q1 0-0 19 Q-B2 — Anderssen.

16 ...	Q—N5

Or 16...P-N4 17 B-B5 Q-Q4 (17... Q-K2 18 P-K6!) 18 KR-Q1 Q-B4 19 QR-Q1 with a winning position — *Chess* 1938.

17 B—N3	Q—QN5
18 Q—K2	P—R3
19 QR—Q1	N—Q5

20 Q-N4 N-K3 21 P-B4 B-N2 22 K-R1 P-R4 23 Q-R3 0-0-0 with complications galore, Zollner-Wright, Manchester 1877. We prefer Black, although White won in that game.

C362:

15 ...	P—QR3
16 QR—B1	

The *Handbuch* suggested 16 N-N5 Q-K2 17 P-K6 P-B3 18 NxRP P-Q3 19 Q-B1 etc. Black can get a powerful counter-attack, however, with 17... BPxP 18 NxRP 0-0-0 19 B-N5 Q-B2 20 BxR NxB.

16 ...	B—N2
17 KR—Q1	B—N3
18 B—K4	N—R4!
19 N—N5	Q—K2
20 BxB	NxB
21 Q—K2	N—B4!

Anderssen's idea was that 21...0-0? loses a piece to 22 Q-K4, while 21... 0-0-0 can be met with 22 P-QR4 and an attack.

However, after the text move Black proposes to consolidate with ...N-K3 etc., and it is unlikely that White can in the long run find sufficient compensation for his pawns. Play might continue, for example, 22 Q-B3 R-Q1 23 B-K3 0-0 24 BxN BxB 25 N-K4 and now either 25...P-Q3 or 25...B-N3!? 26 N-B6+!? K-R1! — analysis.

Finally, it should be noted that after 1 P-K4 P-K4 2 N-KB3 N-QB3 3 B-B4 B-B4 4 P-QN4 BxNP 5 P-B3 B-R4 6 P-Q4 PxP 7 0-0, Black gains nothing by playing instead 7...BxP!?

After 8 NxB PxN:

a) Freeborough and Ranken suggested 9 B-R3!? P-Q3 10 Q-N3 or 10 P-K5.

b) Simplest is 9 Q-N3 when:

b1) 9...Q-K2 10 B-R3 Q-B3 11 P-K5 Q-N3 12 N-N5 — Freeborough and Ranken.

b2) 9...Q-B3 10 P-K5 and now:

b21) 10...NxP? 11 R-K1 (Or 11 NxN QxN 12 BxP+ K-B1 13 B-R3+) 11...P-Q3 12 NxN PxN 13 Q-N5+ P-B3 14 RxP+ N-K2 15 Q-B5 etc. — Ranken.

b22) Better is 10...Q-N3 11 QxBP transposing to line C32 above.

6 The Q—N3 Method

When Black meets the Evans by 5...B-R4, White has the opportunity of avoiding well-known variations by means of an early Q-QN3. We shall see that this idea can take more than one form. In most cases the motive is to draw out the black queen, by the attack on the KBP, into an exposed position and then open lines with P-K5. The disadvantage is that the white queen may itself become an object of attack; ...B-N3 followed by ...N-QR4 has often to be reckoned with.

The Q-N3 Method has been out of fashion for over a hundred years, but is not clearly refuted. The English international postal player M.W. Wills has been consistently successful with the idea, and we are indebted to him for his game scores and comments. The large number of inferior defences, and hence rapid wins by White in this chapter, testify to the great surprise value that the Q-N3 lines have at present. Even when Black knows his danger, it is not easy for him to find his way through the complications.

1	P—K4	P—K4
2	N—KB3	N—QB3
3	B—B4	B—B4
4	P—QN4	BxNP
5	P—B3	B—R4

We divide the material as follows:

A: 6 P-Q4 PxP 7 0-0 P-Q3 8 Q-N3!?
B: 6 P-Q4 PxP 7 Q-N3!?
C: 6 Q-N3!?

A:

6	P—Q4	PxP
7	0—0	P—Q3
8	Q—N3!?*(76)*	

For 8 PxP (8 NxP? KN-K2) see A3 in Chapter 7.

The text move introduces Waller's Attack. Irishman George Waller discussed the move in *The Chess-Players' Chronicle* in 1848, after which it was mentioned in the *Deutsche Schachzeitung* (1849) and Staunton's *Chess-Player's Companion*. Because of this possibility, Black is best advised to play 7...B-N3, heading for the Normal Position (*see* chapter 8), since it will be seen from B below, that Q-N3 is less effective when Black avoids ...P-Q3.

76
B

Black has tried:

A1: 8...Q-Q2
A2: 8...Q-B3
A3: 8...Q-K2

A1:

8	...	Q—Q2

9 P—K5!

9 PxP is not so good, on account of 9...N-Q1! followed by 10...N-K2 — Keres.

9 ... N—Q1

This is probably best, in view of:

a) 9...PxBP 10 R-K1 P-B7 11 P-K6! Kolisch-Rousseau, Paris 1867.

b) 9...PxKP 10 NxP NxN 11 R-K1 P-KB3 12 BxN PxP 13 BxP P-B7 14 RxN+ PxR 15 B-N6+± — *Handbuch*.

10 KPxP BPxP

11 B—KN5! P—QR3

This is better than 11...P-KB3 12 BxN PxB 13 BxP! or 11...N-K2 12 R-K1 N-K3 13 BxN̄ KxB 14 NxP — *Fernschach*.

12 R—K1+ K—B1

13 NxP P—R3?

13...P-N4 was a better chance — *Fernschach*.

14 BxN BxB

15 N—Q2 N—KB3

16 N—K4 NxN

17 RxN P-QN4 18 B-Q5 B-N2 19 QR-K1 B-KB3 (19...BxB 20 QxB R-B1 21 QxQP+!) 20 B-K6! Q-B2 21 BxP QxB 22 N-K6+ K-N1 23 N-N5! ±± Muir-Ormhaug, corres 1958-60.

A2:

8 ... Q—B3

9 P—K5

This is more convincing that 9 PxP B-N3 (9...Q-N3!? — *Handbuch*):

a) 10 B-QN5 B-Q2 11 P-K5 PxP 12 R-K1 KN-K2 13 PxP Q-N3 14 B-Q3 (Staunton & Owen v. Lowenthal & Barnes, 1856) 14...B-KB4 15 N-R4 NxP — *B.C.M.* 1956.

b) 10 P-K5 PxP! 11 PxP Q-N3 e.g. 12 N-KN5 (Or 12 B-R3 B-K3 13 QN-Q2 KN-K2 Thompson-Morphy, New York 1857) 12...N-Q1! (Lowenthal) but not Waller's 12...N-R3 13 P-K6 PxP (Better 13...0-0) 14 BxP BxB 15 NxB∓.

9 ... PxKP

Or 9...Q-N3?! 10 KPxP BPxP 11 N-N5 N-R3 12 R-K1+ K-B1 (Kolisch-Schumov, 2nd match game 1862). The best continuation of White's attack would be 13 R-Q1, with the idea of PxP or B-Q3 to follow.

10 R—K1 *(77)*

Others:

a) 10 PxP? B-N3 see note c2 to White's 9th.

b) 10 B-KN5 (10 B-R3 KN-K2) 10...Q-B4 11 NxKP QxN 12 BxP+ K-B1 — Lowenthal.

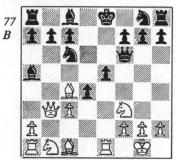

77
B

Black can now consider:

A21: 10...N-R3

A22: 10...B-Q2

A23: 10...B-N3

10...KN-K2? 11 B-KN5 Q-N3 12 BxN NxB 13 NxP Q-N3 14 B-N5+ P-QB3 15 QxP+ K-Q1 16 NxP+! and White won in a game Kolisch-Barnes (from Gossip's *Manual of Chess*).

A21:

10 ... N—R3

11 B—KN5!

Others:

a) 11 B-R3? B-Q2 12 QN-Q2 0-0-0∓ Carstanja-L. Paulsen, Cologne 1862.

b) 11 NxKP!? 0-0! (Not 11...NxN 12 Q-N5+ e.g. 12...K-Q1 13 RxN) 12 NxN PxN and White has no clear attacking line, since 13 B-R3 R-Q1 14 B-K7 fails to 14...R-K1! 15 BxQ RxR+ 16 B-B1 PxB 17 Q-B4 PxP etc.

11   ...   Q—B4
12   Q—R3!

Now White threatens to capture on K5. Not 12 B-Q5 0-0 13 BxN PxB 14 RxP Q-Q6! — *Deutsche Schachzeitung.*

12   ...   P—KB3
13   BxN   PxB
14   B—Q5   BxP

15 NxB PxN 16 BxN+ PxB 17 Q-B5 B-Q2 18 NxKP± — *Sovremenny Debyut.*

A22:

10   ...   B—Q2
11   B—KN5

An Anderssen-Kolisch, Paris 1860, game continued less incisively 11 QN-Q2 KN-K2 12 N-K4 Q-B4 13 B-KN5 and now 13...B-K3 was necessary.

11   ...   Q—B4 *(78)*

78
W

12   QxP!

12 NxKP NxN 13 P-B4 P-KB3 14 QxP!, as played in a game Caldas Vianna v. Silvestre, Rio de Janeiro 1900, is interesting but perhaps unsound. After 14...R-Q1 15 PxN PxB 16 R-KB1 QxP 17 N-Q2 N-K2 18 QR-K1 Q-QB4 19 B-B7+ K-B1 20 B-N6+ B-B4 21 BxB NxB 22 N-K4 Q-N3 23 RxN+ K-N1 White tried the ingenious 24 N-Q6! and even won the game. However, Emanuel Lasker, analysing this combination in his *Manual of Chess,* pointed out 24...

QxQ! 25 NxQBxP 26 NxR BxR and White has few drawing chances.

12   ...   R—N1

Or 12...R-B1 13 B-Q5 R-N1 14 RxP+ QxR 15 BxP+ transposing.

13   RxP+!

Here Keres opines that White has the better game. An old analysis runs 13...QxR 14 BxP+ and now:

a) 14...KxB 15 NxQ+ K-K3 16 Q-R6 KxN 17 N-Q2 or 17 P-KB4 — Berger, 1867.

b) 14...K-B1 15 QxR+ NxQ 16 NxQ PxP 17 B-N3 N-K2 when:

b1) 18 N-B4 B-QN5 19 P-QR3 B-QB4 20 NxP favours White, according to the *Handbuch,* but after 20...P-QR3! (20...N1-B3? 21 N-N5!) 21 N-K4 B-R2 22 R-Q1 K-K1 it seems that White has nothing concrete — analysis.

b2) 18 N-R3 comes into consideration, e.g. 18...B-QN5 19 R-Q1! retaining attacking possibilities. Is the pawn at QB3 really all that strong?

A23:

10   ...   B—N3

To free the QN and protect the QP.

11   B—KN5   Q—B4

Not 11...N-R4? 12 Q-R4+ B-Q2 13 BxQ BxQ 14 BxNP NxB 15 BxR although the win of the exchange still leaves White with much work to do — analysis.

12   NxKP   R—N1 *(79)*

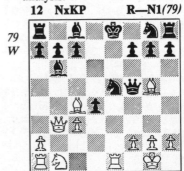

79
W

White has two tries:
A231: 13 P-B4
A232: 13 Q-N5+

A231:
    13 P—B4   PxP+
13...P-KB3 (or 13...PxP+ 14 K-R1
P-KB3) needs to be examined.
    14 K—R1   B—Q5
    15 NxP   K—B1
    16 QR—Q1   NxB
Or 16...P-B4 17 RxB.
    17 QxN   B—K3
    18 QxB   P—KB3
    19 N—K4
Another nice finish is 19 N-N5 QxN
20 RxB PxB 21 P-QR4! Q-R4 22
R1-K1 QxR+ 23 RxQ PxP 24
QxBP+ N-B3 25 Q-QN4+ K-B2 26
R-K7+ K-N3 27 Q-N1+ K-R3 28
Q-B5 QR-Q1 29 P-N4 1-0 Dinic-
Loncarevic, Yugoslavian corres 1967.
    19 ...   P—QN3
Or 19...PxB 20 NxP R-K1 21 R-K5
Q-N5 22 Q-B5+.
After the text move, a game
Morphy-Kipping, Birmingham 1858,
ended 20 N-N3 Q-B4 21 QxQ+ PxQ
22 RxB PxB 23 PxP P-N3 24 P-KR4
K-B2 25 R-K5 P-KR3 26 N-K4 PxP
27 NxP+ K-B3 28 R-K6+ K-B4 29
R-Q5+ K-N5 30 R-K4+ 1-0 (30...
K-N6 31 N-R3).

A232:
    13 Q—N5+   K—B1
Not 13...P-QB3 14 RxN+ B-K3 15
BxB PxB 16 Q-K2 Q-B2 17 N-Q2
K-Q2 18 N-B4 R-K1 19 R-QR5 Q-B1
20 R-N1 BxR 21 RxP+ B-B2 22 Q-K5
R-B1 23 QxQP+ K-K1 24 RxB RxR
25 Q-Q8+ K-B2 26 N-K5 mate;
Kolisch-Lord Cremorne, London
1862.
    14 RxN   Q—Q2
    15 Q—N3   P—KB3
    16 R—Q5   Q—K2
17 B-Q2 P-B3 18 RxP BxR 19 PxB

P-QR4 20 P-QR4 P-R4 with an
unclear position; Cave-Greenwell,
corres (*B.C.M.*, 1891).

A3:
    8 ...   Q—K2
    9 P—K5
As usual, 9 PxP is thought inferior.
Black might consider 9...B-Q2!? in
reply, as suggested in the *Handbuch*.
After 9...B-N3 instead:
a) 10 P-K5? NxP! 11 NxN BxB 12
PxP PxP 13 BxP+ K-B1 14 BxN BxR
15 B-Q5 B-B4∓ was a well-known
**nineteenth-century analysis by A.F.
Svanberg of Uppsala.**
b) 10 B-N2! N-R4 11 Q-B2 NxB 12
QxN B-N5 13 QN-Q2± — *Sovremenny Debyut.*
    9 ...   PxKP(80)

80
W

Now White has:
A31: 10 R-K1
A32: 10 B-R3!

A31:
    10 R—K1   B—Q2
This move was suggested by Heyde-
brand von der Lasa, one of the original
editors of the *Handbuch*. Waller had
only analysed:
a) 10...PxP 11 QNxP BxN 12 QxB
B-K3 13 NxP Q-B3 14 B-KN5 QxB 15
NxN PxN 16 BxB PxB 17 QxBP+ and
wins;
b) 10...B-N3 11 B-R3 Q-B3 12 NxKP
NxN 13 BxP+ K-Q1 14 Q-Q5+ B-Q2

15 RxN P-B3 16 R-K8+ K-B2 17
Q-Q6+ QxQ 18 BxQ+ KxB 19 RxR
e.g. 19...B-K3 20 BxB KxB (Spreckley-
Perigal, London, circa 1845) when
White should have played 21 P-QR4!
instead of 21 N-Q2?!

11 B—Q5!

Improving on von der Lasa's line 11
B-R3 Q-B3 12 NxKP 0-0-0 13 NxKBP
PxP 14 NxQR (14 NxKR P-B7) 14...
NxN 15 Q-B2 N-QB3∓.

11 ... 0—0—0

Or 11...B-N3 12 BxN PxB 13 B-R3
Q-B3 14 RxP+ (14 PxP!? — *Deutsche
Schachzeitung*, 1859) 14...B-K3 15
Q-R4 0-0-0 16 PxP± Lange-Richter,
from *Deutsche Schachzeitung*, 1860.

12 BxN PxB!

Not 12...BxB 13 RxP Q-B3 14 B-N5
Q-N3 15 BxR BxN 16 R-KN5 etc. —
Handbuch.

13 B—N5

White also gets only equality from
13 RxP B-K3 14 Q-R4 B-N3 according
to another old analysis (e.g. *Deutsche
Schachzeitung* 1861).

13 ... N—B3

Not 13...P-B3? 14 RxP and the
bishop cannot be interposed.

14 RxP B—K3
15 Q—R4 B—N3=

Chigorin-Levi, corres 1884; White
finally won after a couple of inferior
moves by his opponent much later on.

A32:

10 B—R3! Q—B3(81)

81
W

11 PxP!

Other promising moves are:
a) 11 R-K1 KN-K2 (11...B-N3 see
A31, note b to Black's tenth.) 12
QN-Q2! (Tartakower) improving upon
12 NxP!? NxN 13 BxN KxB 14 Q-N5
B-N3 of Tartakower-Breyer, Baden
1914, which ended in Black's favour
although White had chances.
b) 11 QN-Q2 when:
b1) 11...B-N3?! 12 QR-K1 KN-K2 13
N-K4 Q-N3 14 BxN KxB 15 N4-N5
P-B3 16 Q-R3+ is±. e.g. 16...N-N5 17
QxN+ P-QB4 18 Q-N3 P-KR3 19
N-B7 B-R6 20 P-N3 BxR 21 NxR RxN
22 BxB Q-B2 23 NxKP PxN 24 RxP+
K-B1 25 B-B4 Q-B2 26 PxP PxP?! 27
Q-KB3+ 1-0 Corzo-Capablanca, 2nd
match game 1901.
b2) 11...KN-K2!? 12 N-K4 Q-N3 13
BxN KxB 14 KR-K1 P-B3 15 B-Q5
B-N3 (15...B-Q2 16 N-B5) 16 BxN PxB
17 PxP± — analysis.

11 ... P—K5

Black is in a quandary. The
plausible move 11...KN-K2, for
example, loses a piece to the familiar
trick 12 P-Q5 and (if the knight moves)
13 Q-R4+ and 14 QxB.

12 N—K5

Or 12 N-N5!? N-R3 13 NxP Q-B4 14
N1-B3 BxN 15 N-N3! with a powerful
attack; Staunton-N.N., London 1847

12 ... N—R3

Or 12...NxP 13 Q-R4+ etc.

13 NxN PxN
14 Q—R4 B—N3
15 N—B3 B—Q2

16 NxP Q-B5 17 N-B5 BxN 18 BxB
N-B4 19 KR-K1+ K-Q1 20 BxP and
White soon won in Fischer-Janush-
kowsky, simul at Davis College, USA
1964.

B:

5 ... B—R4
6 P—Q4 PxP
7 Q—N3(82)

Since Black rarely allows the Waller
Attack, White does best, in our
opinion, to play the Q-N3 Method in

this form. He thus avoids both C1 below, and also various troublesome lines in the next chapter.

82
B

Black's choice is between:
B1: 7...Q-B3
B2: 7...Q-K2

B1:

    7 ...   Q—B3
    8 0—0!*(83)*

Others:

a) 8 P-K5!? NxP (8...Q-N3!) 9 NxN QxN+ 10 K-Q1 Q-R4+ 11 B-K2 Q-N3 12 R-K1+ K-Q1 13 B-R3 P-Q3 14 Q-N5 Q-KB4 and White announced mate in 3; Laldegg-Zeissl, Vienna club 1903.

b) 8 B-KN5 Q-N3 9 0-0 P-Q3 10 PxP N-B3 11 BxN PxB 12 P-Q5 B-R6 13 N-R4 Q-N5 14 PxN QxN 15 PxP R-QN1 (Bradley-Bloodworth, corres 1963-4) 16 QxB   but Black can maybe improve on this.

c) 8 B-N2!? — Schlechter.

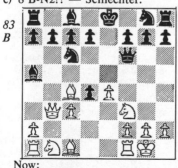

83
B

Now:
B11: 8...P-QN4!?

B12: 8...N-R3
B13: 8...KN-K2
B14: 8...B-N3

Others transpose:
a) 8...P-Q3 see A2.
b) 8...PxP see Chapter 5.
c) 8...BxP also see Chapter 5.
d) 8...P-Q6 see Chapter 1 (Evergreen Game).

B11:

    8 ...   P—QN4!?

Blackburne commented: "I was only too glad to leave the domain of the analyst and try for a counter-attack."

    9 BxNP

9 B-Q5 would transpose to the game Breyer-Schlechter, Baden 1914, when Black played 9...P-KR3! (Preventing B-N5) and White failed to obtain enough compensation for his gambit pawn, viz. 10 PxP KN-K2 11 P-K5 Q-B4 12 QN-Q2 NxB 13 QxN 0-0 14 B-R3 P-N5! 15 B-N2 B-N3 16 Q-N3 (16 N-B4 B-R3; 16 Q-K4!?) 16...P-QR4∓.

    9 ...   R—N1
    10 Q—R4   KN—K2
    11 P—K5   Q—N3

11...NxP 12 QxB NxN+ 13 PxN Q-K4 (Pinning the bishop, guarding the QBP and preventing R-K1) fails narrowly to 14 N-R3 (14 P-QR4!?) 14... P-QB3 15 P-KB4 Q-Q4 16 R-K1! PxB 17 Q-B7 R-R1 18 NxP! and the black knight is doomed.

After the text move, White ought to play 12 PxP with level material and at least equal chances. Steel-Blackburne, London 1881, continued instead 12 B-R3 B-N2! 13 BxN/K7 NxP! 14 N-R4 N-B6+ 15 NxN BxN 16 BxP+ KxB/K2 17 R-K8+ K-B1! (17... K-Q1?? 18 B-R3!) 18 B-R3 B-N3 19 PxP B-B3 20 Q-N4+ K-N1 21 N-B3 P-KR4 22 R-K5 P-R5 23 Q-B4? (23 N-K2 "would have given White a drawing chance" — Blackburne.) 23...BxP! 24 B-B5 B-Q4+ 25 BxQ BxQ 26 B-B2 BxP and Black won.

B12:

8	...	N—R3
9	P—K5	Q—N3
10	B—R3	

Black is unable to bring his king into safety. A Barnes-Owen game, 1857 vintage, continued 10...PxP 11 NxP BxN 12 QxB P-N3 (Black is playing the Compromised Defence with his KN misplaced.) 13 P-K6 BPxP?! 14 BxP B-N2 15 N-R4 Q-B3 16 BxP+ KxB 17 Q-KR3+ K-Q1 18 KR-K1 R-K1 19 QR-Q1+ N-Q5 20 RxN+ QxR 21 RxR+ KxR 22 Q-K6+ forcing mate.

B13:

8	...	KN—K2
9	PxP!*(84)*	

Others are insufficient:

a) 9 P-K5?! (Kipping-Anderssen, Manchester 1857) 9...NxP! e.g. 10 NxN QxN 11 BxP+ K-B1 12 PxP Q-B3 13 B-QB4 B-N3 14 N-B3 BxP∓ — analysis.

b) 9 B-KN5 Q-N3 10 BxN (10 PxP P-B3!) 10...NxB! 11 N-K5 QxKP! 12 NxBP (Or 12 BxP+ K-Q1 13 N-B4 B-N3) 12...R-B1 13 N-Q2 Q-N3 14 N-K5 (14 PxP P-Q4! or 14 N-B3 BxP) 14...Q-R3, and if 15 N-K4 Q-B5 is unconvincing for White — analysis by Botterill and Harding.

84
B

9	...	0—0

Inferior moves:

a) 9...P-Q3? 1Q B-KN5! Q-N3 (10... NxP? 11 BxQ NxQ 12 PxN) 11 P-Q5 N-K4 (11...B-KN5 12 PxN BxN 13

PxP! or 11...P-KR3 12 B-B4) 12 NxN PxN (12...QxB 13 N-KB3) 13 BxN KxB 14 Q-R3+ K-Q1 (14...K-B3 15 K-R1 B-N3 16 P-B4) 15 P-Q6! (15 QxB?? B-R6 16 P-N3 QxKP∓∓)15...B-N3 16 PxP+ KxB 17 N-B3 B-K3? (17... K-N1±) 18 N-N5+ K-B1 19 QR-B1 BxB 20 Q-K7! 1-0 Harding-Day, corres 1973-4.

b) 9...B-N3 10 P-K5 Q-N3 11 B-Q3! Q-R4 12 P-Q5 N-Q1 13 B-R3± — analysis.

c) 9...NxP 10 NxN QxN 11 BxP+ K-B1 (11...K-Q1 12 B-N2) 12 B-R5! P-Q4 (12...P-KN3 13 B-N2 or 12...Q-B3 13 B-N2 and 14 Q-KB3+) 13 PxP! QxQP (13...QxR 14 B-N2 or 13...NxP 14 R-Q1) 14 R-Q1! and 15 R-Q8+ winning — analysis.

10	B—N2	P—Q3

A typical Evans Gambit position has arisen. For his pawn, White has a central pawn duo, which restricts his opponent's mobility and giving opportunities for attack by P-K5 at a suitable moment. The exposed position of Black's queen makes it all the more likely that the position favour White, but practical tests are needed.

White should probably continue 11 N-B3, although 11 QN-Q2 and 11 P-K5 also come into consideration. Not, however, 11 P-Q5? (Shutting out his own KB) 11...N-K4 12 NxN PxN 13 P-B4 B-N3+ 14 K-R1 Q-N3 as in a game Anderssen-Kolisch, Paris 1860.

B14:

8	...	B—N3*(85)*

This move was recommended by Schlechter in his (1913-5) edition of the *Handbuch*. Black prepares ...N-QR4 and removes his bishop from the danger zone.

See diagram next page

9	P—K5	Q—N3

9...Q-B4!? comes into consideration.

10	PxP	NxQP

Others:

a) 10...BxP 11 NxB NxN 12 Q-Q1!
N-QB3 13 N-B3 KN-K2 14 N-QN5 0-0
15 NxBP NxP 16 B-R3! keeping the
initiative; Mnatsakanyan-Vaisman,
USSR Trade Union Ch 1964.
b) 10...N-R4 11 Q-K3 NxB 12 QxN
N-K2 13 B-R3! with pressure for
White.

11	NxN	BxN
12	N—B3	N—R3

12...N-K2 13 B-R3 is also promising
for White.

13 B—K3?
13 B-R3! is correct, and White has
good chances.

13	...	BxKP
14	BxN	QxB
15	P—N3	0—0∓

Bird-Chigorin, Hastings 1895.

B2: 7 ... Q—K2
8 0—0 (86)
8 B-KN5!? (8 B-R3?!) is unclear.
Perhaps Black should reply 8...
Q-B1!?; certainly not 8...QxP+? 9
K-Q1 and 10 R-K1.

Now:
B21: 8...P-KR3?!
B22: 8...N-B3
B32: 8...B-N3!
or:
a) 8...P-Q3 see A3
b) 8...P-Q6? see Chapter 7, A12; note
a to White's 8th move.

B21:
8...P-KR3?! 9 B-R3 P-Q3 10 P-K5
Q-Q2 11 BPxP N-Q1 12 PxP P-QB3 13
N-K5± Harrwitz (blindfold) v. Duke of
Brunswick, Paris 1857.

B22:
8...N-B3 9 P-K5 N-KN5 10 B-R3
P-Q3 11 KPxP BPxP 12 R-K1 N3xP 13
NxN NxN 14 N-Q2 BxP 15 N-K4
BxKR 16 NxP+ K-Q2 17 NxBP BxP+
18 K-R1 Q-K1 19 B-N5+ N-B3 20
Q-Q5+ K-B2 21 B-Q6+ 1-0 Hurdle-
Cock, corres 1963-4.

B23:
8 ... B—N3!
This is probably the toughest
defence to 7 Q-N3. White has now
tried:
B231: 9 B-R3
B232: 9 PxP
9 B-KN5!? Q-B1! and not
9...P-B3? 10 BxN PxB 11 BxP!

B231:
9 B—R3
Dividing once more:
B2311: 9...N-R4
B2312: 9...Q-B3
B2313: 9...P-Q3

B2311:
9...N-R4 10 Q-R4 Q-Q1 (10...Q-B3
11 PxP NxB 12 QxN is very promising
for White.) 11 B-Q3 N-K2 12 PxP 0-0
13 QN-Q2 P-Q3 14 QR-Q1 N4-B3 15
B-N1± Wills-Ruotanen, European
Teams Corres Ch 1973-5.

B2312:

9	...	Q—B3
10	P—K5	Q—N3

Or 10...Q-B4 11 PxP KN-K2 (11... NxP!?; 11...BxP!?) 12 B-Q3 Q-R4!? 13 N-Q2 0-0 with complications, possibly favouring Black — analysis.

11 PxP

If 11 B-R3 N-R4 (11...KN-K2!?) 12 Q-N4!? P-QB4 13 Q-R4 NxB 14 QxN Q-K3.

11	...	NxQP?!

Probably better 11...KN-K2 (Or even 11...N-R4) 12 B-Q3 with balanced chances.

12	NxN	BxN
13	N—B3	BxN
14	QxB	N—K2
15	QR—Q1	P—N3
16	KR—K1	

Not 16 P-K6 because after 16... BPxP 17 BxP PxB 18 BxN (Staunton) comes 18...B-N2! 19 P-B3 Q-B2∓ — Schlechter.

16	...	B—N2
17	P—B3	P—QB4

Or 17...N-B3 when:

a) 18 B-Q3 eventually won in a consultation game of 1854 in which **Staunton led the White team and Lowenthal the Black.**

b) Staunton discovered a sacrificial win here by 18 RxP KxR 19 BxP QxB 20 P-K6+ QxP 21 QxP+ N-K2 22 RxQ KxR 23 QxN+.

The text move has been suggested as Black's last chance of a free game; Schlechter even considered that Black should stand better. However 18 R-Q6 Q-B4 19 R1-Q1 B-B3 (19...R-Q1 20 P-K6! BPxP 21 BxP!) 20 B-N2 (To meet castling by 21 P-K6) keeps a strong grip for White — analysis.

B2313:

9	...	P—Q3*(87)*

87
W

10 PxP

Also possible is 10 B-N5 (10 P-K5 N-R4) e.g. 10...B-K3? (A common error in such positions.) 11 Q-R4 B-Q2 12 PxP P-QR3 13 N-B3 Q-B3 14 P-K5 Q-N3 15 PxP PxP 16 KR-K1+ K-Q1 17 N-Q5 B-R4? (17...B-B2 was necessary; then, in view of the ...B-R6 threat, White's best is 18 N-B4 and 19 P-Q5.) 18 BxN BxR 19 RxB 1-0 Cafferty-Corbyn, Birmingham 1963.

10	...	NxP

10...N-R4 is also quite playable, although we know of no examples from master practice. White cannot hope for more than equality.

11	NxN	BxN
12	N—B3	N—B3
13	BxBP+?!	

13 QR-Q1! is stronger. If 13...B-N3 (Or 13...B-QB4) 14 P-K5, or if 13...BxN 14 QxB 0-0 15 P-K5!? (Or 15 P-B4) or here 14...NxP 15 QxNP, in each case with chances for White — analysis.

After the text move, the game **Lobigas-Balinas, Manila international** tournament 1968, continued 13...QxB 14 Q-R4+ B-Q2 15 QxB/Q4 0-0 16 P-B4 (16 P-K5?! leads to a strong Black counter-attack.) 16...B-B3 17 R-B3 (Or 17 P-K5 PxP 18 PxP Q-N3 19 Q-B2 N-Q2 20 BxR RxB 21 Q-N3 QxQ 22 PxQ NxP) 17...QR-K1 18 R-K1 P-QR4 ∓ .

B232:

9 PxP *(88)*

This is critical, since 9 B-R3 has been seen to be unsatisfactory.

88
B

After 9...N-R4 10 Q-B2 NxB 11 QxN, White will continue with N-QB3-Q5 and B-K3 or B-KN5, with more space and pressure against points like QB7, as in some lines of the **Normal Variation** (*see* **Chapter 9**).

9 ... **NxP**
10 NxN **BxN**
11 N—B3

Once again, admittedly at the cost of two pawns instead of one, White has that familiar plan, with B-R3 and N-QN5 as additional options. There can follow:

a) 11...P-QB3? 12 R-Q1! B-B4 13 N-R4 P-Q3 14 NxB PxN 15 BxP+ QxB 16 R-Q8+ K-K2 17 B-N5+ N-B3 18 RxR P-KR3 19 P-K5 B-K3 20 RxR BxQ 21 RxP+ K-K1 22 RxQ BxR 23 PxN and White won; Pfleger-Mendes, Lourenco Marques 1973.

b) 11...N-B3 (11...BxN!?; 11...P-KR3!?) is interesting:

b1) 12 N-N5!? is hard to justify for White. After 12...BxR 13 NxBP+ (If 13 B-R3 P-Q3 protects QB2) 13...K-Q1 14 NxR B-K4 White still has to rescue his knight and deal with the ...N-N5 threat, e.g. 15 B-R3 P-Q3 16 R-B1 N-N5 17 P-N3 (17 P-R3? NxP! 18 KxN B-Q5+!) with complications probably favouring Black.

b2) 12 B-N5!? is more hopeful, e.g.:
b21) 12...0-0 13 N-Q5 Q-Q1 14

QR-Q1 B-K4 15 P-B4
b22) 12...P-QB3! 13 QR-Q1 Q-B4! or 13 P-K5 BxP 14 QR-K1 0-0 (15 N-K4? P-Q4) seems good for Black.
b23) 12...BxN 13 QxB NxP 14 QxNP QxB 15 QxR+ K-K2 16 KR-K1+
b24) 12...P-KR3 13 N-Q5 Q-Q1 14 NxN+ (14 QR-Q1 first may be better.) 14...PxN 15 BxBP+ K-B1 16 QR-Q1 and White keeps the attack going — analysis.

b3) 12 B-R3! P-Q3 13 BxBP+!? QxB 14 Q-R4+ B-Q2 15 QxB with interesting play for the pawn.

C:

6 Q—N3 *(89)*

This is the form in which Wills has preferred to play the Q-N3 Method.

89
B

Now:
C1: 6...N-R3!
C2: 6...Q-K2
6...Q-B3 7 P-Q4 B-N3!? (7...PxP 8 0-0 see B1) 8 PxP Q-N3 9 0-0 N-R4 10 Q-R4 NxB 11 QxN N-K2 12 B-R3 Q-K3 13 Q-Q3 0-0 14 P-B4 with chances for White — analysis

C1:

6 ... **N—R3!**

This seems best, but has not been tested in practice.

7 P—Q4 **0—0!**

This is the point. Black accepts the weakening of his K-side pawns, as he would thereby gain the two bishops.

How is White to continue?
1) 8 PxP? N-KN5.
b) 8 P-Q5 N-N1! 9 QN-Q2 is probably
∓, while if 9 NxP Q-K2 keeps the extra
material.
c) 8 0-0 Q-K2 or 8...N-KN5!? 9
P-KR3 N-B3 with complications.
d) 8 BxN PxB 9 PxP (But 9 0-0!? —
compare Chapter 2, B.) 9...**Q-K2 and**
Black's position is no worse after, for
example, 10 QN-Q2 NxP 11 NxN QxN
12 0-0 B-N3 13 K-R1 P-Q3 14 P-B4=.

C2:

> **6 ...   Q—K2**
> **7 P—Q4***(90)*

Not 7 B-R3 P-Q3 8 P-Q4 PxP 9 0-0
B-N3 10 P-K5 (Kipping-Anderssen,
Manchester 1857) 10...N-R4! and if 11
Q-R4+ B-Q2.

90
B

After 7 P-Q4, Black has:
C21: 7...B-N3
C22: 7...NxP
   7...PxP see B2.
   7...P-Q3 see chapter 3.

C21:

> **7 ...   B—N3**
> **8 NxP**

This is better than 8 B-KN5?! P-B3!
9 BxN N-R4! 10 Q-B2 RxB∓.

> **8 ...   NxN**
> **9 PxN   P—Q3!**
> **10 0—0!**

White gets nothing with 10 PxP
QxP+ 11 K-Q1 BxP, nor with 10 B-R3
QxP 11 BxBP+ K-B1 12 0-0 N-R3 —
Wills.

> **10 ...   PxP**
> **11 B—R3   Q—B3**
> **12 N—Q2   B—Q2**

13 B-Q5 N-K2 (13...B-B3 14 N-B4 or
14 P-QB4) 14 P-QB4 B-Q5 15 QxP
R-QB1 16 QR-N1 0-0 17 N-B3 KR-K1
18 NxB PxN 19 P-B4 NxB 20 P-K5
Q-KN3 (Interesting complications
follow 20...B-B3 21 QxR! RxQ 22 PxQ
N-K6 23 R-B2 NxBP 24 B-B5 P-Q6.)
21 PxN B-B4 22 R-N2 B-K5 23 QxRP
BxQP 24 QxQP Q-K3 25 R1-B2 R-R1
26 QR-Q2 P-QB3 (Wills-Hopewell,
British Corres Ch 1969-70) and now 27
B-N2 RxP 28 P-B5 (Hopewell) would
have kept winning chances for White.

C22:

> **7 ...   NxP**
> **8 NxN   PxN**
> **9 0—0   B—N3***(91)*

9...BxP 10 NxB PxN 11 B-R3 P-Q3
12 P-K5 B-K3 (Wills-Cunliffe, London
1970) 13 QxP±± as analysed by Wills:
a) 13...Q-Q1 14 PxP PxP 15 B-N5+
K-B1 (15...B-Q2 16 BxB+) 16 BxP+;
b) 13...R-Q1 14 B-N5+ K-B1 15
QxRP
c) 13...R-B1 14 B-N5+ etc.

91
W

> **10 P—K5!**

Not 10 B-N2 P-Q6! — Wills.

> **10 ...   P—Q3**

Wills suggests that 10...N-R3!?
might be better.

Not 10...QxP? 11 BxP+! K-B1 12
N-Q2 N-B3 13 B-R3+ P-Q3 14 N-B3
Q-K2 15 B-B4±± Wills-Jones, Essex v.
Bedfordshire 1969.

11	**KPxP**	**BPxP**
12	**B—Q2**	**B—K3**

Wills also analysed 12...N-B3? 13 R-K1 N-K5 14 BxP+ QxB (14...K-B1 15 B-Q5) 15 RxN+ K-B1 16 R-B4.

13	**PxP**	**0—0—0**

Or 13...BxP 14 N-B3 0-0-0 15 QR-N1± .

14	**P—Q5**	**B—KB4**
15	**N—B3**	**N—R3**
16	**N—R4**	**B—Q5**

17 QR-B1 K-N1 18 B-QR6 N-N5 (Wills-Bramwell, Essex Ch 1971) and now 19 R-B4! would have won rapidly.

We conclude that in the present state of knowledge one cannot make categorical judgements about the value of the Q-N3 Method. Clearly there are several complicated lines to be analysed and tested. What is still more to the point, the wealth of little-known material in this chapter helps to refute the common allegation that the Evans was played out long ago.

7 Other Lines after 5...B—R4

1	P—K4	P—K4
2	N—KB3	N—QB3
3	B—B4	B—B4
4	P—QN4	BxNP
5	P—B3	B—R4

A variety of defensive methods based on this retreat remain to be considered. The most important of these, the 'Normal' variation, is discussed separately in chapters 8-10 as it is really the main line after 5...B-B4. Of the lines in the present chapter, some are theoretically important, although little-known, which is why White may choose to avoid them by employing some form of the Q-N3 Method. We look at:

A: 6 P-Q4
B: 6 0-0

A:

6   P—Q4 *(92)*

92
B

A1: 6...PxP (Remaining lines)
A2: 6...B-N3
A3: 6...P-QN4!?
A4: 6...Q-K2
6...NxP?! has been played

sometimes, but Black should lose material after 7 NxP! N-K3 8 NxBP Q-B3 (8...KxN 9 Q-R5+ and 10 QxB) 9 BxN and 10 NxR — Keres.

6...N-B3? 7 PxP N-KN5 (7... KNxP? 8 Q-Q5) 8 B-KN5 or 8 BxP+ KxB 9 N-N5+±.

6...Q-B3 7 P-Q5? (7 0-0 see B1.) 7...N-N1 8 Q-R4 B-N3 9 B-KN5 Q-N3 10 QN-Q2 N-KB3∓ Kopylov-Romanovsky, Leningrad 1938.

A1:

6	...	PxP
7	0—0	

A11: 7...KN-K2
A12: 7...P-Q6
A13: 7...P-Q3
A14: 7...P-QN4
7...B-N3 (7...N-B3 see B21.) 8 Q-N3? (8 PxP is correct; see chapter 8.) 8...N-R4! 9 BxP+? (9 Q-R4) 9...K-B1 10 Q-R3+ (10 B-R3+ N-K2! or 10 Q-Q5 N-KB3 and the bishop falls.) 10...KxB (Or 10...Q-K2 with a good ending.) 11 N-N5+ K-K1 and White should have insufficient attack for the piece — analysis.

A11:

7	...	KN—K2 *(93)*

This is one of the soundest defences that Black can adopt against the Evans. He makes ready to return the pawn by ...P-Q4, the traditional freeing move in open games, which makes room for his Q-side pieces to come out, and blunts the threats to his KBP. In the nineteenth century this defence was not popular, because Black generally feared the opening of the K-file that can result, and the few modern games with 7...KN-K2 have also been inconclusive evidence from a theoretical point of view. Best play probably leads to balanced chances.

93
W

White plays either:
A111: 8 N-N5 or
A112: 8 PxP

    8 Q-N3 0-0 9 PxP P-Q3 (Or 9... B-N3!?) could lead to positions somewhat like those in Chapter 10, and might be worth further consideration. What if now 10 N-N5 NxP? 11 BxP+ K-R1 12 Q-B4 P-KR3 (12...N2-B3? 13 B-N8!) 13 QxN PxN 14 B-QB4 for example? Better is 10...Q-K1, intending ...B-N3.

A111:
    8 N—N5   P—Q4
    Others:
a) 8...0-0? 9 Q-R5 P-KR3 10 NxP and Black must give up the exchange.
b) Rellstab mentioned 8...N-K4 in *Schach-Echo,* 1971. The continuation 9 NxBP (9 Q-R5 P-KN3) 9...NxN 10 BxN+ KxB 11 Q-R5+ and 12 QxB retains some attack for White.
    9 PxP
    Not 9 BxP? NxB 10 Q-R5 P-KN3 11 Q-R6 B-K3! 12 NxB PxN 13 PxN QxP 14 B-N5 R-KB1 15 PxP NxP 16 N-Q2 R-B4! and wins, Estrin-Kondali, corres 1970-2.

    9 ...   N—K4
    Not 9...NxP? 10 NxBP KxN 11 Q-R5+ K-K3 12 R-K1+ — *Handbuch.*
    After 9...N-K4 White has a glum choice between:
A1111: 10 QxP
A1112: 10 R-K1
A1113: 10 P-Q6
A1114: 10 B-N3

A1111:
    10 QxP   P—KB3...
    Not 10...NxB? 11 QxNP R-B1 12 NxRP N-KN3 13 B-N5!±±.
    Black protects his knight, and threatens 11...PxN, or else just to develop his pieces with useful threats. Thus:
a) 11 B-N3 B-N3 12 Q-K4? B-KB4 and Black soon wins material (13 Q-K2 B-Q6).
b) 11 B-QN5+ P-B3 12 PxP PxP 13 Q-K4 B-B4.
c) 11 R-K1 B-N3 12 B-QN5+ P-B3 13 PxP PxP 14 Q-K4 PxB 15 QxR PxN etc.
d) 11 N-K4 NxB 12 QxN QxP with a steady win for Black.

A1112:
    10 R—K1   NxB!
    10...P-KB3 is not good here, because of 11 RxN! PxR 12 Q-R4+ P-B3 13 PxBP NxP 14 N-B7 with a strong attack for White.
    11 Q—R4+   P—QB3!
    12 QxN
    12 PxP? meets with the pretty refutation 12...P-N4! 13 QxP N-Q3∓.
    12 ...   QxP!
    After 12...PxP 13 Q-K2! White keeps some attack.
    13 QxQ
    The ingenious queen sacrifice 13 B-R3!? QxQ 14 RxN+ fails; White's attack is repulsed after 14...K-Q1 (14...K-B1 15 RxBP+! K-N1? 16

R-B8 mate) 15 NxBP+ QxN 16 RxQ R-K1! (16...PxP? 17 NxP!) e.g. 17 K-B1 B-K3 (threatening ...B-B5+) or 17 N-Q2 BxP or 17 R-B8 PxP (18 NxP RxR!)∓∓ — analysis.

13 ... PxQ
14 B—R3 B—Q1
15 PxP P—KR3

16 N-QB3 (16 N-KB3 B-K3 17 N-B3 0-0∓—*Handbuch*) 16...PxN 17 BxN BxB 18 NxP B-K3 19 NxB (Or 19 N-B7+?! K-Q2 and Black gets two bishops for a rook.) 19...KxN 20 P-Q5 KR-Q1 and Black has winning chances — analysis.

A1113:
10 P—Q6

a) 10...PxQP? 11 B-QN5+ B-Q2 12 BxB+ QxB 13 PxP N-B5?! (White has succeeded in muddying the waters.) 14 N-R3 P-Q4 (14...R-QB1!?) 15 NxN PxN 16 NxBP! 0-0 17 N-K5 etc., eventually drawn; Khristov-Yurdanov, Bulgarian corres 1956-7.
b) Black can do better with 10...QxP e.g. 11 B-QN5+ (11 Q-R4+ B-Q2!) 11...P-QB3 12 QxP (12 PxP loses a piece after 12...N-N5!) 12...B-B2 and Black keeps his extra pawn with a good position — analysis.

A1114:
10 B—N3

This looks as if it ought to be too slow:
a) 10...0-0? 11 PxP N-N5 12 B-R3 NxQP?! 13 BxR±± Anderssen-S. Mieses, Breslau 1867.
b) 10...P-Q6?! 11 R-K1 P-KB3 12 B-R3!± — analysis.
c) 10...PxP (10...BxP!?) 11 Q-Q4 P-KB3 12 NxBP B-N3 with a good game for Black — analysis.

A112:
8 PxP P—Q4

The traditional freeing move is clearly essential here.

9 PxP N2xP*(94)*

The 1939 edition of *M.C.O.* mentions 9...P-QN4!?, a suggestion of one F.J. Wallis. Then:
a) 10 BxP QxP 11 Q-R4 B-Q2 when:
a1) 12 B-R3? R-QN1! (Wallis gave 12...P-QR3∓.) 13 B-B4 NxP!∓
a2) 12 B-QB4 Q-KB4 13 Q-Q1 B-K3= — Unzicker.
b) Unzicker suggests 10 B-N3 N2xP (10...N-N5 11 B-Q2!±) 11 Q-K2 N3-K2 12 QxP+ P-B3= .
c) We think this line is based on a false premise, because White can play 10 PxN PxB 11 Q-R4 with advantage:
c1) 11...B-N3 12 R-K1 0-0 13 B-R3 B-K3 (13...R-K1 14 QxBP B-K3 15 RxB!) 14 P-Q5 winning the exchange.
c2) 11...Q-Q4 12 B-R3 B-K3 (12...B-R3 13 BxN KxB 14 N-R3 threatening KR-K1+; or 12...NxP 13 QN-Q2 BxN 14 NxB B-K3 15 KR-K1) 13 B-B5! B-N3 14 N-B3 QxBP 15 QxQ+ NxQ 16 BxB RPxB 17 P-Q5 wins material.

94
W

A1121: 10 Q-N3
A11122: 10 B-R3

Keres tried 10 B-KN5!? Q-Q3 11 Q-N3 and won in a simul. game. Instead of 11...N3-K2? 12 B/N5xN etc., Black should have played 11...B-K3 and if 12 QN-Q2 (12 QxP? R-QN1) 12...BxN! with good chances.

A1121:
10 Q—N3

This move is favoured by Euwe.

10 ...   B—K3!?

Most sources give only 10... N3-K2=, by analogy with the Guioco Piano. This line is worth testing in practice, e.g. 11 B-R3 P-QB3 12 QN-Q2 0-0 13 KR-K1 with pressure. P-QB3 12 QN-Q2 0-0 13 KR-K1 with pressure to compensate for the missing pawn.

11 QxP!

11 B-R3!?, to cut across Black's natural development, is interesting:

a) 11...B-N3?! 12 N-B3! (12 R-K1 N-R4 13 Q-R4+ Q-Q2) 12...NxN 13 BxB PxB (13...N-K7+ 14 K-R1 PxB 15 QxP threatening QxN and KR-K1) 14 QxN! NxP 15 KR-K1 P-β4 (15... NxN+ 16 QxN Q-B1 17 Q-R5+±±) 16 NxN QxN 17 RxP+ K-Q2 18 Q-R3 or 18 QxQ+!? PxQ 19 R-Q6+ K-K1! 20 R-K1+ K-B2 21 R-Q7+ — analysis.

b) 11...Q-Q2! when:

b1) 12 R-Q1!? 0-0-0 13 N-K5? (13 QN-Q2? N-B6!) 13...NxN 14 PxN Q-B3! 15 B-N2? (His position is already bad.) 15...N-B5 16 BxB+ PxB 17 P-B3 Q-N3+ 0-1 Selfe-Harding, corres 1974-5.

b2) 12 QxNP? R-QN1 13 Q-R6 R-N3∓∓or 12 BxN BxB! 13 R-K1+ K-Q1 14 QxNP NxP! etc. while if 12 B-N5 N4-K2! Perhaps 12 QN-Q2 or 12 B-N3 are playable.

11 ...   N4—N5
12 B—QN5   B—Q2

The *Handbuch* recommended this, but our analysis seems to refute it. A game Anderssen-S. Mieses, Breslau 1867, went instead 12...0-0 (Given a ! in von Gottschall's book on Anderssen) 13 BxN R-N1 14 QxRP N-B3 15 Q-B5 B-Q4 16 B-R3 R-K1 17 QN-Q2 R-K7 18 KR-Q1 Q-Q2 19 N-B1 and White won in 78 moves. Botterill's suggestion 12...B-Q4! may refute White's play after all.

13 R—K1+   K—B1

14 N—K5!

Perhaps Anderssen had seen this clever way to save his queen. Now:

a) 14...R-QN1? 15 NxB+ QxN 16 QxR+ NxQ 17 BxQ threatening R-K8 mate.

b) 14...NxN 15 RxN when:

b1) 15...R-N1 16 QxRP BxB (16... P-QB3 17 Q-B5+ or 16...B-N3 17 Q-R4 BxP 18 QxN+ P-QB4 19 RxP!) 17 QxB QxP (17...N-B3 18 Q-R3+) 18 QxN+ QxQ 19 B-R3 P-QB4 20 BxQ PxB 21 N-Q2 with an ending that is possibly slightly in White's favour, as the QNP is weak.

b2) 15...P-QB3 16 B-QB4 R-QN1 17 QxRP B-N3 18 Q-R3 or 18 Q-R4.

b3) 15...P-KB3 16 BxB! and now:

b31) 16...PxR? 17 Q-B3+ K-K2 (17...Q-B3 18 QxR+) 18 B-N5+ KxB 19 BxQ QRxB 20 N-R3 and White ought to win.

b32) 16...R-QN1 17 Q-B3:

b321) 17...QxB 18 RxB N-B7 19 B-R3+ K-B2 20 N-Q2 NxR 21 Q-B3 and White has (after capturing the knight) two pieces for a rook.

b322) 17...N-B7 18 R-K8+ QxR 19 BxQ NxR 20 B-R3+ KxB 21 Q-K4+ K-B2 is not altogether clear, as White has back rank worries.

A1122:

10 B—R3   B—K3
11 B—N5

White cannot allow 11...N-K6 12 PxN BxB.

11 QN-Q2 comes into consideration:

a) 11...BxN? 12 QxB when Fine wrote in his 1942 book, *Chess the Easy Way:* "To castle on the Q-side would be highly dangerous for Black, as White has two powerful open files for his rooks. But to castle on the other side he must first block the diagonal of the bishop at QR3 and this can be done only at the expense of a pawn."

Fine analyses 12...N3-K2 (A nine-teenth-century game Neumann-Loyd, Paris 1869, varied here with 12...Q-B3 13 B-N5 and White stood better.) 13 KR-K1 P-QB3 (13...0-0? loses the excahnge to 14 B4xN.) 14 N-N5 0-0 (14...Q-Q2 15 B/R3xN and 16 P-B4 etc.) 15 NxB PxN 16 RxP and White retains the pawn with the better position.
b) However 11...B-QN5! or 11...N-B6, playing for exchanges, need further investigation.

| 11 | ... | B—QN5 |
| 12 | BxB | |

Or first 12 BxN+ transposing, but not 12 Q-R4 Q-Q3 13 N-K5 0-0!∓ Muravlev-Tanin, RSFSR corres 1968.

| 12... | ... | N4xB |
| 13 | BxN+ | PxB |

Or 13...NxB (This could be avoided at move 12.) 14 N-B3 N-K2 15 N-KN5 0-0 16 Q-N1= — Levenfish.

13	...	PxB
14	Q—R4	Q—Q3
15	N—B3	0—0
16	N—K4=	

After 16...Q-B5 17 N4-N5 or 16...Q-K2 17 N-B5 White's play is at least as valuable as Black's extra doubled isolated QBP — Levenfish in *Sovremenny Debyut*.

A12:

| 7 | ... | P—Q6*(95)* |

This line is not recommended for Black.

95
W

8 R—K1!
This move is recommended by Pachman in his *Modern Chess Tactics*. Such has been the influence of the Evergreen Game, however, that most opening books only consider 8 Q-N3 here, which move also gives White good chances (and White needs to know it if he plays the Q-N3 Method instead of 7 0-0). After 8 Q-N3:
a) 8...Q-K2 9 P-K5! B-N3 10 B-R3 N-R4 11 Q-R4 Q-Q1 12 BxQP N-K2 13 Q-K4 P-Q4 14 PxPep PxP 15 R-K1! B-QB4 16 BxB PxB 17 N-R3 B-K3 18 QR-Q1 Q-B2 19 N-QN5 Q-N3 20 N-Q6+ K-B1 21 NxBP! amd wins; Rozhlapa-Pletiukhova, USSR Women's Ch 1963;
b) More usually, Black has replied 8...Q-B3 9 P-K5 (9 B-KN5 has not done so well in practice.) 9...Q-N3 transposing to the Evergreen Game, Anderssen-Dufresne, in Chapter 1 (page 19). Although Keres and Unzicker prefer White's chances, the reader should take a look at Black's suggested improvements at moves 10 and 11. White could consider 9 R-K1!? e.g. 9...KN-K2 10 B-KN5 Q-N3 11 BxN KxB (11...NxB 12 N-K5) 12 P-K5 (Anderssen-Rosenthal, Vienna 1873) 12...R-K1.

| 8 | ... | B—N3 |

Others:
a) 8...N-B3? 9 P-K5 as usual;
b) 8...KN-K2 9 N-N5 0-0 10 Q-R5 etc.;
c) 8...P-Q3 9 Q-N3 Q-K2 (9...Q-Q2 loses a piece after 10 P-K5! PxP 11 NxP NxN 12 RxN+.) 10 P-K5! PxP 11 B-R3 Q-B3 12 NxP! NxN 13 Q-N5+ K-Q1 14 QxN QxQ 15 RxQ B-N3 16 B-B8! gaining decisive material advantage — Euwe.

9 P—K5!
It is very hard to complete Black's development; he must stop N-N5.

9	...	P—KR3
10	QN—Q2	KN—K2
11	N—K4	0—0
12	QxP	

With a threat of 13 BxRP.

| 12 | ... | NxP! |

The best defensive try.

| 13 | NxN | P—Q4 |
| 14 | BxRP! | B—KB4! |

Pachman gives these variations:

a) 14...NPxB 15 N-B6+ K-N2 16 Q-R7+! KxN 17 B-Q3! B-KB4 18 BxB NxB 19 N-N4+ K-N4 20 R-K5!±.

b) 14...QPxB 15 N-B6+ PxN 16 Q-N3+.

c) 14...PxN 15 BxBP+:

c1) 15...K-R2 16 QxP+ B-KB4 17 Q-KR4 PxB 18 QR-Q1 with a fierce attack;

c2) 15...K-R1 16 BxP+ KxB 17 Q-N3+ K-B3 (Or 17...K-R2 18 Q-R4+ K-N2 19 Q-N5+ K-R2 20 R-K4) 18 Q-R4+! KxN 19 RxP+ K-Q3 20 Q-B6+ K-B4 21 R-QB4+ K-N4 22 R-N1+ K-R4 23 Q-K5+ etc. — a pleasant king-hunt!

| **15** | **N—B6+!** | **K—R1** |

Not 15...PxN 16 Q-N3+ N-N3 17 NxN BxN 18 BxR and White should win.

16	Q—N3	PxB
17	Q—B4	K—N2
18	N5—N4	BxN
19	RxN!	

Another finesse! After 19 NxB N-N1! Black could defend.

| 19 | ... | PxB |

Forced, in view of 19...QxR? 20 QxB+ K-R1 (Or 20...KxN 21 Q-R4+ K-K3 22 R-K1+) 21 Q-R4 K-N2 22 N-R5+.

| **20** | **QxB+** | |

After 20 NxB? Q-Q3! it is not so clear that White can win. In the game Prins-Fuderer, Rogaska Slatina 1948, White went on to spoil his hitherto brilliant play and even lost.

After the text move, Pachman

shows that Black is defenceless:

a) 20...KxN 21 R1-K1! (Threatening to force mate by 22 R1-K6+! etc.) 21...Q-B1 22 R-Q7 (Threatens R-K4) 22...R-K1 23 Q-B4+ and mates;

b) 20...K-R1 21 Q-B5 K-N2 22 N-R5+ and it's all over once again.

A13:

| 7 | ... | P—Q3 |
| **8** | **PxP***(96)* | |

We recommend 8 Q-N3: see line A in Chapter 6.

96
B

| **8** | ... | **N—B3!?** |

Others:

a) 8...B-N3 see chapters 8-10;

b) 8...B-Q2 9 B-N2 Q-K2 10 N-B3 0-0-0 11 R-K1 (Threatening N-Q5) 11...BxN 12 BxB± Harding-W. Smith, Southport 1972.

c) 8...B-KN5!? is relatively untested; compare B in Chapter 4.

The text was Steinitz's latest, and relatively most successful method, against Chigorin's Evans.

| **9** | **Q—R4** | |

9 P-K5!? PxP (9...N-KN5 or 9...N-K5 10 Q-R4 is unclear:

a) 10 B-R3 B-K3! 11 B-N5 Q-Q4 12 Q-R4 0-0-0 (Better 12...B-Q2! 13 PxP P-QR3∓ Chigorin-Steinitz, St Petersburg 1896) 13 BxN BxN 14 B-B5 B-N3 (Chigorin-Steinitz, Hastings 1895) 15 N-K5 with a good attack — Grekov.

b) 10 Q-N3!? e.g. 10...Q-Q2 11 PxP or 10...Q-K2 11 P-Q5 and 12 Q-R4+.

9 ...   B—Q2

Or 9...P-QR3 10 B-Q5! B-N3 11 BxN+ PxB 12 P-K5! "This was my intention though 12 QxP+ B-Q2 13 Q-B3 also yields a pretty strong attack for White" wrote Chigorin.

10 B—QN5

Or 10 P-Q5 (Chigorin also tried 10 Q-R3 without success.) 10...N-K4! 11 QxB NxB 12 Q-N4 N-N3 13 P-QR4 P-QR4 (13...P-B4 14 Q-N3 Q-B2 15 P-R5 N-B1 16 B-N2 N-R4 17 N3-Q2!+ — Chigorin) 14 Q-Q4 0-0 15 B-N5± (but drawn in 99 moves after White missed several opportunities) Chigorin-Steinitz, St Petersburg 1895-6.

10 ...   B—N3
11 P—K5

11 B-N5 is also strong — von Gottschall.

After the text, a game Anderssen-Saalbach, Leipzig 1855, continued 11...P-QR3 (Perhaps 11...PxP 12 PxP N-Q4 is better.) 12 PxN PxB 13 R-K1+ (13 PxP looks even better.) 13...B-K3 (13...K-B1!?) 14 PxP R-KN1 15 Q-Q1! P-Q4 16 B-N5 Q-Q2 (Slightly better 16...Q-B3 17 B-B6 N-K2± — von Gottschall.) 17 B-B6 B-R4 18 QN-Q2 B-QN5 19 N-N5 B-K2 20 NxB PxN 21 Q-R5+ K-Q1 22 Q-B7 1-0.

A14:
7 ...   P—QN4

This counter-sacrifice has been played at several junctures, always with the idea of diverting the bishop from its classical attacking diagonal. After 8 BxNP PxP (or 8...KN-K2 9 PxP 0-0 10 P-Q5 N-N1 11 B-N2± Zukertort-Schulten, 1869) 9 BxN PxB 10 Q-R4 B-N3 11 QxBP+ B-Q2 12 QxP/B3 Q-B3 13 P-K5 Q-N3 (13... Q-QB3 14 P-K6! PxP 15 QxP) and now instead of 14 B-R3 (Tartakower-Johner, Baden 1914), Fine recommended 14 P-K6! to open lines

(14...PxP 15 N-K5 Q-B3 16 B-K3 or 16 N-Q2 with a promising game).

A2:
6 ...   B—N3
7 PxP *(97)*

If 7 0-0 P-Q3 and Black has got Lasker's Defence! 7 P-QR4?! is worse, as after 7...PxP 8 0-0 P-Q3 9 PxP we have line B22 of chapter 8, which is an inferior form of the Normal variation, while ideas based on P-QR5 do not work against careful defence.

So White must take the pawn. 7 NxP NxN 8 PxN N-K2 (8...Q-K2 9 Q-Q5!) would be less dangerous to Black than the text, e.g. 9 B-B4 0-0 10 0-0 N-N3 11 B-N3 Q-K2 as Black here does not have to worry about B-KN5.

97
B

7 ...   KN—K2!

7...Q-K2!? may be playable, but as White does not yet really threaten B-KN5 or N-N5, ...P-KR3 would be a waste of time. The game Tartakower-Chajes, Karlsbad 1923, illustrates this: 7...P-KR3? 8 Q-Q5 Q-K2 9 B-R3 Q-K3 10 Q-Q3 NxP (Black's difficulties increase after 10...Q-N3 11 0-0 KN-K2 12 QN-Q2 0-0 13 B-Q5! R-K1 14 N-B4.) 11 NxN QxN 12 P-B4! Q-KR4 (12...QxBP 13 R-B1 Q-K6+ 14 QxQ BxQ 15 RxP!±) 13 N-Q2 P-Q3 14 B-N5+! .

Tartakower said that 7...P-Q3 or 7...KN-K2 would be better, "But in all cases Black's game is difficult". White must be careful nonetheless and, virtually no attacking ideas being available, must hang on to his regained pawn in the hope that it will restrict Black's development. Sometimes the doubled isolated KP can be worse than useless in the Evans, as testified by a game of Capablanca's:

8 0—0

The immediate 8 B-B4 might be more precise.

8 ...   0—0

If 8...N-N3 9 B-KN5.

9 B—R3?!

Probably White's correct plan is 9 B-B4, e.g. 9...N-N3 10 B-KN3 Q-K23 11 Q-Q5 followed by the attempt to manoeuvre the QN to KB5. Whether correct play gives more than balanced chances is unclear; there are no practical examples of this line.

9 ...   P—KR3

Not 9...R-K1? 10 BxP+! KxB 11 N-N5+ K-N3 12 Q-N4 NxP 13 Q-N3±. Nor 9...N-N3 10 BxR QxB 11 Q-Q5 Q-K2 12 QN-Q2 KNxP 13 N-Q4±.

10 QN—Q2   R—K1
11 N—N3   N—N3

White's front KP is doomed. In the game Blanco-Capablanca, Havana 1913, White tried to blast his way out by 12 BxP+!? KxB 13 Q-Q5+ R-K3 14 N/N3-Q4 N-B5 15 NxR (15 Q-N3? N-R4) but instead of 15...NxQ (when White would get fair compensation for the exchange) Capablanca played 15...PxN 16 QxQ (16 Q-B4 Q-Q6 or 16 Q-N3!? P-N4! 17 QR-Q1 Q-N1) 16...NxQ 17 N-Q4 N-B3 with the superior ending (0-1, 38). This line of defence was typical of the economical style of the future World Champion.

A3:

6 ...   P—QN4!?
(98)

A counter-gambit which was recommended by P.S. Leonhardt in *British Chess Magazine,* 1906.

98
W

7 B—Q5!

Leonhardt's idea was that 7 BxNP can be met by 7...NxP attacking the bishop, and if 8 NxN (Or 8 NxP NxB 9 Q-Q5 Q-B3! 10 QxR N-K2) 8...PxN 9 QxP N-B3 (Better than 9...Q-B3 10 P-K5±) with complications.

7 ...   PxP
8 Q—N3

Possibly even better is 8 NxP e.g. 8...Q-B3 9 0-0 KN-K2 and now:
a) 10 P-K5 Q-N3 11 P-KB4 B-N3? (But 11...NxN 12 BxRN-B7 is correct.) 12 K-R1! (Not 12 P-B5? NxN 13 PxQ N-K7+ 14 K-R1 N-N6+ 15 PxN PxP+ which Leonhardt analysed.) 12...NxN 13 BxR N-B7 14 P-KN4! following Purdy's analysis in *Chess World* 1948.
b) 10 NxP! 0-0 (10...B-R3 11 P-QR4!, but 10...P-QR3 11 N5-R3 BxP might equalize.) 11 B-K3 P-QR3 12 N-Q4 B-N3 (12...NxB 13 PxN N-K4 14 N-Q2! P-Q3 15 N/Q4-N3 B-N3 16 BxN PxB 17 P-KB4 N-N3 18 Q-B3) 13 N-B2!± Purdy-Goldstein, 2nd Australian Corres Ch 1946-8.

8 ...   Q—B3

Or 8...Q-K2 9 0-0 and Black has difficulties: 9...N-B3? 10 B-R3 P-N5 11 PxNP BxP 12 BxN winning a piece; Cafferty-Morry, Birmingham 1968.

9 P—K5

This move was recommended by Maroczy. 9 0-0 transposes to line B11 in chapter 6.

9 ...	Q—N3
10 N—N5	N—R3
11 P—K6	

With advantage to White, following Collijn's *Larobok*. After 11...BPxP 12 NxKP! (Threatening 0-0 and R-K1) Black's king is fatally vulnerable in the centre. If Black plays 11...0-0, White's best plan seems to be 12 B-K4 Q-B3 (12...Q-R4 13 QxP threatening **BxP+, NxP+, QxQ**) 13 NxRP QxKP 14 QxQ BPxQ 15 NxR KxN but the position remains difficult as Black's Q-side pawns provide compensation for the exchange — analysis.

A4:

6 ...   Q—K2(99)

This is another idea that cannot be completely written off.

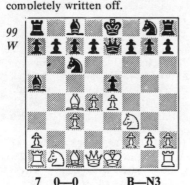

99
W

| 7 0—0 | B—N3 |

Not 7...P-Q3? 8 P-Q5 and 9 Q-R4+.

8 B—R3

Other moves seem inadequate:
a) 8 NxP NxN 9 PxN QxP 10 Q-N3 Q-KR4 11 B-R3 N-K2 12 P-K5 N-B3 13 N-Q2?! NxP 14 KR-K1 P-Q3∓ Barden-Gereben, Hastings 1958-59.
b) 8 P-QR4 P-QR3 9 P-R5 B-R2 10 B-N5 N-B3 11 P-Q5 N-Q1 12 P-Q6

QxP! 13 QxQ PxQ 14 BxN PxB 15 R-Q1 (15 N-R4!?; this sort of position is known from the Guioco Piano — but then White has a QNP!) 15...P-Q4 16 RxP K-K2 17 QN-Q2 P-Q3 18 N-R4 N-B3 19 R-N1 R-QN1 and Black eventually won in Kopylov-Dubinin, Leningrad ½-final 17 USSR Ch 1949. He has the long-term advantage of an extra pawn and the bishop pair, and White's QRP is becoming weak.

8 ...   Q—B3

Now 8...P-Q3 fails to 9 B-N5! B-Q2 10 BxN and 11 NxP.

9 PxP	NxP
10 NxN	QxN
11 Q—N3	N—R3
12 N—Q2	B—B4!

Best, in view of 12...P-Q3 13 B-N5+ B-Q2 14 BxB+ followed by 15 Q-R4+ and 16 N-B4±.

| 13 N—B3 | Q—K2 |
| 14 B—B1! | 0—0 |

Or 14...P-QN3 15 B-KN5 P-KB3 16 BxN PxB 17 P-K5 — Ragozin.

15 B—KN5!

In the game Ragozin-Levenfish, 17 USSR Ch 1949, the game stood level after 15 P-K5 R-K1 and after further inaccuracies by both players a draw resulted. The text move was recommended at the time by the players.

After 15 B-KN5 White has good attacking chances. A possible continuation is 15...QxP!? 16 BxN PxB 17 QR-K1 Q-N3!? 18 N-K5 Q-N2 19 NxBP! RxN 20 R-K3 (Inviting Black to open the KB-file by ...BxR.) 20...P-Q4 21 BxP P-B3 22 BxR+ QxB 23 R-N3+ K-B1 24 R-B3 B-B4 25 P-N4 and White wins — analysis.

B:

6 0—0

A last look at this old-fashioned continuation. Black can reply, besides the lines seen in Chapter 4, with:

B1: 6...Q-B3
B2: 6...N-B3
    6...KN-K2!? 7 N-N5 P-Q4 8 PxP
NxP 9 P-Q4 and now:
a) 9...PxP 10 NxBP! KxN 11 Q-B3+
— *Handbuch.*
b) 9...0-0 10 PxP B-K3 11 Q-R5
P-KR3 12 NxB PxN 13 B-KR6 R-B2
(13...PxB 14 Q-N6+) 14 R-Q1± —
Handbuch.
c) 9...P-KR3 10 PxP (10 NxP KxN 11
Q-B3+ K-K3 12 R-K1! R-KB1 13
Q-K4 B-N3 is too speculative.)
10...PxN 11 BxN B-K3! (11...NxP 12
R-K1 P-KB3 13 BxP) 12 BxB QxB
13 RxQ PxB 14 BxP NxP and Black
has play for the pawn — Unzicker.

B1:

   6   ...   Q—B3
   7   P—Q4*(100)*

100
B

Now Black has tried:
B11: 7...KN-K2
B12: 7...N-R3
B13: 7...P-KR3

B11:

   7   ...   KN—K2
   8   B—KN5
Others:
a) In the first game of the 1889 World
Championship match, Chigorin
played 8 N-N5 N-Q1 9 P-B4 but,
although he won, he never repeated
that idea.
b) In his notes, Chigorin seemed to

think that the best move-order was 8
P-Q5 N-Q1 9 Q-R4 B-N3 10 B-KN5
Q-Q3 (as in the 15th game), thus
avoiding Black's alternatives at move
10 below.

   8   ...   Q—Q3
   9   P—Q5
Not 9 Q-N3 0-0 10 N-R3 (Or 10
R-Q1 B-N3 as in the fifth game of the
1889 match) 10...P-QR3 11 BxBP+
(11 QR-Q1 P-N4!) 11...RxB 12 N-B4
Q-K3! and Black won in 39 moves;
Lyublinsky-Holmov, Moscow ½-final
16 USSR Ch 1948.

   9   ...   N—Q1
  10   Q—R4   B—N3
Steinitz also tried:
a) 10...P-QN3 11 N-R3 P-QR3 12
B-Q3 (12 B-N3 failed in the ninth
game.) 12...BxP 13 QR-N1 (Chigorin
even considered 13 N-B4!? Q-N5 14
Q-B2 BxR 15 B-Q2.) 13...B-N2 14
N-B4 Q-B4 15 B-K3 and White won
in 31 moves (eleventh game).
b) 10...P-KB3 11 B-B1 B-N3 12 N-R3
P-B3 (thirteenth game) and now
Chigorin said he should have played
13 R-Q1.
  11   N—R3   P—QB3
  In the seventh game, Steinitz had
tried 11...Q-N3 12 BxN KxB 13 NxP
Q-KB3 14 N-B3 QxP but there fol-
lowed 15 P-K5 P-QB3 16 P-Q6+
K-B1 17 B-N3 P-KR3 18 Q-R4 P-N4
19 Q-R5 Q-Q6 20 QR-Q1 (20 NxP
Q-N3) 20...Q-R2 (20...Q-N3 21 QxQ
PxQ 22 P-K6 K-N2 23 KR-K1! —
Chigorin) 21 N-B2 (Steinitz feared 21
P-K6 NxP 22 BxN BPxB 23 N-K5 but
Chigorin pointed out 23...R-KN1 24
R-Q3 P-N5! and 25...R-N4.) 21...
K-N2 22 N2-Q4 Q-N3 23 Q-N4
P-KR4 24 N-B5+ K-B1 25 QxNP
QxQ 26 NxQ P-R5 27 K-R1 R-R4 28
P-B4 N-K3 29 P-N4 PxPep 30 NxNP
R-R3 31 NxP! KxN 32 P-B5 K-K1 33
PxN PxP 34 N-K4 1-0. However the
text move does not do much either to

alleviate the paralysis of Black's Q-side.

12 QR—Q1   Q—N1

Or 12...P-B3 13 PxP QxP 14 N-N5 PxB 15 NxKP Q-B4 16 N-Q6+ K-B1 17 QxQP! — Chigorin.

The top left corner of the board, with the black pieces heaped clumsily upon each other, resembles an automobile junkyard rather than a World Championship chess game position (and after only twelve moves!).

13 BxN   KxB
14 P—Q6+   K—B1
15 Q—N4!

After 15 NxP P-B3 16 N-B3 B-B4! as in the 15th game, Black starts to get counterplay.

15 ...   P—B3
16 B—N3

Chigorin later suggested 16 K-R1!, to meet 16...P-N3? by 17 NxP PxN 18 P-B4 K-N2 19 PxP.

16 ...   P—N3

In a consultation game Chigorin & Pons v. Steinitz & Gavrilan, held at Havana after the match, 16...N-B2 was refuted by 17 N-R4 P-N3 18 K-R1 B-Q1 19 P-B4 PxP 20 BxN! KxB 21 P-K5! PxP 22 RxP+! K-N2 23 N-B5+! PxN 24 RxP R-N1 25 R1-KB1 P-N4 26 Q-N4+ and mate in 4.

17 N—B4   K—N2
18 P—QR4   N—B2
19 NxB   PxN

20 BxN KxB 21 NxP+! and White regained his pawn with the superior game, since taking the knight would allow an attack like that in the previous note (e.g. 22 P-KB4 etc.). The seventeenth Chigorin-Steinitz game was finally drawn, however, after 21...K-N2 22 N-B4 P-QN4 as White missed some chances later on.

B12:

7 ...   N—R3

8 B—KN5   Q—Q3

Bogoljubow thought that Black could have equalized by returning the pawn: 8...Q-N3!? 9 P-Q5 N-QN1 10 BxN QxB 11 NxP 0-0 12 P-Q6 N-B3 but Vasyukov's book on Chigorin then gives 13 N-N4 Q-N3 14 R-K1±.

9 P—Q5   N—Q1

9...N-K2 is no better: 10 Q-R4 B-N3 11 N-R3 N-N5!? 12 P-R3 NxBP 13 RxN BxR+ 14 KxB Q-N3+ 15 B-K3 Q-N7+ 16 N-B2± Chigorin-Markov, corres 1890.

10 Q—R4   B—N3
11 N—R3   P—QB3

Or 11...0-0 12 B-Q3 Q-N3 13 N-B4 P-KB3 (13...P-Q3 14 B-K7!) 14 NxB PxN 15 B-K3± — Vasyukov.

12 B—K2!

a) 12...B-B2 see Chap. 1 (p. 27) for the Chigorin-Steinitz telegraph match game;

b) 12...B-B4 13 N-B4 Q-B1 14 BxN KxB (14...P-QN4 15 Q-R5 PxN 16 PxP) 15 N4xP P-B3 16 PxP (Steinitz) **e.g. 16...PxN 17 PxQP BxQP 18** QR-Q1 Q-K2 19 NxP B-Q3 20 NxB QxN 21 RxB++— Chigorin.

B13:

7 ...   P—KR3 *(101)*

8 B—K3

Other playable replies:
a) 8 B-QN5 (Gunsberg also tried 8 Q-R4.) 8...KN-K2 9 B-R3! PxP 10 PxP (Better than 10 P-K5 of

Gunsberg-Steinitz, fourteenth game, 1891) and White has the advantage according to Pachman. In a game Chigorin played as Black, against consultative partners at Havana 1891, 10...P-R3 and won in 31 moves after 11 P-K5?; 11 B-QB4 first looks more troublesome. If 10...NxP White presumably plays 11 QN-Q2 NxN+ 12 NxN 0-0 13 P-K5 (Or possibly other moves) with good attacking chances in return for the two pawns.
b) 8 PxP!? NxP 9 NxN QxN 10 Q-N3 Q-R4 (10...Q-B3 11 P-K5 QxKP 12 BxBP+) 11 P-K5 N-K2 12 B-R3 N-B3 13 N-Q1 B-N3 14 QR-K1 N-R4 15 Q-R4 K-Q1 (15...NxB 16 P-K6! BPxP 17 RxP+ K-B2 18 R-K7+) 16 B-Q3 R-K1 17 N-B3 R-K3 (17...N-B3 18 Q-KB4) 18 P-R4 P-KB3 19 PxP PxP 20 RxR PxR 21 B-N6! B-Q2 22 R-Q1 1-0 Ciocaltea-Brzozka, Romania v. Poland 1958.

8 ...   B—N3
Or 8...KN-K2 9 P-Q5 and 10 Q-R4 — Levenfish.

9 PxP   Q—N3
Or 9...NxP 10 NxN QxN 11 B-Q4! BxB 12 PxB Q-K2 13 P-K5 (Chigorin) or 13 N-B3 (Bogoljubow) with good chances for White.

10 QN—Q2   BxB
Chigorin v. Zybin & Otto, St Petersburg 1893, went instead 10... N-R4? 11 N-R4 Q-R2 (11...Q-QB3 12 B-Q5 QxP 13 BxBP+!) 12 N-B5 P-Q4 13 PxPep BxN 14 BxB BPxB 15 PxB QxP (15...0-0-0 16 Q-N4 N-B3 17 Q-B4) 16 Q-K2 K-B1 17 KR-K1 P-KR4 18 N-B3 R-R3 (18...NxB 19 QxN Q-B4 20 N-K5!) 19 QR-Q1 N-B3 20 P-Q7 1-0 (20...N-K2 21 QxN+!).

After the text, White has good chances, despite his peculiar pawn structure. Chigorin gave the line 11 PxB KN-K2 12 N-R4 Q-N4 13 BxP+ K-Q1 14 R-B4 NxP 15 N-B3 NxN+ 16 QxN and if 16...Q-QB4 17 B-B4 N-B3

18 R-B5 etc.

B2:
6 ...   N—B3
For some light on the history of this variation, we refer to Zukertort's article on the Evans, entitled "Forty Years in the Life of a Favourite", published in the *Westminster Papers,* 1874. Apparently 6 N-B3 first appeared in 1836 and was "specially practised by the English chess leaders". La Bourdonnais, in the *Palamede* (1838) condemned this on account of 7 N-N5, "entirely oblivious of the fact that George Walker published, a year before, a perfectly satisfactory defence against this move, invented by Mr Burnett of Edinburgh" Zukertort then claims that the Evans Gambit was almost given up because of unfavourable results in the following years, although "the redoubtable defence", as he calls 6...N-B3, could be avoided by 6 P-Q4 as pointed out, for example, by Stanley in the *American Magazine,* 1847. While after 6 0-0 N-B3 the improvement 7 P-Q4 is generally known as the Richardson Attack, after another American amateur, but we have been unable to trace the origin of this line.
7 P-Q4*(102)*
7 N-N5?! is best met by 7...0-0 8 P-B4 P-Q4 (Or 8...P-Q3 — *Sovremenny Debyut*) 9 PxP NxP (Jaenisch quoted a drawn game Shottisbrooke-Delhi, with 9...B-N3+.) 10 B-R3 (10 Q-N3 B-K3! or 10 P-Q4 P-KR3) 10...NxKBP! 11 NxBP (Or 11 RxN QxN 12 R-B1 B-N3+ 13 K-R1 N-R4 14 BxR NxB∓ — *Handbuch*) 11...RxN 12 BxR+ KxB 13 P-N3 Q-N4 14 K-R1 B-K3 15 Q-B3 Q-Q1 16 Q-R5+ K-R1 17 PxN Q-B3 and Black has a murderous attack for the exchange — Wormald.

102
B

B21: 7...PxP?
B22: 7...NxKP
B23: 7...0-0
    7...P-Q3 see Chapter 4, line A.

B21:
    7 ...   PxP?
    8 B—R3!
    For 8 PxP P-Q3 see A13 above, while 8 P-K5?! P-Q4! was good for Black in the first Morphy-Anderssen match game, Paris 1858. Zukertort comments that after this game Morphy declared he would never again play the Evans in a serious contest, "yet six months later this celebrated defence was totally demolished by B. Suhle" in the *Schachzeitung* for July 1859! The French player Arnous de Riviere, later a great friend of Morphy's, had played 8 B-R3! as early as 1848. Ideas did not travel as quickly in those days as they do now!
    8 ...   P—Q3
    Or 8...P-Q4 (8...NxP 9 Q-N3 P-Q4 10 BxP N-Q3 11 BxP+!) 9 KPxP NxP 10 Q-N3 B-K3 11 QxP N4-K2 12 B-N5 B-Q2 13 B/N5xN BxB 14 Q-R6 BxN 15 R-K1 P-QB4 16 BxP 0-0 17 BxN±± — *Handbuch.*
    9 P—K5!   PxKP
    Others:
    a) 9...N-K5 10 PxP (10 R-K1 — Blackburne) 10...NxQP 11 R-K1+ N-K2? (11...K-B1 may be tenable.) 12

N-N5 0-0 13 Q-R5 B-B4 14 NxBP NxN 15 RxN B-N3 16 QxKB — Levenfish.
    b) 9...P-Q4 (Morphy-Greenaway, blindford simul., London 1859) 10 PxN PxB 11 R-K1+ K-Q2 12 PxNP R-N1 13 NxP±.
    c) 9...N-KN5!? 10 KPxP BPxP 11 R-K1+ N5-K4! (Mlotkowski in *B.C.M.*) and now we suggest 12 PxP! (Instead of the unclear line 12 NxN PxN 13 N-Q2 B-B4! 14 Q-B3) 12...BxR 13 QxB (13 PxN B-QN5!) 13...NxP! 14 NxN/Q4 since the minor pieces will be superior to rook and two pawns after 14...0-0 15 B-Q5 with Q-N4 coming to win the QP.
    10 Q—N3   Q—Q2?
    11 N—N5!
    The books quote de Riviere-Zurni, Paris 1848, which went instead 11 R-K1 P-K5 12 QN-Q2? (12 N-N5!) 12...BxP 13 NxKP BxKR 14 RxB but now, instead of the feeble move 14...K-Q1?, 14...NxN 15 RxN+ K-Q1 16 N-N5 NxN (16...N-R4 17 NxQ!) 17 RxN P-QB3 would put up a strong resistance — analysis.
    The text move was suggested by Levenfish. A possible continuation is 11...N-Q1 12 R-K1 B-N3 (12...N-N5 13 P-R3) 13 RxP+ N-K3 14 NxN PxN 15 BxP winning material.

B22:
    7 ...   NxKP*(103)*

103
W

B221: 8 PxP
B222: 8 NxP
8 P-Q5!? is a neglected possibility. It is worth looking closer at 8...N-K2 (8...N-N1!?) not 8...N-Q3?? 9 PxN NxB 10 Q-Q5) 9 NxP 0-0 (9... NxQBP? 10 Q-B3) 10 B-Q3 N-Q3 (10...N-KB3!?) 11 Q-R5 P-KN3 12 Q-R3 NxP 13 N-N4 with the idea of P-QB4 and B-N2 and some attack for the two pawns, since Black's bishop is out on a limb at QR4 — Botterill and Harding.

B221:
8 PxP
This leads to sharp open play, but Black's chances are probably to be preferred.
8 ...   0—0
Others:
a) 8...NxQBP? 9 NxN (9 Q-N3 — Unzicker) 9...BxN 10 Q-N3 BxR 11 BxP+ K-B1 12 B-N8! RxB 13 N-N5 NxP (13...QxN 14 BxQ BxP 15 Q-KB3+) and now La Bourdonnais-**Jay (from a blindfold exhibition,** *circa* 1835) continued 14 P-B4!? with an eventual White win; Cozens gives 14 NxP+ as a quick win.
b) 8...N-B4 9 B-KN5 (9 Q-Q5!? — *Handbuch*) 9...N-K2 10 N-Q4 N-K3 11 B-R4 and White has a strong attack — Chigorin.
9 B—Q5
Other attempts:
a) 9 Q-B2 P-Q4 10 R-Q1 (Or 10 B-R3 R-K1 11 R-Q1 B-K3 Brosztel-Charousek, Kassa 1892) 10...B-K3 e.g. 11 B-K3 P-B4 12 BxQP BxB 13 P-B4 N-N5 14 Q-N2 P-B5 15 B-Q4 B-K3∓ — Wormald.
b) 9 Q-Q3 (Or 9 Q-Q5 NxQBP 10 Q-Q3 — Löwenthal — 10...P-Q4!∓) 9...N-B4 10 Q-Q5 N-K3 11 B-R3 R-K1 12 N-Q4 B-N3 13 N-B5 Q-N4! Neumann-Seidl, Vienna 1897.
c) 9 B-R3 P-Q3 (Staunton, 1847) 10

Q-B2 N-B4 11 BxN PxB 12 QN-Q2 Q-K2 13 QR-K1 B-K3 14 BxB PxB 15 N-K4 P-KR3 16 N-N3 QR-Q1 17 R-K4 R-Q4 18 P-B4 R-Q2∓ — *Sovremenny Debyut.*
d) 9 R-K1 NxQBP (9...N-B4!? and ...N-K3) 10 NxN BxN 11 N-N5 NxP (11...BxKR 12 Q-R5) 12 RxN BxR/K4 13 Q-R5 P-KR3 14 NxP RxN 15 QxR+ K-R1 16 B-KN5! B-B3 17 BxB PxB 18 R-K1 1-0 Steinitz-Devide, friendly, New York 1890.
9 ...   **N—B4!**
Others:
a) 9...NxQBP? 10 NxN BxN 11 N-N5! and wins much as in the Steinitz game.
b) 9...BxP 10 BxN BxR 11 BxP+:
b1) 11...K-R1 12 N-N5 P-KN3 13 Q-N4 BxP (13...K-N2 14 Q-KR4) 14 Q-KR4 K-N2 15 N-K6+! PxN 16 Q-R6+ K-B2 17 BxP+ K-K2 18 Q-R4+ R-B3 19 B-R3+! P-Q3 20 Q-R7+ K-B1 21 Q-R8+ K-K2 22 Q-N7+ R-B2 23 QxR mate; Chigorin-Alapin, St Petersburg 1883.
b2) 11...KxB 12 N-N5+ when:
b21) 12...K-N3 13 Q-N4 (13 Q-Q3+ P-B4 leads to a draw.) 13...P-B4 14 PxPep N-K4! 15 Q-N3! KxP 16 P-B4 K-K2 (16...N-N3 17 P-B5 N-K4 18 N-K4+ or 16...N-B3 17 N-K4+ K-K2 18 P-B5) 17 R-K1 P-Q3 18 N-QB3! BxN 19 QxB B-B4 20 PxN K-Q2 21 P-K6+! 1-0 Chigorin-Rosenkrantz, St Petersburg 1897.
b22) 12...QxN 13 BxQ BxP (A Steinitz idea) 14 B-K3! P-KN3 (Or 14...P-Q3 15 P-B4 B-B3 16 Q-R5+ as in an earlier Chigorin-Manko game) 15 P-B4 B-B3 16 P-B5 P-Q3 17 P-N4 B-Q2 18 Q-B3 P-KN4 (18...N-K4 19 Q-R3+ K-N1 20 N-B3 and if 20... N-B6+ 21 RxN BxN then 22 P-B6) 19 P-KR4 QR-K1 20 PxP RxB 21 Q-R1+ K-N1 22 PxB N-K4 23 Q-R4 1-0 Chigorin-Manko, 8th *New Time* corres tourney, Russia 1901-02. The

original suggestion of the 11 BxP+ coup was apparently due to Berger's 1876 *Deutsche Schachzeitung* analysis (of which Chigorin was somewhat critical).

10 N—N5*(104)*

104
B

Alapin analysed this position in 1893 and concluded that Black ought to be able to repulse the attack. Whatever contemporary players thought, his opinion is generally accepted nowadays.

10 ...   Q—K2

Others:

a) 10...P-KR3 11 NxP RxN 12 BxR+ KxB 13 Q-Q5+ N-K3 14 P-KB4 B-N3+ 15 K-R1 N-K2 16 Q-B3 P-N3 17 P-B5!± Heinrichsen-Walbrodt, 1897.

b) 10...N-K3 11 Q-R5 P-KR3 (Or 11...NxN 12 BxN Q-K1 13 B-KB6! N-K2 14 QN-Q2± Chigorin-Shabelsky, corres 1884-5) 12 N-K4 P-Q3 13 BxRP! NxP 14 P-KB4 P-KN3 15 Q-K2±± Chigorin-Weber, St Petersburg 1898.

c) 10...NxP!? 11 P-KB4 P-QB3! (11... P-KR3? 12 PxN PxN 13 Q-R5 or 13 R-B3 — Chigorin) 12 PxN PxB 13 Q-R5 (Or 13 QxP B-N3 14 K-R1 Q-K2!) 13...P-KR3 14 NxP Q-K1 and White's attack peters out — Berger.

11 Q—B2

Alapin looked at 11 Q-R5 P-KR3 12 N-B3 P-Q3! e.g.:

a) 13 B-N5 PxB 14 NxP B-B4 15 P-N4

N-K5! 16 NxN BxN 17 BxB P-KN3 18 Q-R6 QxP∓.

b) 13 PxP QxP 14 BxN (14 R-Q1 B-K3 15 B-N3 Q-K2) 14...QxB 15 B-R3 B-N3 16 N-Q4 Q-N3!∓.

11 ...   P—KN3
12 P—KB4   B—N3
13 K—R1   P—Q3
14 P—B5   NxP

a) 15 PxP PxP 16 NxP B-K3!∓ — Hardin;

b) 15 Q-B2 Q-B3 16 Q-R4 P-KR4 17 N-Q2 BxP 18 N2-K4 NxN 19 BxN N-N5 20 BxB N-K6 21 BxN BxB∓ — Alapin.

c) 15 P-B6 Q-Q1 16 P-KR3 (16 Q-B2 N/B4-Q6 17 Q-R4 P-KR4 or 16 Q-Q2 N-N5) 16...B-K3 17 Q-Q2 (Chigorin) is critical. Can Black improve upon 17...BxB 18 NxRP N-K5 19 Q-R6 N-N6+ 20 K-R2 NxR+ 21 K-R1 N-N6+ drawing?

B222:

8 NxP   0—0*(105)*

Others:

a) 8...P-Q4? 9 NxP! KxN 10 Q-R5+ K-K2 11 BxP P-KN3 12 B-R3+ N-Q3 13 Q-N5+ K-B1 14 Q-R6+ K-K1 15 Q-N7 R-B1 16 BxN+ PxB 17 R-K1+ and wins — Berger.

b) 8...NxN 9 PxN and now:

b1) 9...P-Q4 10 BxP BxP 11 NxB NxN 12 BxP+ KxB 13 Q-B3+ K-N1 14 QxN± — von Bardeleben.

b2) 9...0-0 10 Q-Q5 BxP 11 NxB NxN 12 Q-B3 N-R5 13 Q-KN3 K-R1 (13... P-Q4!?) 14 B-KN5 Q-K1 15 KR-K1 N-N3 16 B-B6! R-KN1 17 B-Q3 PxB and now both 18 Q-R4 and 18 PxP lead to mate — Levenfish.

See diagram next page

9 B—R3

Or:

a) 9 NxP?! RxN 10 BxR+ KxB 11 P-Q5 N-K2! 12 Q-R4 (Berger overlooked that 12 Q-R5+ K-N1 13 P-Q6

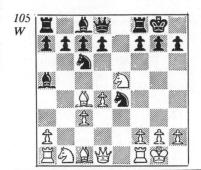

105
W

is met by 13...PxP! guarding the bishop!) 12...BxP 13 NxB NxN 14 Q-QB4+ N2-Q4 15 B-Q2 P-QN4! 16 Q-N3 (Anderssen) 16...Q-R5! 17 BxN Q-QB5! and Black has winning chances (quoted by Chigorin).
b) 9 Q-R5!? NxN (9...P-Q4? 10 NxP! RxN 11 BxP Q-K2 12 R-K1) 10 QxN P-Q4! (10...BxP 11 NxB NxN 12 P-Q5 N-R5 13 B-KN5 Q-K1 14 Q-N3) 11 BxP NxQBP 12 B-QB4! P-B4 (12... P-QN4 13 B-Q2! PxB 14 QxB NxN 15 QRxN= Alapin-Chigorin, Ostend 1905.

9	...	**P—Q3**
10	**NxN**	**PxN**
11	**Q—R4**	

Berger's suggestion 11 Q-B3 can be met by 11...Q-K1 12 R-K1 N-N4!, as indicated by Chigorin.

11	...	**BxP**

Most sources follow this analysis from Berger's article. However, a postal game Heinrichsen-Chigorin (1899-1900) went instead 11...Q-N4!? 12 P-B4 (12 B-B1!?) 12...Q-N3 e.g.:
a) 13 R-K1 B-R6 14 B-B1 B-N3 15 QxBP B-KB4 16 B-B1 QR-K1 17 N-Q2 R-K3 with complications.
b) If instead 13 QxB, then after 13... B-R6 14 P-N3 NxNP 15 Q-KN5 QxQ 16 PxQ BxR 17 BxB N-K5 18 B-B1 P-B3! (Chigorin's analysis) White may be too slow in the development of his Q-side.

12	**NxB**	**NxN**

13 QxBP   B—K3
14 B—Q3   N—Q4
15 B-K4 N-N3 16 Q-B2 R-N1 17 BxRP+ and White, having regained his pawn and still possessing the bishop pair, certainly does not stand badly.

B23:

7	...	**0—0** *(106)*

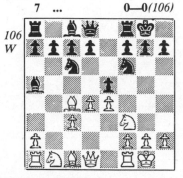

106
W

B231: 8 Q-B2?!
B232: 8 B-R3!
    8 PxP see B221 and 8 NxP see B222.
    8 B-KN5 P-Q3 9 P-Q5 N-K2 10 BxN PxB 11 N-R4 N-N3 12 NxN? (12 N-B5!) 12...RPxN 13 P-KB4 B-N3+ 14 K-R1 K-N2 and Black occupied the KR-file; Zukertort-Anderssen, Breslau 1864.
    8 Q—B2?!   Q—K2!
Not 8...P-Q3 (8...P-Q4!? 9 KPxP P-K5) 9 PxP when:
a) 9...QNxP 10 NxN PxN 11 B-R3 R-K1 12 R-Q1 N-Q2 13 Q-N3 Q-B3 14 R-Q3 Q-KN3 15 R-N3 Q-R4 16 Q-R4!±± Dufresne-Anderssen, Berlin 1851.
b) 9...PxP 10 B-R3 R-K1 11 R-Q1 N-Q2 (11...B-Q2 12 N-N5) 12 Q-N3 Q-B3 13 N-N5±— Levenfish.

9	**PxP**	**NxP**
10	**NxN**	**QxN**
11	**B—Q3**	**N—N5∓**

a) Another Dufresne - Anderssen game went 12 P-N3 B-N3 13 N-R3

P-Q4 14 B-KB4 Q-KR4 15 P-KR4 P-KR3! etc.

b) An American postal game of 1905, Philbrook-Viele, concluded catastrophically 12 P-KB4 Q-R4 13 P-KR3 B-N3+ 14 K-R1 Q-R5 15 Q-K2 N-B7+ 16 K-R2 P-KR4 17 P-B5 (The threat was ...N-N5+ and ...Q-N6.) 17...P-QB3! 18 B-B2 B-B2+ 19 K-N1 Q-N6 20 QxP N-R8! 21 R-B3 Q-K8+ 0-1 (If 22 R-B1 QxR+ wins a rook).

B232:
    8 B—R3!   R—K1

8...P-Q3!? 9 PxP KNxP is possible, but then comes 10 B-Q3 and if 10... N-B4 11 BxN PxB 12 Q-B2 P-KR3 13 QN-Q2 with good compensation for the pawn — Botterill and Harding.

    9 P—Q5   N—N1
  10 P—Q6!   PxP

10...N-QB3! looks like the last chance.

  11 BxQP   NxP
  12 NxP   NxB
  13 QxN±

a) 13...R-K2 14 NxBP! RxN 15 Q-Q5± Kolisch-Winawer, London 1883 (friendly).

b) 13...B-B2 14 BxP+ (14 NxBP is also good.) 14...K-R1 15 BxR (15 N-N6+ PxN 16 QxNP BxP+ is not so clear.) 15...BxQ 16 N-B7+ K-N1 17 NxQ etc.

8 5...B—B4 Defence: Introduction

It is now time to consider what happens if, after the opening moves **1 P-K4 P-K4 2 N-KB3 N-QB3 3 B-B4 B-B4 4 P-QN4 BxNP 5 P-B3,** Black chooses the less popular retreat **5...B-B4***(107)*. Most players nowadays consider this move to be inferior to 5...B-R4, or at best equivalent to it — as after ...B-N3 in some cases (e.g. the Normal Variation) it will make no difference in the long run which fifth move Black chose. There was no such consensus in the nineteenth century, however. Lasker played 5...B-B4 in his two games with Chigorin (see **Chapter 4).** Zukertort, in the *Westminster Papers* (1874), argued that 5...B-R4 was best, because it was just as good as 5...B-B4 if Black wanted to play the Normal line, but it also gave him the opportunity of adopting other defences, notably the Compromised, which he and Anderssen favoured at that time.

H.E. Bird, a strong English master who held many independent views on the openings, argued in reply that Zukertort's article ignored the contributions of British players to the theory of the Evans. In his *Modern Chess,* he wrote: "Zukertort strongly expresses his views and that of other foreign masters in favour of retiring the bishop to R4, whilst the English players preferred B-B4. I have always supported the latter move, and in recent play Zukertort has declined the Evans attack altogether...It appears not unlikely that he has lost confi-

dence in the defence he so long advocated, and probably would not like to admit his conversion to English ideas..." Bird went on to elaborate upon his preferred method, commencing 5...B-B4 6 P-Q4 PxP 7 PxP B-N3 which was wont to lead to the Normal Position. "I have no doubt" he concluded, "that the line of defence indicated, though difficult to conduct properly to a successful issue, should constitute a solid and trustworthy defence to the formidable Evans Gambit attack".

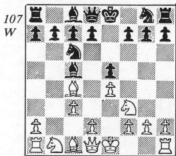

107
W

Since 5...B-R4 can also lead to the Normal, it is not easy to see what Bird was driving at. It is true that 5...B-B4 avoids the Q-N3 Method, and this may be why Lasker chose that move-order as a way of reaching his own defence, but this was not one of the arguments Bird used.

From a technical point of view, there can be no other virtue in 5...B-B4, since the bishop is exposed and unguarded on that square and it does not pin White's QBP. Moreover, after 5...B-B4 6 P-Q4 Black is more or less obliged to play ...PxP, which is not the case with the bishop at R4. We have already seen that, by and large, White gets more attack in those lines where Black's KP disappears from K4.

6 P—Q4!

After 6 0-0 P-Q3 7 P-Q4 Black often transposed to the Normal line (B5 below) by 7...PxP 8 PxP B-N3. Simply 7...B-N3!, transposing to the Lasker Defence, is best, avoiding the complications and equalizing as we have already seen. It is a mystery why Chigorin did not play the text move!

6 ... PxP*(108)*

6...B-N3 transposes to the Capablanca line in the previous chapter.

Not 6...N-R4? 7 BxP+! KxB 8 NxP+ and White wins a pawn.

Now White has:

A: 7 PxP!?

B: 7 0-0

Not 7 N-N5? N-R3 8 BxP+ NxB 9 NxN KxN 10 Q-R5+ P-KN3 11 QxB because of 11...P-Q4 (11...P-Q3!? or 11...R-K1!? — Bird) 12 KPxP (12 QxP/5+ B-K3!) 12...R-K1+ 13 K-B1 R-K4 14 P-QB4 Q-R5 15 B-Q2 Q-K5 16 P-B3 Q-K7+ 17 K-N1 R-N4! 18 P-N4 N-K4∓∓— Lange.

A:

7 PxP!?

This is of course impossible when a bishop at a5 pins the pawn.

7 ... B—N5+!?

This obvious move is possibly not best. Bird advocated 7...B-N3, after which 8 0-0 P-Q3 would transpose immediately to the Normal Position. If White defers castling, playing instead 8 P-Q5 N-R4! or 8 N-B3 or 8 B-N2, the game is still quite likely to **transpose into Chapter 10 in the end.** These lines have been relatively little-examined in the twentieth century, but the old authorities considered 7...B-N3 followed by an early ...N-R4, to be a sufficient defence for Black.

A line worth looking into is 7...B-N3 8 B-N2!? N-B3 (Instead of 8...N-R4) 9 P-K5 (Not mentioned in the *Encyclopaedia of Chess Openings!)* 9...N-K5 (9...P-Q4? 10 PxN PxB 11 P-Q5! — Bird) 10 B-Q5 N-N4 11 0-0 as Harrwitz played in an 1864 game. Bird considered this position good for White. For example 11...0-0 could be met by 12 NxN followed by N-QR3-B4.

After 8...N-R4 9 P-Q5 N-K2 (9... NxB 10 BxP P-KB3 11 BxR Q-K2 12 0-0 N-R3 13 P-K5!) 10 B-Q3 P-Q3 11 N-B3 P-QB4 in a consultation game Blackburne & Herington v. Bird and Chapman, Hastings 1896, White tried an unusual plan of avoiding castling: 12 N-K2 0-0 13 R-QB1 P-B3 14 N-R4 N-N3 15 NxN PxN 16 P-KR4! Q-K1 17 P-R5 P-B5 18 B-N1 and the White team won, but the defence made several errors so, from a theoretical point of view, this game can be no more than food for thought.

8 K—B1

This move is stronger here than in the analogous Krakow Variation of the Guioco Piano (1 P-K4 P-K4 2 N-KB3 N-QB3 3 B-B4 B-B4 4 P-B3 N-B3 5 P-Q4 PxP 6 PxP B-N5+ 7 K-B1!?) chiefly because of the additional chance here of bringing the QR into the attack speedily along the second rank. However, White's king remains somewhat exposed and his KR is hard to employ usefully, so the variation is on a knife-edge.

It is worth considering these rare moves:

a) 8 B-Q2 Q-K2 9 0-0 BxB 10 QxB Q-N5 (It is not easy to find a sound plan for Black.) 11 Q-N5 P-KN3 12 QN-Q2 and White won quickly; Spielmann-Razinger, Ebensee 1933.

b) 8 QN-Q2!? Q-K2 (8...B-B6? 9 BxP+) 9 0-0 BxN 10 BxB P-Q3 (Podgorny recommended 10...N-B3 in *Ceskolovensky Sach.*) 11 R-K1 B-N5 12 Q-N3 0-0-0 13 QR-N1± Skok-Luskac, Czechoslovakia 1956.

8 ... Q—K2

Others:

1) 8...B-K2 9 Q-N3 N-R4 10 BxP+ K-B1 11 Q-B3 (11 Q-R4 P-B3 12 BxN P-QN4! Mlotkowski-Kohler, Philadelphia 1911) 11...KxB 12 QxN P-Q3 13 B-N2 with fair prospects for White; Lasker-Raimond, blindfold exhibition in New York, 1892. Zak gives 13...P-B3! 14 Q-R4 N-KB3 as critical now.

b) 8...N-B3 when:
b1) *M.C.O.* (8th edition) suggested 9 Q-N3 but then 9...Q-K2 looks strong.
b2) Not 9 N-N5 0-0 10 P-K5 P-Q4 11 PxN PxB 12 Q-R5 B-KB4 13 PxP QxP! 14 PxR=Q+ RxQ 15 P-N4 B-N3 0-1 Winter-G. Wood, *Sunday Chronicle* tourney, England 1946.
b3) The *Handbuch* suggestion 9 P-QR3 (Or immediately 9 P-Q5) looks best. Black has to decide whether to put his bishop on K2 and QN on QR4 — or vice versa! Freeborough and Ranken (1893) give 9 P-QR3 B-R4 10 P-Q5 N-K2 11 P-K5±.
c) 8...P-Q3? 9 P-Q5 and 10 Q-R4+ etc.

9 P—K5

9 P-QR3 B-R4 10 R-R2, as played by Blackburne in a blindfold game,

also deserves consideration. This, given in fact by Jaenisch in 1843, may be best!

9 ... P—B3!? *(109)*

Black has also tried 9...P-Q3, when:
a) 10 P-Q5, as recommended by Kan in his *Shakmatnye Vstrechi* (1962), would fail to 10...NxP 11 Q-R4+ (Or 11 NxN QxN and the QR is en prise) 11...K-B1! 12 QxB/N4 NxN 13 PxN B-R6+ 14 K-N1 Q-B3 15 B-Q3 QxP∓∓— Freeborough and Ranken.
b) 10 P-QR3 B-R4 11 P-Q5 NxP 12 NxN QxN 13 R-R2 is promising:
b1) After 13...K-B1 (13...K-Q1!?) 14 R-K1 Q-B4 15 Q-R4 B-Q2 16 QxB/R5 QxN 17 Q-B3 White threatens 18 R-N2 or 18 B-R2 or 18 B-Q3 with good attacking chances — analysis.
b2) The counter-sacrifice 13... B-KN5?! 14 P-B3 0-0-0 proved inadequate after 15 PxB R-K1 16 N-Q2! (Not 16 R-K2?? Q-B3+ 17 R-B2 Q-Q5! 18 QxQ R-K8 mate) 16...N-B3 17 N-B3 Q-K2 (17...Q-B6 18 R-QB2) 18 R-K2 in a 1974-5 postal game Harding-Mayne.

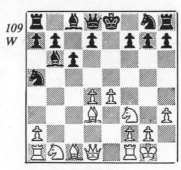

10 P—QR3!

This improves upon 10 PxP? KNxP 11 B-KN5 P-QN3 12 P-QR3 B-Q3 13 R-R2 Q-B1 of Minchin-Steinitz, London 1866, which Black eventually won.

| 10 | ... | **B—R4** |
| 11 | **Q—N3** | **PxP** |

This is relatively the best move. 11...N-R3 could be met by 12 BxN PxB 13 N-B3 (Kan) or 12 PxP QxBP 13 B-KN5 Q-Q3 14 N-B3 (Levenfish).

12	**BxN**	**P—K5**
13	**B—N5**	**Q—B1**
14	**B—Q5**	**PxN**

15 N-B3! Q-KB4! 16 R-K1+ K-B1 17 BxN QxB 18 BxBP P-Q3 19 P-KR4 Q-N3 (19...Q-Q7 20 Q-R4! — Kan) 20 R-K3! (20 Q-N5 would be met by 20... BxN 21 B-R5 B-Q2!) 20...BxN 21 QxB P-B3 22 P-R5 Q-N8+ 23 R-K1 Q-N4+ 24 K-N1 P-KR3 25 Q-K3 B-B4 26 R-R4 K-N1 27 R-B4 R-KB1 28 P-N4 P-N4 29 RxB RxR 30 Q-K8+ 1-0 Kan-Kots, Moscow Ch 1931.

B:

7   0—0*(110)*

After this move, Black's best plan is to head for the Normal Position.

110
B

Now:
B1: 7...P-Q6?!
B2: 7...P-Q3

Others can be disposed of briefly:
a) 7...PxP? 8 BxP+ (8 Q-N3 and 8 NxP are also strong.) 8...KxB 9 Q-Q5+ K-B1 10 QxB+ Q-K2 11 QxBP and if 11...QxP 12 B-N2 — Euwe.
b) 7...KN-K2? 8 PxP B-N3 9 N-N5 P-Q4 (9...0-0? 10 Q-R5 P-KR3 11

NxP±±) 10 PxP QNxP (10...BxP 11 PxN BxR 12 BxP+ wins the queen first and then mates; or 10...KNxP 11 R-K1+ N3-K2 12 B-R3) 11 B-N2 N5-B4 12 Q-R5 P-N3 13 Q-K2 and White has a winning attack.
c) 7...N-B3? 8 PxP B-N3 9 P-K5 N-KN1 (9...N-K5 10 Q-K2 or 9...P-Q4 10 PxN) 10 P-Q5 N-R4 (10...N3-K2 11 P-Q6 PxP 12 PxP N-QB3 13 R-K1+ K-B1 14 Q-Q5 Q-B3 15 B-KN5 Q-N3 16 N-R4±) 11 B-KN5 N-K2 (Or 11... P-KB3 12 PxP NxP 13 P-Q6 NxB 14 Q-K2+ K-B1 15 QxN±) 12 P-Q6 PxP 13 PxP P-B3 14 PxN Q-B2 15 B-Q5 PxB 16 NxP and White must win — *Handbuch.*
d) 7...N-R4?! 8 PxP (8 BxP+ is not clear.) 8...NxB 9 PxN should favour White, e.g. 9...P-QN4 10 P-QR4! or 9...Q-B3 10 P-K5 Q-K2 11 Q-Q5 etc. If the knight retreats, B-N2 gives White strong pressure on the long black diagonal — analysis.
e) 7...B-N3! 8 PxP N-R4 (8...P-Q3 see **B2.**) 9 B-Q3 (*M.C.O.,* 7th ed., gave 9 B-KN5 but 9...N-K2 or 9...P-B3 would be good replies.) 9...P-Q3 (9...N-KB3 10 P-K5!) and now White has probably nothing better than 10 **N-B3 transposing to Chapter 9, E3.**

B1:

| 7 | ... | **P—Q6?!** |
| 8 | **N—N5!** | |

In the third Anderssen-Steinitz match game, London 1866, White played 8 QxP? and eventually lost. Anderssen's choice was all the more surprising since, according to Bachmann's biography, the German master had already condemned the move in the *Deutsche Schachzeitung!* The text move is very old, being recommended for example in Wormald's *Chess Openings* (1875).

| 8 | ... | **N—R3** |

9 NxBP!   NxN
10 BxN+   KxB
11 Q—R5+   P—KN3

11...K-B1 12 QxB+ P-Q3 13 Q-Q5 Q-B3 14 QxP/Q3 B-K3 15 P-KB4 also led to a win for White, in Wills-Iqbal Ahmad, corres 1964-5.

12 QxB   P—Q3
13 Q—Q5+

Or 13 Q-QN5 (To tie down the QB) 13...N-K2 14 N-Q2 R-K1 15 P-KB4 K-N1 16 QxQP B-K3 17 B-N2 P-Q4 18 P-B4! Ragozin v. Ilin-Zhenevsky, match 1930.

13 ...   B—K3
14 QxP/Q3

White has regained his pawn and achieved a promising attacking position — P-KB4 will be followed by N-Q2-B3 or B-N2 and P-QB4. This position first occurred in a game Duhrssen-Kramer, Ebensee 1930, and the assessment was confirmed in Sokolsky-Kopayev, Chernovice 1946.

B2:

7 ...   P—Q3
8 PxP   B—N3*(111)*

Thus arises the so-called Normal Position of the Evans Gambit, which can also come about by 5...B-R4 6 P-Q4 PxP 7 0-0 B-N3 8 PxP P-Q3. The defensive set-up that Black is adopting was known as early as the La Bourdonnais v. McDonnell match, and was termed 'normal' by the first editors of the *Handbuch*. Although by no means as popular now as it was in the nineteenth century, the Normal still offers a real challenge to White's attacking prowess. True, he has the classical pawn centre, but Black is ready for counter-blows like ...N-QR4 and ...B-KN5 and, if allowed to castle, will set about advancing his Q-side pawn majority. Keen open play is certain to result.

111
W

The two most usual moves for White here are discussed in separate chapters, *viz.* 9 N-B3 in Chapter 9, and 9 P-Q5 in Chapter 10. The other possibilities, of which at least one merits serious consideration, are dealt with now. These are:

B21: 9 B-R3
B22: 9 P-QR4
B23: 9 R-K1
B24: 9 B-KN5
B25: 9 P-K5
B26: 9 B-N2
B27: 9 P-KR3

B21:

9 B—R3   B—N5

Also possible are:
a) 9...N-R4 10 B-Q3 N-K2 11 P-K5 0-0 "White's QB is out of play, and he has no attack" — Wormald.
b) 9...N-B3? (But 9...KN-K2!?) 10 P-K5! PxP? (10...N-KN5 is much better.) 11 Q-N3 Q-Q2 12 PxP N-QR4 13 PxN!±± Staunton-Cochrane, 1842.

10 B—QN5

10 P-K5 (10 P-Q5? N-K4 or 10 Q-R4 B-Q2 11 Q-N3 N-R4) 10...PxP 11 Q-N3 Q-Q2 12 NxP NxN 13 PxN B-K3 and White's attack was broken; Strauss-Steinitz, Vienna 1860.

10 ...   BxN
11 BxN+   PxB
12 PxB   N—K2

13 K-R1 N-N3 14 R-N1 0-0 15 N-B3 R-K1 16 R-N3 Q-B3 17 N-K2 P-B4!∓

Johner-Fahrni, Baden Gambit Tourney 1914.

B22:
9 P—QR4
A move occasionally seen in the nineteenth century, but which does nothing to further White's development. Black can reply:

a) 9...N-R4 10 B-R2 and now 10...B-K3 would transpose to D43 in chapter 4. Other possibilities are 10...B-N5 11 P-K5 or 10...N-KB3 11 Q-B2 in either case with good prospects for White according to Wormald.

b) 9...B-N5, and if 10 B-QN5 P-QR3! scotching the threats to Black's bishop, should be a complete defence. See D45 in Chapter 4.

B23:
9 R—K1
Another obsolete move, whose intention clearly is to open the K-file.
9 ... N—R4!
Others are not so clear:

a) 9...N-B3 (Zukertort) could be met by 10 B-KN5 or 10 P-Q5 N-K2 11 B-KN5 (Levenfish) or possibly 10 P-K5 PxP 11 P-Q5 (Wormald).

b) 9...B-N5 10 B-QN5 BxN 11 PxB Q-R5 (11...K-B1 12 B-N2 and White has compensation — Wormald) 12 B-K3 KN-K2 with complications, as in a nineteenth-century game Burn-de Vere.
10 B—Q3
White should have some positional compensation for his pawn, but we cannot see any immediate use for the rook on K1. Attempts to open the game immediately should not be successful:

a) 10 BxP+?! KxB 11 N-N5+ K-B1 12 P-K5 is best met by 12...P-KR3! (and if 13 Q-B3+ N-KB3) as suggested in *Sovremenny Debyut;* White will run out of attack and remain at least a pawn down.

b) 10 P-K5 NxB 11 Q-R4+ P-QB3! 12 QxN P-Q4 — Wormald.

c) 10 N-B3 NxB 11 Q-R4+ B-Q2 12 QxN N-K2∓ as Black has not played the weakening ...P-KB3 by comparison with lines in the next chapter.

B24:
9 B—KN5
This rare move, by comparison with 9 N-B3, allows Black a tempo to get castled, but that may not be the last word.
9 ... KN—K2
9...P-B3 10 B-K3! KN-K2 11 N-B3 N-R4 12 P-KR3 (and if 12...NxB 13 Q-R4+) is discussed in the next chapter.
10 N—B3 B—N5
Or 10...0-0 11 N-Q5 B-K3 as in a 1932 game played by Lilienthal in Spain.
11 N—Q5 0—0
12 P—QR4 P—QR4
13 NxB PxN
14 P-Q5 N-K4 15 B-K2 BxN 16 BxB NxB+ with equality, e.g. 17 QxB P-B3 18 B-K3 N-N3 19 KR-N1 N-K4 20 Q-K2 R-R3 21 R-N5 N-Q2 — *Sovremenny Debyut.*

B25:
9 P—K5 PxP
Why not 9...P-Q4! e.g. 10 B-QN5 KN-K2∓.
10 Q—N3
This unsound line was successful in a German correspondence game of the 1950s. However, instead of 10...NxP?, Black should have played 10...N-R4! and after 11 BxP+ K-B1 12 B-R3+ N-K2 13 Q-Q5! not the risky 13...P-B3 14 QxKP KxB 15 N-N5+ but 13...QxQ 14 BxQ P-B3! 15 B-K4 N-B5 relieving the pressure — analysis.

B26:

9   B—N2(112)

This is a reasonable move, but one hardly seen nowadays, for White cannot do better with it than transpose lines discussed in Chapter 10.

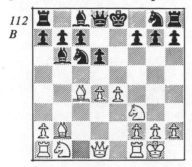

9 ...   N—B3

Others:

a) 9...KN-K2 10 N-N5? (10 P-Q5 N-R4 see Chap. 10; 10 N-B3 gives the QB a misplaced look.) 10...P-Q4 11 PxP N-R4 12 P-Q6 NxB 13 PxN Q-Q4 14 N-B3 QxN (Or 14...NxB 15 NxQ NxQ 16 QRxN P-QB3∓ — Unzicker) 15 Q-R4+ P-QB3 16 QxN B-R6∓ — Keres.

b) 9...P-B3 (Mayet-Hanstein, 1841) is unnecessary, and exposes Black's king on the white squares. The *Handbuch* now gives 10 P-K5!, e.g. 10... QPxP 11 BxN RxB 12 Q-N3 R-B1 13 PxP PxP 14 NxP NxN 15 BxN and Black is stripped naked.

c) 9...B-N5!? 10 P-Q5 N-K4 11 B-N5+ K-B1 12 QN-Q2± — *Sovremenny Debyut.*

d) 9...N-QR4 10 P-Q5 *see* Chapter 10.

10   P—Q5

This is more consistent than:

a) 10 Q-K2 0-0 11 P-K5 (Dufresne-Harrwitz, Berlin 1848) 11...N-K1.

b) 10 Q-N3 0-0 11 P-K5 N-QR4 12 Q-B2 NxB 13 PxN NxB 14 PxP R-K1 15 QxN Q-B3 (15...KxP? 16 N-B3)∓

— Sokolsky.

c) 10 P-K5 PxP 11 B-R3 (11 PxP QxQ 12 RxQ N-KN5) 11...B-K3! 12 BxB PxB 13 Q-N3 Q-Q4 — *Handbuch.*

d) 10 QN-Q2 P-Q4 11 PxP KNxP 12 B-R3 B-K3 13 N-K4 (Erkel-Szen, Budapest 1845) 13...Q-Q2 followed by Q-side castling, with a good position for Black — *Sovremenny Debyut.*

10 ...   N—K2

10...N-QR4 transposes to chapter 10, in a form favourable to White.

11   P—K5

Others:

a) 11 BxN PxB 12 P-QR4 (Wormald suggested 12 N-R4 followed by 13 N-Q2.) 12...0-0 13 K-R1 P-KB4 14 N-N5 P-KR3 15 N-KR3 PxP 16 R-R3 N-N3 17 R-KN3 (Bird-Steinitz, London 1883) and now Steinitz said he should have played either 17... Q-R5 or 17...K-N2 18 Q-R5 BxN 19 PxB (19 RxB Q-N4) 19...Q-B3 followed by ...QR-K1 with a good game.

b) 11 N-B3 0-0 12 Q-B2 proved too slow for White in Gunsberg-Steinitz, Hastings 1895.

11 ...   PxP

12   BxP   0—0

13   BxN   PxB

14 N-B3 N-N3 15 N-K5 B-N5 16 Q-N3 and now instead of 16...BxN (Staunton-Cochrane, 1842) Black could probably get the better of things by 16...N-K4!

B27:

9   P—KR3(113)

With this move, preventing defensive lines based on ...B-N5, White shows that he is confident of building up an attack at his leisure. This old move has attracted renewed attention lately, especially since grandmaster Gligoric lost against it in 1971.

113
B

Black's principal replies are:
B271: 9...N-B3
B272: 9...P-KR3
B273: 9...N-R4
    9...Q-B3 10 B-N2 N-R3 11
QN-Q2 0-0 12 P-K5 gave White a
strong attack in Anderssen-Hillel,
Breslau 1856.

B271:
    9 ...   N—B3
    Now White can play:
B2711: 10 N-B3
B2712: 10 R-K1
    10 B-KN5 would not achieve
much after 10...P-KR3 11 B-R3 N-K2
12 BxN PxB — *Handbuch*.

B2711:
    10 N—B3   0—0
10...P-KR3, with play similar to
B272, may be better.
    11 B—KN5   N—K2
Or 11...P-KR3 12 B-R4 P-N4 13
NxP! PxN 14 BxNP BxQP 15 N-Q5!
B-K3 (15...BxR 16 QxB±±) 16 R-N1
R-N1 17 R-N3 K-R2 18 BxN BxB 19
Q-R5+ K-N1 20 R-N3+ 1-0
Löwenthal-Anderssen, London 1851
(Sources differ on who was White in
this game!).
    12 P—K5   PxP
    13 PxP   N—Q2
Others lose a piece. Now 14 N-Q5
could be met by 14...B-B4 — Morphy.

    14 P—K6
"Strong as White's attack looks, it
is not easy to discover any move which
is more advantageous than this." —
Morphy. The game Bird-de Riviere,
London 1858, continued 14...PxP 15
BxP+ K-R1 16 N-Q5 N-KB3 17 BxN
PxB 18 BxB RxB 19 N-B4 QxQ 20
QRxQ QR-Q1? (20...KR-Q1 is
critical.) 21 N-K6 RxR 22 RxR R-K1
23 R-Q7 N-Q4? (23...N-B3 —
Morphy) 24 N-Q8 N-B5 25 N-B7+
K-N1 26 N-R6+ K-R1 27 N-R4
R-K8+ 28 K-R2 BxP and White
announced mate in 5 (29 R-Q8+ etc.)

B2712:
    10 R—K1   P—KR3
10...0-0 11 B-KN5 would be
unpleasant for Black.
    11 B—R3
11 P-K5 PxP 12 P-Q5 N-K2 would
be inconclusive.
    11 ...   0—0
    12 N—B3   R—K1
    13 R—QB1   N—R2
Chances are balanced in this complicated position. We shall follow the
game Mariotti-Gligoric, Venice 1971:
14 R-K3 N-R4 15 B-Q3 B-K3 16
Q-K2 N-B1 (The more active 16...
N-N4 was suggested in *Shakhmaty v
SSSR*.) 17 N-QR4! N-N3 18 NxB
RPxN 19 P-Q5! B-Q2 20 B-N2 N-B5
21 Q-B2 P-QB3 22 Q-B3 P-B3 23 PxP
PxP 24 B-B1 P-QB4 25 N-R4 P-Q4?
(25...N-B3 was correct; now White
takes the initiative.) 26 PxP NxQP 27
RxR+ QxR 28 Q-KN3 Q-K5 29
R-Q1! (29 B-Q3 Q-B5 30 Q-N6 is
unclear.) 29...R-K1 30 B-Q3 Q-QR5
31 B-R7+ KxB 32 RxN R-K2 33 BxP!
Q-K5 34 N-N6! QxN (34...QxR 35
NxR Q-B2 36 Q-Q3+ K-R1 37 QxB
PxB 38 Q-Q8+) 35 BxR B-K3 36
R-Q6 Q-B2 37 RxP N-B5 (37...QxB
38 Q-K3) 38 R-N7 B-B4 39 R-B7
B-N3 40 BxP Q-B3 41 B-N4 1-0. This

is an excellent example of the validity of nineteenth-century methods in modern chess.

B272:

9	**...**	**P—KR3**(114)

White's B-KN5 is also prevented, and the buck is returned.

114
W

10	**R—K1**	

Plans based on P-Q5 and B-N2 are comparable to chapter 10, but the slight difference should be in White's favour (weakness on g6 if Black plays ...P-KB3).

10	**...**	**KN—K2**

10...N-B3 could transpose to Mariotti-Gligoric.

11	**N—B3**	**0—0**
12	**B—K3**	**N—R4**
13	**B—Q3**	**P—Q4**

14 Q-B1!? (Envisaging sacrifices on KR6) 14...PxP 15 NxP N-B4 16 Q-B3 N-B3 17 P-Q5 NxB (17...QxP may be playable, e.g. 18 BxB RPxB 19 B-B4 Q-R4!) 18 PxN N-Q4 19 Q-K5 PxP 20 QR-Q1 and White had compensation for the two pawns sacrificed; B.

Sigurjonsson-Gunnarsson, Reykjavik Ch 1969.

B273:

9	**...**	**N—R4**
10	**B—Q3**(115)	

115
B

10   ...   N—K2

Only in this way can Black really hope to avoid the necessity for ...P-KR3.

11   N—B3

11 P-Q5 puts White a tempo down on lines in Chapter 10, since P-KR3 is not much use in Anderssen's line.

11	**...**	**0—0**
12	**Q—B2**	

12 B-KN5 looks better, with the idea of inducing a weakening--pawn move.

12	**...**	**N—N3**
13	**N—Q5**	**N—B3**
14	**NxB**	**RPxN**

15 B-QN5 B-Q2 16 B-N5 QN-K2 17 B-QB4 with a complicated position, eventually won by Black; Purdy-Fell, New South Wales Ch 1947.

9 Normal Variation: with Morphy's 9 N—B3

The most direct and economical attacks in the Normal line arise from the move 9 N-B3, which has already been mentioned in connection with Morphy in Chapter 1. White maintains his central pawns abreast and develops his pieces according to the rule 'knights before bishops', since it is not yet clear where the white QB belongs. White will soon be ready to attack the black king, which will generally be forced to remain in the centre. The resulting variations were extensively played and analysed in the latter half of the nineteenth century, but some of the discoveries made at that time are no longer common knowledge so the treatment of the Morphy line in most books is quite misleading. Although analysis suggests that best defence leads to a draw (at least against the methods which Chigorin was wont to employ) White's undoubted positional compensation for his pawn, together with the many possibilities for speculative sacrifices leading to king-hunts, means that the Morphy line is still White's best practical chance of winning.

116

Diagram 116 is reached by the sequence 1 P-K4 P-K4 2 N-KB3 N-QB3 3 B-B4 B-B4 4 P-QN4 BxNP 5 P-B3 B-B4 6 P-Q4 PxP 7 0-0 P-Q3 8 PxP B-N3 9 N-B3. There is no immediate threat involved in this move, so Black has a fairly wide choice of moves, although only two should be considered seriously:
A: 9...KN-K2?
B: 9...B-Q2?!
C: 9...N-B3?!
D: 9...B-N5
E: 9...N-R4
   9...QN-K2 10 Q-N3 (10 N-KN5 N-R3 — Steinitz.) 10...P-KB3 11 P-K5! opening the centre.

A:

9 ...	KN—K2?
10 N—KN5	P—Q4

Not 10...0-0? 11 Q-R5 etc.

| 11 NxQP | BxP |
| 12 NxBP! | Q—Q2 |

Or 12...KxN 13 NxP+ K-B1 14 Q-B3+ B-B3 15 QxB+! PxQ 16 B-R6 mate!

After the text move a game Harrwitz (blindfold) against consulting amateurs, played at Brighton in 1848, concluded vigorously: 13 NxR BxR 14 Q-R5+ P-KN3 15 QxRP N-Q1 16 N-B6+! BxN 17 B-B7+ NxB 18 QxN+ K-Q1 19 Q-B8+ Q-K1 20 R-Q1+ N-Q4 (20...B-Q2 21 N-B7+ K-B1 22 QxQ+ BxQ 23 R-Q8 mate) 21 QxB+ Q-K2 22 RxN+ B-Q2 23 N-B7+ K-K1 24 R-K5 QxR 25 NxQ 1-0.

B:

9 ...   **B—Q2?!**
10 P—K5

10 N-KN5 does not work now, because of 10...N-R3.

10 ...   **PxP**
11 R—K1

Clemenz-Eisenschmidt, Dorpat 1862, concluded 11...KN-K2 12 N-KN5 B-K3 13 BxB PxB 14 NxKP Q-Q3 15 NxNP+ K-B1 16 Q-N4 BxP 17 N-K4 Q-N5 18 N-K6+ K-K1 19 N-B6+ K-B2 20 N-N5+ K-B1 21 **B-R3!** QxB 22 Q-K6 N-Q1 23 Q-B7+! NxQ 24 N-K6 mate.

C:

9 ...   **N—B3?!**
10 P—K5

10 B-KN5 is also good, according to Euwe.

10 ...   **PxP**

Or 10...P-Q4 11 PxN PxB 12 PxP R-KN1 13 R-K1+ B-K3 14 P-Q5 Q-B3 15 B-KN5 QxN 16 PxB Q-Q6 17 PxP+ KxP 18 R-K7+ K-N3 19 Q-K1 Q-Q4 20 R-Q1 N-Q5 21 RxN! BxR 22 Q-N1+ 1-0 de Riviere-Morphy, Paris 1858.

Also 10...N-KN5 11 P-KR3 N-R3 12 B-KN5 Q-Q2 13 P-K6 PxP 14 BxP QxB 15 R-K1 — Euwe.

11 B—R3!*(117)*

White has a strong attack, and ought to win.

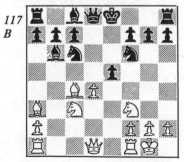

117 B

11 ...   **N—QR4**

Others:
a) 11...BxP 12 Q-N3! Q-Q2 (12... **B-K3 see Morphy-Stanley, p. 23**) 13 N-KN5 (13 NxB NxN 14 Q-N2 Q-B3 15 B-N5! — Sokolsky) 13...N-Q1 14 QR-Q1 P-KR3 (14...N-K3 15 BxN PxB 16 N-N5 threatening NxKP and/or KR-K1) 15 RxB! with a terrific attack — analysis.
b) 11...PxP 12 R-K1+ B-K3 13 Q-N3! N-QR4 14 BxB! NxQ 15 B-KB5+ etc.±±— Euwe.
c) 11...NxP 12 NxN (Also possible is 12 NxP!? B-K3 13 Q-R4+ following a Blackburne exhibition game.) 12... BxN13 Q-N3 R-B1 14 QR-Q1 P-B3? (Black's position is uncomfortable anyway.) 15 N-K2 B-N5 16 NxB BxR 17 RxB Q-B2 18 N-B5 R-KN1 (Following a Taubenhaus game) 19 BxP+!±±
d) 11...B-N5 12 Q-N3 (12 NxP NxN!) 12...B-KR4 13 KR-K1 (13 PxP N-QR4!; Euwe gives 13 N-KN5.) 13...N-Q2 14 NxP N3xN 15 RxN+! NxR 16 Q-N5+ P-QB3 17 QxN+ K-Q2 18 QxB±±Cafferty-Parry, Birmingham v. Nuneaton 1969.

Unzicker, in the *Encyclopaedia of Chess Openings,* gives the text move an exclamation mark, and says the game is unclear. We wonder what improvement he can have in mind over the following:
a) 12 R-K1 NxB 13 Q-R4+ P-B3 14 QxN B-K3 15 RxP Q-Q2 16 RxB+ PxR 17 N-K5±±following Wormald, or
b) 12 NxP NxB 13 Q-R4+ B-Q2? (13...P-B3!) 14 QxN B-K3 15 P-Q5! BxQP 16 Q-R4+ P-B3 17 QR-Q1 N-Q2 18 NxN QxN 19 NxB PxN 20 RxP! 1-0 Lehmann-Muller, West Germany v. Switzerland 1952.

D:

9 ...   **B—N5***(118)*

Historically, this was the next move

to be tried for Black. It is still recommended by most books as a sound equalizing line.

118
W

White can reply:
D1: 10 Q-R4
D2: 10 B-QN5!

10 Q-N3 BxN 11 BxP+ K-B1 12 BxN RxB 13 PxB NxP 14 Q-Q1 Q-B3 15 P-B4 P-N4! 16 P-B5 P-N5 17 N-Q5 Q-R5 18 B-B4 N-B6+ 19 K-R1 P-N6! 20 BxNP RxB 0-1 Weiss-Recsi, Budapest 1862.

D1:
10 Q—R4
This move was introduced by G.B. Fraser, and subsequently analysed by the English player Mortimer. It always produces an exciting game, but the piece sacrifice which it involves is incorrect.
10 ... B—Q2
This is the only satisfactory way to save the QN:
a) 10...K-B1 11 P-Q5 N-QR4 (Or 11...N3-K2 12 N-K2 N-N3 13 N3-Q4 Wisker-Bird) 12 B-K2 BxN 13 BxB B-KR3 14 B-K2 N-KB3 15 K-R1 Q-K1 16 Q-B2± Fraser v. consulting amateurs (from Wormald *Chess Openings*).
b) 10...BxN 11 P-Q5! B-N5 (11... Q-B3 12 PxN 0-0-0 13 N-Q5) 12 PxN PxP 13 QxBP+ (Fraser's first idea 13 P-K5 is met by 13...B-Q2.) 13...B-Q2 14 Q-Q5 B-K3 15 B-QN5+ K-B1 16

Q-Q3 N-K2 17 K-R1! (The *Handbuch* gave 17 B-N5 P-KB3 18 B-K3 K-B2 19 P-KB4 P-KB4 20 BxB RPxB 21 B-B4=.) 17...P-QB3 18 B-R4 P-B3 19 P-B4 K-B2 20 P-B5 B-B1 21 B-N3+ K-K1 22 Q-B4 R-B1 23 B-R3 B-N2 24 QR-Q1 N-B1 25 Q-K2 Q-K2 26 Q-R5+ K-Q1 27 P-K5! QxP (27...BPxP 28 N-K4) 28 QxP R-K1 29 QxP P-Q4 30 NxP! 1-0 Noakh-Fishzon, Leningrad 1937.

11 Q—N3
The only consistent continuation.
11 ... N—R4
12 BxP+ K—B1
13 Q—B2!
This was Mortimer's improvement. Earlier in 1862, some games were played with Fraser's suggestion 13 Q-Q5?! N-KB3 14 Q-KN5 KxB 15 P-K5, after which Black can play 15... N-N5 (Steinitz), 15...KR-K1 (following *Chess Monthly*) or possibly other moves.
13 ... KxB
14 P—K5(119)

119
B

This attack is by no means as silly as it may look. Black must try to find a good way of returning the piece to break White's initiative and get his king into safety. He can choose between:
D11: 14...B-N5?
D12: 14...K-B1!
D13: 14...P-KR3!?
D14: 14...N-QB3

14...N-KB3 (Or 14...P-N3 or 14...N-K2, both met by 15 P-K6+) 15 P-K6+! BxKP 16 N-KN5+ K-K2 17 R-K1 K-Q2 18 NxB Q-KN1 19 Q-B5 Mortimer-Rosenthal, casual game played in Paris, 1865.

D11:

    14 ...   **B—N5?**
15 R-K1 BxN 16 Q-B5+ N-KB3 17 QxB R-K1 18 B-N5 N-B3 19 PxN RxR+ 20 RxR PxP 21 Q-R5+ K-N1 22 B-R6 Q-Q2 23 R-K4 K-R1 24 Q-R4 Q-B2 25 N-Q5 Q-N3 (25...BxP was relatively better.) 26 N-B4 Q-B4 27 Q-N3 Q-Q2 28 N-R5 1-0 Blackburne-Steinitz, London 1862.

D12:

    14 ...   **K—B1!**
Anderssen's idea, to take the sting out of P-K6.

    15 R—K1   N—QB3!
Steinitz suggested 15...N-R3?, whilst a Kolisch-Hirschfield match game went 15...Q-B1?! 16 P-Q5 B-KB4 17 Q-Q2 N-R3 18 Q-B4 N-N5 19 P-K6 BxBP+ 20 K-R1 BxR 21 QxB+ N-B3 22 N-K4 K-K2? (*Chess World* suggested 22...B-B6! 23 NxB Q-K1 with chances of holding the game.) 23 B-N5 Q-B1 24 RxB R-K1 25 R-QB1 K-Q1 26 N-K5! PxN 27 P-Q6 N-B3 28 RxN!PxR 29 NxN PxN 30 BxP+ K-B1 31 P-K7+ 1-0. It can be hard to silence White's guns! The text is critical.

    16 B—N5   Q—K1
    17 P—K6   Q—N3!
    18 QxQ   PxQ
    19 PxB   N—B3∓
Analysis from the *Handbuch;* if 20 BxN PxB 21 N-Q5 K-B2 22 R-K4 QR-Q1 etc. As is often the case, the best defence against heavy sacrifices is to give back nearly all the extra material to break the force of the attack.

D13:

    14 ...   **P—KR3!?**
    15 P—Q5   **N—KB3!**
Most other moves allow 16 P-K6+ with a strong attack, while 15...PxP 16 NxP+ is very promising for White.

    16 P—K6+
If 16 PxN QxP 17 N-K4 B-KB4 or even 17...QxR!? — Wormald.

    16 ...   **BxKP!?**
After 16...K-N1 17 PxB QxP White is only one pawn down and may have some play for it.

    17 PxB+   KxP
This position was known from Mortimer's analysis. Does White have an attack strong enough to compensate for the two pawns sacrificed? It is possible.

D14:

    14 ...   **N—QB3**
    15 P—K6+   **K—B1**
    16 PxB   **QxP**
    17 N—Q5
White's open lines and chances against Black's exposed king may be sufficient compensation for the sacrificed material — analysis.

D2:

    10 **B—QN5!**(*120*)
This move, apparently introduced by Morphy and revived by Blackburne, gives White good chances without the risks attendant upon the Fraser-Mortimer Attack.

Black may reply:
D21: 10...B-Q2?
D22: 10...BxN
D23: 10...K-B1!
Chigorin proposed the refinement
10...P-QR3 11 B-R4 K-B1 which is
worth looking into further, since
White cannot then advance his QRP.

D21:
10 ...   B—Q2?
11 P—K5!   PxP
Or 11...KN-K2 12 B-N5 when:
a) 12...0-0 13 N-Q5!Q-K1 14 N-B6+!
PxN 15 BxP with a strong attack;
Kolisch-Rosenthal, match, Paris 1864
b) 12...P-KR3 13 P-K6! PxP 14
BxN/K7 QxB 15 P-Q5 N-K4 16 NxN
PxN 17 Q-R5+±.
c) 12...PxP (12...Q-B1!? has been
suggested.) 13 N-Q5 Q-B1 14
BxN/K7 NxB 15 NxN KxN 16 R-K1!
(Better than exchanging bishops, as in
a 1901 Schlechter game) 16...BxB 17
RxP+ K-B1 18 RxB±. These analyses
stem from *Deutsche Schachzeitung*,
1873, and have been reproduced in
most twentieth-century sources. It is
not easy to demonstrate a forced win
for White after 10...B-Q2, because the
number of possible sub-variations is
so large, but there is no doubt that
Black's game is very difficult to play.
12 P—Q5!
12 R-K1 KN-K2 13 P-Q5 (Neu-
mann, 1864) is also promising. If 12...
N-N1 13 NxP N-K2 14 Q-N4!
12 ...   N3—K2
12...N-N1 and 12...N-Q5 are also
inadequate.
13 BxB+   QxB
14 NxP   Q—B4
15 Q-R4+ K-Q1 (Black could not
have relished 15...P-QB3!? 16 PxP
0-0-0!) 16 B-B4 N-N3 17 P-N4! Q-B1
(17...Q-B3 18 Q-Q7 mate) 18 KR-K1
NxN 19 BxN P-KB3 20 BxQBP+!
KxB 21 N-N5+ K-Q1 22 N-Q6 Q-Q2

23 R-K8+ QxR 24 QxQ+ K-B2 25
N-N5 mate; Hirschfield-Kolisch,
match 1864.

D22:
10 ...   BxN
11 PxB
In a 1968 German postal game,
Felbecker-Unger, White won with the
incredible move 11 Q-R4?! Black
should have replied 11...B-N5 12
P-Q5 P-QR3 13 B-Q3 KN-K2.
11 ...   K—B1
11...Q-B3 12 B-K3 0-0-0 13 N-Q5
— Chigorin — favours White.
12 B—K3!   KN—K2
Or 12...N-B3 (12...QN-K2 13
K-R1) 13 P-QR4 P-QR3 14 BxN PxB
15 P-R5 B-R2 16 N-K2 P-KN4? 17
N-N3 P-KR4 18 Q-B2 P-N5 19 QxP
and White won; Fichtl-Dietze, Prague
1943.
13 P—Q5   N—QN1
14 K—R1±
Analysis from *Sovremenny Debyut*; if
14...N-N3 15 P-B4 etc. while White
intends to pile up pressure on the
KN-file.

D23:
10 ...   K—B1!
As recommended by Anderssen in
1867.
11 B—K3!
This is generally considered to be
the best play for both sides after
9...B-N5. As Black cannot castle,
White should have good play for his
pawn; still, there are relatively few
weaknesses in the Black position.
11 ...   KN—K2
Or 11...QN-K2 12 B-QB4 (More
dynamic than 12 P-KR3 of Morphy-
de Riviere, Paris 1858) 12...N-B3 13
Q-N3 BxN 14 PxB Q-K1 15 P-QR4
B-R4 16 N-K2 R-QN1 17 K-R1 P-B3
18 R-KN1± Schlechter-Meitner,
Vienna 1898.

12   P—QR4*(121)*

121
B

12   ...   P—QR4!?
Others:
a) 12...P-Q4? 13 BxN NxB (13...PxB? 14 P-R5) 14 NxP — Chigorin.
b) 12...N-R4 13 P-Q5 BxB 14 PxB N-N3 (Chigorin-Gunsberg, fifth match game 1889) and now Chigorin recommended 15 Q-K1 and if 15...BxN 16 PxB±.
c) We think Black should try 12... P-QR3, and possible continue with ...P-KR4!? — note that Hirschfield was playing 11...P-KR4?! in 1861.
   13   B—QB4
White now threatens 14 BxP.
   13   ...   B—R4
In the game Estrin-R. Angelov, Lenin Memorial Corres 1970-3, Black played 13...Q-K1!?:
a) 14 B-QN5 (Threatening P-Q5), 14 P-Q5 at once, or 14 R-K1 with the idea of N-Q5 all come into considera-tion — Cafferty.
b) **The game continued 14 N-QN5 P-B4!? 15 P-R3 P-R4 16 PxB** (But 16 PxP! e.g. 16...NxBP 17 R-K1 Q-N3 18 B-Q3 BxRP 19 N-R4 and wins — Cafferty) 16...RPxP 17 N-N5 P-Q4 18 PxP Q-R4 19 P-B4 N-N5 20 NxBP? (20 K-B2) 20...BxN 21 N-K6+ K-B2 22 NxB N-B1! 23 P-Q6+ K-N3 24 B-N3 N-Q6! 25 QxN P-N6 0-1.
   14   R—B1!
Chigorin-Gunsberg, Hastings 1895, went instead 14 K-R1 N-N5 15 P-Q5

(Sokolsky suggested 15 Q-N3.) when instead of 15...BxB? Black could have equalized by 15...N-N3! 16 BxB PxB as shown by Levenfish. The text move gives White a more lasting initiative, e.g. 14...Q-Q2 15 B-QN5 Q-B1 16 B-K2 P-R3 17 P-Q5 BxB 18 PxB N-R2 19 N-Q4 BxB 20 QxB Q-Q2 21 Q-KB2 N-N3 22 N3-N5 NxN 23 NxN 1-0 (23...R-B1 24 NxQP) Cafferty-Cadden, corres 1967-8. The combined pressure on the KB- and QB-files is the key to White's plan.

E:

9   ...   N—R4*(122)*

122
W

White has played a number of moves here, although only the last is ever seen nowadays. We look at:
E1: 10 N-KN5
E2: 10 B-N2
E3: 10 B-Q3
E4: 10 B-KN5!
   and these dubious moves, in brief:
a) 10 R-K1 NxB 11 Q-R4+ P-QB3 13 QxN N-K2 13 B-N5 0-0 14 P-Q5 P-B3 15 PxP+ K-R1 (Johner-Spielmann, Baden 1914) and now 16 PxP= — Korn, *MCO*, 7th edition.
b) 10 BxP+? KxB 11 N-KN5+ (11 P-K5 P-KR3 — Wormald — or 11...K-B1 12 P-Q5 B-N5 — *Sovremenny Debyut*) 11...K-K1 12 R-K1 N-K2 13 Q-KB3 R-KB1 14 Q-R5+ P-KN3 15 QxRP BxQP∓— Wormald.

c) 10 P-K5 (Robey-Steinitz, London
1865) 10...NxB 11 Q-R4+ P-QB3 12
QxN P-Q4∓.

E1:

10   N—KN5

This move was played on several
occasions by Morphy.

10   ...   NxB
11   Q—R4+   Q—Q2!

Or 11...P-B3 12 QxN Q-B2 —
Blackburne.

12   QxN   P—KR3
13   N—B3   N—K2
  ∓   —   *Handbuch*

E2:

10   B—N2   N—K2

10...NxB is also playable.

11   B—Q3   0—0
12   P—Q5   N—N3

The game thus transposes into line
C of the next chapter.

E3:

10   B—Q3   N—K2

Now White's best play is possibly
11 P-Q5 0-0 12 B-N2 with the same
outcome as in E2. Note also that other
tenth moves for Black are not reliable,
e.g. 10...P-QB4?! 11 P-Q5 B-N5 12
N-K2 Q-B3 13 B-KN5 Q-N3 (Steinitz-
Bird, skittles game 1870) when White
could have tried 14 P-K5.

11   P—K5!?

Others:

a) 11 B-KN5 P-KB3 12 B-R4 N-N3 13
P-K5 NxB led to a draw in Burden-
Steinitz, London 1866.

b) 11 N-Q5 0-0 (11...N4-B3!?) 12 NxB
(By no means forced) 12...RPxN 13
P-Q5 N-N3 14 Q-B2 P-QB4! 15 R-N1
B-N5 16 B-K2 R-K1 and now, instead
of 17 B-QN5? BxN! 18 BxR N-R5!
(Bird-Chigorin, London 1899), *Sov-
remenny Debyut* gave 17 P-KR3 and
White has a good game. This line may
merit further attention.

11   ...   PxP

Or 11...B-N5 12 PxP QxP 13 N-K4
Q-Q2 14 N4-N5 P-KR3 15 NxP!
R-KB1 16 R-K1!±±Zollner-Downey,
Manchester 1880. But surely Black
should try to keep lines closed, e.g.
11...P-Q4!?

12   PxP

12...B-R3 is not effective here, e.g.
12...BxP 13 Q-B2 N4-B3 14 QR-Q1
B-N5 Munich-Stuttgart, corres 1902.

The text was played in one of
Blackburne's exhibition games in
1862. After 12...B-N5 13 B-KN5
N4-B3 14 R-K1 0-0 15 R-K4 Black
could have got a good game with
15...Q-Q2! Instead 15...B-KB4? allowed the grandmaster one of his
typical finishes: 16 Q-Q2! BxR 17
NxB N-Q5 18 N-B6+! PxN 19 BxP
NxN+ 20 PxN Q-Q5 21 R-KB1 etc.

E4:

10   B—KN5! *(123)*

This has usually been known as
Goring's Attack, since its appearance
in an article in the *Deutsche Schachzeitung* in 1871, but the move was not
completely new then. It had, for
example, been played by Minckwitz
against Steinitz in the 1870 Baden-
Baden tournament. According to
Zukertort, it was played in several
Goring-Minckwitz games in 1869.

Black may reply:
E41: 10...Q-Q2

E42: 10...P-B3
E43: 10...N-K2

E41:

10 ... Q—Q2

There is an apocryphal story that some chess-players at a seance tried to call up the shade of Morphy to ask whether this was the best defence in the Normal Variation, but had no success. In an article entitled *The Ghost Variation,* published in *Correspondence Chess* in the 1950s, Dr M.G. Sturm tried to imagine what Morphy might have played in this position. He came up with an interesting, but ultimately unsound, sacrificial idea.

11 B—N5!?

Probably better in fact is 11 B-Q3 e.g.:

a) 11...P-KB3 12 B-R4 N-K2 13 P-K5! BPxP 14 PxP 0-0 15 P-K5 Q-K1 16 R-K1 N4-B3 17 B-K4 B-R4 18 R-QB1± — Minckwitz, *Deutsche Schachzeitung,* 1871

b) 11...P-KR3 12 B-R4 N-K2 13 BxN QxB 14 R-K1 (Bachmann suggested 14 P-K5 in *Schachmeister Steinitz.*) 14...P-QB3 15 P-Q5 (±says Pachman) 15...B-N5 16 P-K5 and now, instead of 16...QPxP? in the Minckwitz-Steinitz game, Fine in *All the World's a Chessboard* (1948) said that 16...0-0!gives Black at least equality. 10...Q-Q2 is by far the least-known of Black's three moves in diagram 123, and clearly needs further investigation.

11 ... P—QB3

12 P—K5?!

This is Sturm's idea. Others:

a) 12 B-Q3 (A tempo down on the previous note) 12...P-KR3 13 B-R4 13...N-K2 14 P-Q5!? 0-0 15 P-QR4 Q-K1 Q-Q1 16 R-N1 is interesting.) 13...N-K2 14 **P-Q5!?** 0-0 15 P-QR4 (Riemath-Austin, corres 1956) and

now Black should play 15...PxP 16 PxP Q-Q1 or 15...N-N3 16 B-N3 Q-K2.

b) 12 B-QR4 comes into consideration, e.g. 12...N-K2 13 BxN QxB 14 P-K5 0-0 (14...P-Q4? 15 NxP) 15 PxP QxP 16 N-K4 Q-N5 17 B-B2 N-B5 18 Q-Q3 P-KB4 19 N-B5!threatening 20 B-N3 — analysis.

12 ... PxB

13 PxP P—B3

14 R—K1+ K—B1!

Not 14...K-B2? 15 Q-K2 Q-Q1 16 Q-K2 Q-Q1 16 QxP N-B3 17 Q-Q5+ K-B1 (Black has lost a fatal tempo) 18 B-B4 B-Q1 19 N-N5 R-B1 20 N-B7 P-N4 21 NxP! PxN 22 BxP BxN 23 BxQ BxB 24 R-K7! BxR 25 PxB+ KxP 26 R-K1+ K-Q1 27 Q-N5+ N3-K2 28 P-Q5 R-B4 29 Q-K5 N-N3 30 Q-N8+ R-B1 31 QxRP R-B7 (31... K-B2 32 R-N1) 32 QxP N-R3 33 Q-N6+ K-B1 34 R-N1 B-N4 35 QxB K-B2 36 Q-N6+ K-Q2 37 Q-K6+ 1-0 Sturm-Magee, corres 1950.

After the text, Sturm gave 15 N-K5 **(15 B-B4!?)** 15...PxN 16 RxP N-QB3 17 Q-B3+ N-B3? but Black can safely play 17...Q-KB2∓∓.

E42:

10 ... P—KB3*(124)*

124
W

Now White has tried:
E421: 11 B-R4?!
E422: 11 B-B4

In addition, Maroczy suggested 11
B-K3 e.g. 11...N-K2 12 P-KR3 B-Q2
13 B-N3 NxB 14 QxN Q-B1 15 P-QR4
B-K3 16 Q-R3 with pressure for
White. However, Black can play
better by 11...NxB leading to play
similar to E422.

E421:
   11   B—R4?!
This would only be good if P-K5
could be forced in all lines.
Now:
E4211: 11...N-R3
E4212: 11...NxB
E4213: 11...N-K2

E4211:
   11   ...   N—R3
12 P-K5 P-N4 13 NxP B-N5 14 PxBP!
BxQ 15 R-K1+ K-Q2 16 B-K6+
K-B3 17 P-Q5+ and the wandering
king is doomed; Schiffers-Nolde,
1872.

E4212:
   11   ...   NxB
   12   Q—R4+   Q—Q2
   13   QxN   Q—B2
This queen manoeuvre is typical;
Black shores up the weakened K-side.
   14   N—Q5
Wormald gave only 14 P-Q5?
P-B3∓.
   14   ...   N—R3!
According to Pachman, Black
stands better now. We shall follow the
hard-fought game Chigorin-Yaku-
bovich, corres 1879: 15 QR-Q1 (15
P-QR4!?) 15...B-N5 16 Q-B1! BxN 17
PxB 0-0!18 K-R1 (18 NxKBP+?!PxN
19 QxN Q-N3+ with White's bishop
badly placed for the ending.)
18...Q-R4 19 Q-B4! but now instead
of 19...K-R1 Black should have played
19...P-B3!e.g. 20 NxP+ RxN 21 BxR
PxB 22 QxBP N-B2 because the two
pieces should overcome White's rook.

E4213:
   11   ...   N—K2
   12   R—K1!   B—N5
Why not 12...P-B3 by analogy with
E4222 (Motzko-Vidmar)?
   13   P—K5!?
13 N-Q5 (Schlechter-Englisch,
Vienna 1895) should have been met
by 13...BxN — Spielmann.
   13   ...   QPxP
   14   PxP   QxQ
   15   QRxQ   NxB
If 15...P-KB4 then 16 B-K6!
   16   PxP   PxP
   17   BxP
Black's position is satisfactory after
17 N-Q5!? 0-0-0!
   17   ...   K—B2!
   18   BxN   BxN
   19   PxB   B—R4
a) 20   R-Q7?! N-N3! 21   RxP
KR-QB1! 22 RxP BxN∓ Pollock-
Chigorin, Hastings 1895.
b) 20 R-K4 is critical. Levenfish gave
20...BxN 21 RxN B-K4 as a sufficient
defence, but then, as Vasyukov and
Nikitin have pointed out, 22 P-B4!
KR-KN1+ 23 K-B1 leaves something
to play for (23...R-N5 24 B-N5! threatening 25 P-KR3).

E422:
   11   B—B4(125)
This is better than B-R4 as it
attacks the QP, making a subsequent
...P-B3 by Black into a serious self-
weakening.

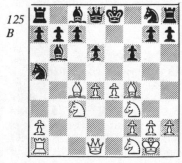

125
B

Now:
E4221: 11...NxB
E4222: 11...N-K2!

E4221:
11 ...   NxB
12 Q—R4+   Q—Q2
This is better than 12...K-B2 13
QxN+ B-K3 14 P-Q5! B-Q2 (14...
B-N5 15 N-Q4 or 15 P-K5 BPxP 16
NxP+ PxN 17 BxP) 15 N-K2 (15
P-K5!?) 15...Q-K1 (15...N-K2!?) 16
P-QR4! N-K2 17 B-K3!± Chigorin-
Pollock, New York 1889.
13 QxN   Q—B2
Sovremenny Debyut quotes a postal
game Yevgenev-Hogan: 13...P-N4!? 14
B-N3 P-KR4 15 P-KR4 Q-N2 16
N-Q5 B-N5 17 Q-R4+ B-Q2 18 Q-R3
R-B1 19 KR-K1 P-N5 20 P-K5 K-Q1
"with double-edged play." It looks
good for White after 21 NxB RPxN 22
N-Q2 threatening Q-R7 etc.; sacri-
fices might also be playable.
14 N—Q5   B—K3
Chigorin-Steinitz, London 1883,
went 14...P-N4?! 15 B-N3 B-K3
(Slightly better 15...P-KR4 16 QR-B1)
16 Q-R4+ B-Q2 (16...Q-Q2 17 NxB
BPxN 18 QxQ+ KxQ 19 P-Q5 B-B2
20 N-Q4±) 17 Q-R3 R-B1 18 KR-K1±
and White won.
15 Q—R4+
A little-known game Vidmar-
Poljanec, Lubliana 1901, is worth
study: 15 KR-K1!? BxN (15...P-B3 16
Q-R4! or 15...K-B1 16 P-QR4!) 16
PxB K-B1 17 R-K6 P-N4 18 B-N3
R-K1 19 R1-K1 N-K2? (19...RxR 20
PxR Q-K1 21 P-Q5 N-K2 22 N-Q4
P-KR4 23 P-B3) 20 N-R4! (Threa-
tening 21 N-B5!) 20...P-KB4 (20...
PxN 21 BxRP gives White a strong
attack.) 21 N-B3 P-KR3 22 B-K5!PxB
23 NxP Q-N2 24 N-Q7+ K-B2 25
P-Q6 1-0.
15 ...   B—Q2

15...Q-Q2 16 NxB BPxN 17 Q-R3
P-Q4 18 PxP BxQP 19 KR-K1+
K-B2 20 QR-B1 gives White an initia-
tive — Larry Evans.
16 Q—B2!
This move, which improves upon
Chigorin's original idea 16 Q-R3,
gives White the advantage. Thanks to
his safer king and more harmonious
development, he has play on both
sides of the board. The game
Chigorin-Dorrer, corres 1884, was
decided on the Q-side: 16...R-B1
(16...B-R3 17 N-K3 and P-QR4, or 17
NxB RPxN 18 P-Q5 B-R5 19 Q-B3) 17
P-QR4 B-R4 18 KR-N1 N-K2 (18...
P-QN3 19 N-K3 and N-B4) 19 NxN
QxN 20 RxP 0-0 21 RxRP B-N3 22
R-R6 R-R1 23 P-R5!RxR 24 Q-B4+
K-R1 25 QxR BxRP 26 QxB QxP 27
QxP QxB 28 QxB R-QN1 29 Q-R7
1-0.

E4222:
11 ...   N—K2! *(126)*
This improvement has escaped
inclusion in many openings books.

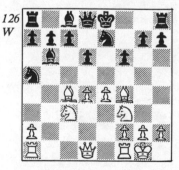

126
W

12 P—KR3
Best, according to Chigorin. Other
moves in practice favoured Black:
a) 12 B-Q3 0-0 13 P-KR3 14 K-R2
N4-B3 15 N-K2 P-Q4 16 P-K5 PxP 17
PxP N-B4 18 B-KN5 Q-K1 19 BxN
BxB 20 QxP P-KR3! 21 B-R4 P-N4!

and Black won in 39 moves; Yankovich-Chigorin, All-Russian tourney, Moscow 1900-01.

b) 12 R-K1 P-B3 13 Q-Q3 (13 B-Q3, trying for P-K5, may be slightly better.) 13...B-B2 14 P-QR4 NxB 15 QxN N-N3∓ Motzko-Vidmar, corres 1910.

>   **12   ...   P—B3**

Others:

a) 12...NxB 13 Q-R4+ P-B3 14 QxN P-Q4 15 PxP NxP 16 KR-K1 K-B2 17 N-K4± — Chigorin.

b) 12...N-N3 13 B-KN3 NxB 14 Q-R4+ Q-Q2 15 QxN Q-B2 16 N-Q5 0-0 17 P-QR4 B-K3! 18 P-R5 P-B3 = Chigorin & Polner v. Hardin & Alapin, St Petersburg 1888.

>   **13   B—QN3   N—N3**
>   **14   B—N3   Q—K2**
>   **15   R—K1   NxB =**

We have been following a game Asharin-Chigorin, Riga 1892. Asharin now played 16 QxN B-K3 17 P-Q5 (17 N-Q5!? Q-Q1! 18 Q-R3 0-0 19 N-K3! was an idea of Chigorin's.) 17... B-KB2 18 N-QR4 0-0 19 NxB PxN 20 QxP (20 N-Q4!? — Steinitz) 20...R-R3 21 Q-N2 P-QB4 and Black gradually got the better of it.

E43:
>   **10   ...   N—K2*(127)***

Black, hoping for a quick draw, encourages White to sacrifice.

127
W

E421: 11 N-Q5
E422: 11 BxP+!?

Maybe 11 B-Q3 0-0 12 P-K5, hoping to keep some K-side attack, is playable.

E431:
>   **11   N—Q5   P—KB3**

Others:

a) 11...N4-B3 12 N-R4 B-K3 (12...0-0 13 N-B6+) 13 NxB winning a piece.

b) 11...NxB 12 BxN Q-Q2 13 B-B6 when:

b1) 13...0-0 14 Q-B1 Q-N5 15 N-K7+ K-R1 16 Q-R6 B-B4 17 NxB±± — *Sovremenny Debyut.*

b2) 13...Q-N5 14 P-KR3 Q-N3 15 B-R4 P-KB3 16 Q-R4+ P-KB3 17 QxN PxN 18 QxP± — Chigorin.

b3) 13...K-B1 14 Q-B1 N-R4 15 B-K7+ and 16 Q-N5±±.

>   **12   BxP   PxB**
>   **13   NxKBP+   K—B1**
>   **14   N—N5*(128)***

128
B

>   **14   ...   N—N1?!**

Or:

a) 14...N-B4? 15 N5xP+ RxN 16 NxR+ K-N2 17 Q-N4+ KxN 18 PxN NxB 19 Q-N6+ K-R1 20 P-B6 Q-B1 21 QR-K1 N-K4 22 PxN PxP 23 R-K4 1-0 Taylor-Zukertort, London 1874.

b) 14...NxB! forces White to take perpetual check, vis:

b1) 15 Q-B3!? (Blackburne-Leverson, 1898) 15...N-B4!∓ — Blackburne.

b2) 15 Q-R5! K-N2 16 Q-B7+ (16

N-B7 Q-B1! 17 NxR QxN/3₹) 16...
K-R3 when:

b21) 17 Q-R5+ etc. draws.

b22) Not 17 N5xP (17 N6xP? Q-N1!)
17...BxP 18 P-N4 BxN 19 NxB Q-B1
20 P-N5+ KxP 21 P-B4+ K-R3 and
White has nothing — analysis.

15 N5xP+!

Black had been following an
analysis by Berger in *Deutsche
Schachzeitung* which gave only 15
N6xP+ K-N2 16 Q-R5 N-R3 (not
however 16...Q-K2 17 B-B7!).

15 ...   K—N2
16 BxN!   RxN

If 16...RxB, 17 Q-R5 was analysed
to a win by Chigorin, e.g.:

a) 17...BxP 18 Q-N5+ K-R1 (18...
K-B2 19 Q-Q5+) 19 Q-R6;

b) 17...R-R1 18 Q-N5+ etc.;

c) 17...N-B3 18 P-K5 PxP 19 PxP
threatening 20 N-N5 and 20 QR-Q1.

17 NxR   Q—R5

If 17...QxB 18 N-N5 K-N3 19 N-B3
and the attack continues — Chigorin.

18 Q—B3!   KxB
19 N—B6+   K—N2
20 N—R5+   K—N3

21 N-B4+ K-R2 22 N-Q5! B-K3 (22...
BxP 23 Q-B7+ B-N2 24 NxP R-N1 25
N-K6 Q-R3 26 Q-B7 N-B3 27 QR-B1
etc.) 23 NxB RPxN 24 P-Q5 B-N1 25
QR-B1 Q-K2 (25...P-B4 26 P-K5! PxP
27 Q-B5+) 26 Q-KR3+ 1-0 (26...
K-N2 27 Q-QB3+ or 26...K-N3 27
R-B3) Chigorin-Urusov, corres 1884.

E432:
11 BxP+!?   KxB
12 N—Q5

This sacrificial line was proposed
by Schiffers in 1887.

12 ...   R—K1!

This is safer than 12...N4-B3? 13
BxN NxB 14 N-N5+ K-N3 (14...K-N1
15 Q-N3!; 14...K-B1 15 Q-B3;
14...K-K1 15 Q-R5+) 15 **N-B4+!**
K-B3 16 P-K5+ and White should

win, although in the ninth Chigorin-
Gunsberg match game 1890 he blundered and eventually lost.

13 BxN

Slower methods ought to fail, e.g.
13 Q-Q2 B-K3! 14 Q-B4+ (14 BxN
RxB 15 N-N5+ K-N1 and Black is
alright.) 14...K-N1 15 NxN+ RxN 16
Q-R4 K-B2 17 QxP Q-R1₹ —
analysis.

13 ...   RxB
14 N—N5+   K—N1
15 Q—R5(129)

15 ...   P—N3?

Chigorin had been prepared for
15...P-KR3! 16 Q-N6! PxN 17 N-B6+
K-B1 18 N-R7+ K-N1 with perpetual
check (not 19 NxP?! B-K3! 20 NxB
Q-K1!), and this probably is the
legitimate result after 11 BxP+.

Gunsberg proposed the text move
as a possible refutation of White's
idea, but our analysis shows that
White should probably win:

16 N—B6+!   K—N2!

16...K-R1? 17 Q-R6±± e.g. 17..
BxP 18 N5xP! and mates.

17 QxRP+   KxN
18 P—K5+!   PxP

This is necessary, to pin the KBP,
as becomes clear from:

a) 18...K-B4?? 19 Q-R3+ KxN 20
P-B4 mate.

b) 18...KxN 19 P-B4+ K-B4 20
Q-R3+ K-K5 21 Q-KB3+ KxQP 22
QR-B1! threatening 23 KR-Q1 mate.

19   N—K4+!!

19 PxP+ is probably a failure, e.g.
19...KxN 20 P-KR4+ K-B5 21
Q-R6+ K-B6 22 QR-K1 Q-Q6! 23
R-K3+ BxR 24 PxB+ K-K7∓ —
Botterill.

19   ...   K—K3

Not 19...K-B4? 20 Q-R3+ KxN 21
Q-KB3+ KxP 22 KR-Q1+ K-B4 23
QR-B1+ and 24 RxQ etc.

20   QxP+   K—Q2

20...K-Q4 is met by 21 N-B6+!
K-K3 (21...K-Q3 22 PxP+ or 21...
K-B5 22 QR-B1+) 22 P-Q5+ QxP
(22...K-Q3 23 N-K4+) 23 NxQor 23

Q-N8+ and with the K-side passed
pawns and exposed black king, White
should win.

21   PxP!   B—Q5

Others:

a) 21...Q-K1? 22 KR-Q1+ B-Q5 23
RxB mate;

b) 21...N-B3 22 KR-Q1+ N-Q5 (22...
B-Q5 23 N-B5 mate) 23 QR-B1!
threatening N-B5+ to expose the king
(23...P-B3 24 RxN+!).

22	**KR—Q1**	**P—B4**
23	**Q—Q6+**	**K—K1**
24	**N—B6+**	**K—B2**
25	**QxQ±±**	

10 Normal Variation: with Anderssen's 9 P—Q5

In this chapter, we discuss the rather old-fashioned lines that arise from 1 P-K4 P-K4 2 N-KB3 N-QB3 3 B-B4 B-B4 4 P-QN4 BxNP 5 P-B3 B-B4 6 P-Q4 PxP 7 0-0 P-Q3 8 PxP B-N3 9 P-Q5!?*(130)*. This move, which was at the height of its popularity in the 1860s due to the example of Anderssen, is hardly ever played nowadays although many defenders would be hard put to find Black's correct line over the board.

130
B

The theoretical objection to 9 P-Q5 is, according to Tarrasch, that it "prematurely uses up the strength of White's centre and closes the attacking diagonal of his KB". Furthermore, Black is given a free tempo to attack White's KB, he is allowed to castle and can soon commence the advance of his numerous Q-side pawns. White plays for a gradual but massive K-side offensive, principally against KN7, and hopes he can blockade Black's Q-side for long enough to press home his attack. Careful play by Black

should probably give him the advantage, but 9 P-Q5 remains a good practical chance, at least at club-players level, particularly when you remember that your opponent is more likely to be prepared for 9 N-B3.

After 9 P-Q5 Black may play:
A: 9...N-K4?
B: 9...N3-K2
C: 9...N-R4!

9...Q-B3? 10 PxN QxR 11 Q-N3 (11 BxP+ K-B1! is not so clear.) 11...Q-B3 12 P-K5 QPxP 13 R-K1 PxP 14 B-KN5 Q-Q3 15 NxP B-K3 16 NxKBP! KxN 17 RxB±± Kolisch-Shumov, 1863.

A:

9	...	N—K4?
10	NxN	PxN
11	B—R3!	

This move was proposed by Chigorin in *Shakhmatny Listok,* 1877. Steinitz, in 1860, had played 11 B-N2 P-KB3 12 K-R1 followed by P-B4 and this also turned out well for White! La Bourdonnais played 11 N-Q2.

11 ... N—K2

Or 11...B-Q5?! 12 N-Q2 BxR 13 QxB following ancient analysis. Black must be lost, e.g. 13...P-KB3 14 P-B4 PxP 15 RxP N-K2 16 P-K5 N-N3 17 PxP! NxR 18 Q-K5+ Bennett-Moseley, Brisbane 1929.

12 N—Q2 0—0

Otherwise White has moves like N-N3, K-R1 and P-B4.

13 Q—R5 B—Q5

14 QR—N1±

White will continue N-B3 or R-N3-KB3/N3.

B:

9 ...   N3—K2

A passive move, which also impedes the development of the K-side.

10 P—K5!*(131)*

Von der Lasa played 10 B-N2 P-B3 11 P-QR4 — also a good plan, but 10...N-KB3 is an improvement for Black.

131
B

10 ...   N—R3!?

One of Steinitz's ideas. Others:

a) 10...B-N5 (Anderssen) 11 Q-R4+:

a1) 11...Q-Q2 12 B-QN5 P-QB3 13 P-K6 PxP 14 QxB PxB 15 PxP Q-B2 16 QxP N-N3 17 B-N2± — Euler & Neumann.

a2) 11...B-Q2 12 Q-N3 N-N3 13 N-B3 NxP 14 NxN PxN 15 P-Q6 PxP 16 BxP+ K-B1 17 BxN RxB 18 B-R3 B-B3 19 QR-Q1 B-B2 20 KR-K1 Q-N4 21 N-K4 BxN 22 RxB± — *Handbuch*.

b) 10...N-N3 (Steinitz, 1862) 11 P-K6! PxP 12 PxP N1-K2 13 N-N5 (13 N-B3 P-KR3) 13...0-0 14 N-QB3 (14 Q-R5 P-KR3 15 QxN!? — Wormald) 14... N-K4 15 B-N3 P-B3 16 N-R4 P-Q4 (16...B-B2 17 P-B4 N4-N3 18 P-B5!) 17 NxB QxN 18 B-R3 N4-N3 19 B-B2± — *Handbuch*.

c) 10...PxP 11 NxP N-KB3 12 B-QN5+ K-B1! (12...P-B3 13 PxP! or

12...N-Q2 13 Q-N4!) 13 N-QB3 N2xP 14 B-R3+ with compensation for the pawns — Unzicker.

11 N—B3   0—0

12 BxN!   PxB

13 Q—Q2!

Improving upon the 13 N-K4!? of earlier games.

13 ...   K—N2

Or 13...PxP 14 QR-K1± Neumann-Steinitz, Paris 1867.

14 QR—K1   PxP

15 RxP   B—N5

So far Anderssen-Winawer, Baden-Baden 1870. Now Anderssen said he should have played 16 Q-B4! with the evidently superior piece co-ordination and strong pressure against Black's weaknesses (e.g. 16...BxN 17 QxB N-N3 18 R-R5 R-K1 19 P-Q6 — analysis).

C:

9 ...   N—R4!*(132)*

132
W

10 B—N2

Here 10 B-Q3 will transpose back to the text next move. Others:

a) 10 B-K2 N-K2 11 B-N2 P-KB3 12 Q-Q2 0-0 with play similar to the main line; Staunton & Barnes v. Bird & Owen, London 1858.

b) 10 N-B3 NxB (Others could transpose to the main line.) 11 Q-R4+ B-Q2 12 QxN P-KB3 (12...N-K2 13 P-K5 PxP 14 P-Q6) 13 KR-K1 N-K2 14 P-K5 QPxP 15 NxP 0-0! 16 N-B3

N-N3 and Black won in 25 moves; Winawer-Chigorin, Warsaw 1882.

c) 10 P-K5?! (Played by Steinitz in his early years) 10...NxB (10...N-K2 of Kolisch-Anderssen, Paris 1860, should also be playable.) 11 Q-R4+ B-Q2 12 QxN N-K2 (12...PxP 13 NxP± — Wormald) 13 P-K6 PxP 14 PxP B-B3 15 N-N5 0-0 16 Q-K2 N-N3 17 Q-R5 P-KR3 18 QxN PxN 19 BxP Q-K1∓ — *Handbuch*.

d) 10 B-QN5+ P-B3 (10...B-Q2 11 BxB+ and N-Q4) 11 B-R4 N-K2 12 B-N2 might give White some Q-side play — Ulvestad.

10 ...   N—K2!

Keres says that 10...N-KB3!? 11 B-Q3 0-0 (11...B-N5 12 N-B3 P-B3 — Freeborough & Ranken) 12 N-B3 P-B3 is "possibly good". Black would need to improve upon the continuation suggested by Anderssen: 13 N-K2 B-N5 14 Q-Q2 R-B1 15 Q-N5 BxN 16 PxB PxP 17 K-R1! N-B5? (White has a promising attack anyway.) 18 R-KN1 N-K1 19 QxNP+! NxQ 20 **RxN+ K-R1 21 R-N8+!±±.**

11   B—Q3

Not 11 BxP? R-KN1 12 B-B6 because of 12...NxB 13 Q-R4+ Q-Q2 14 QxN RxP+! 15 K-R1 (O4 15 KxR Q-N5+ etc.) 15...Q-R6 16 QN-Q2 B-N5 17 Q-N3 0-0-0 and 18...R-N1 — Anderssen.

11 ...   0—0
12   N—B3   N—N3*(133)*

The study of the 9 P-Q5 N-QR4 line is bedevilled by cross-transpositions and subtle differences between apparently similar lines. A number of other moves have been played by Black at this point, although the text seems the most logical, as it fights for control of e5, f4 and h4 and gives the queen some scope.

The others:

a) 12...P-QB4? 13 P-K5! e.g.:
a1) 13...N-N3 14 PxP QxP 15 N-KN5

Q-B5 16 Q-R5 P-KR3 17 NxP RxN 18 BxN±.

a2) 13...PxP 14 NxP N-N3 15 Q-R5 Q-Q3 16 QR-K1 B-B2 17 N-K4!± — Zukertort.

b) 12...P-KB4? 13 N-KN5 (Neumann-de Riviere, 1866) 13...Q-K1± — Wormald.

c) 12...B-N5!? 13 N-K2 (13 P-KR3!?) 13...BxN 14 PxB N-N3 15 P-B4 Q-R5 16 N-N3 P-KB3 "with a safe position" — Wormald. 15 K-R1, reserving options, is playable.

d) 12...P-KB3 13 N-K2 P-QB4 14 N-Q2 (14 Q-Q2 or 14 R-B1 compare text lines below.) 14...N-N3 15 K-R1 P-QR3 16 P-B4 (de Vere-Taylor, Westminster 1868) and Emanuel Lasker thought that White's position was to be preferred. For example, 16...B-B2 17 N-KB3 P-N4 18 P-B5 N-K4 19 N-B4 and as it takes at least seven moves for Black's pawns to reach their destination, White's attack with P-N4-5 will come first; *(Common Sense in Chess)*. The position does not seem all that clear to us, but a World Champion's judgement is to be respected.

e) 12...P-QB3 is interesting, though it was not well thought of in the nineteenth century. White can reply:

e1) 13 Q-Q2 PxP (13...N-N3 see note to Black's 13th) 14 NxP N-N3 15 NxB QxN 16 QR-N1 Q-Q2 17 Q-B2 (17 B-B3!? intending R-N5 — Bachmann, *Schachmeister Steinitz*) 17...P-B3 18 N-Q4 N-B5 19 QR-Q1 (19 QR-K1!?) 19...B-Q2 (Minckwitz, Neumann & L. Paulsen v. Blackburne, Steinitz & de Vere, Baden-Baden 1870) and now 20 Q-Q2 would be best. Three days later, the Blackburne-Steinitz game was played in the tournament and Steinitz did not exchange pawns at move 13!

e2) 13 N-K2 P-KB4?! 14 R-B1 KBPxP 15 BxKP B-KB4 16 BxB RxB

17 PxP PxP 18 N2-Q4 (Anderssen-Steinitz, first match game 1866) and now 18...R-KB1 would be relatively best.

133
W

13 N—K2?　　P—QB4

Getting the pawns under way thus seems a good idea. But again several moves have been tried by Black: Reasonable candidates are:

a) 13...P-QB3 14 Q-Q2 B-N5 15 N-N3 R-B1 and the chances seem equally divided; Blackburne-Steinitz (by transposition).

b) 13...P-KB3 seems unnecessarily passive. White might well reply 14 N3-Q4 (14 Q-Q2 or 14 N-N3 P-QB4 see below), intending to proceed more or less as Lasker suggested. A game Zukertort-Schulten continued 14... R-B2!? 15 K-R1 P-QB4 16 N-K6 Q-K1 17 P-B4 BxN 18 PxB R-B2 19 B-B3 P-B5 20 B-B2 R-Q1 21 P-B5 N-K4 22 N-B4 QN-B3 23 N-Q5 R2-B1 24 R-QN1 and White has secured the superiority over the whole board!

14 Q—Q2(134)

14 R-B1 is playable, but has little independent significance, if traditional sources are to be believed. But consider:

a) 14...R-N1 15 P-K5!? B-B2 16 N-B3 P-QR3 17 N-K4 P-QN3 18 N3-N5 P-R3 19 N-B6+ PxN 20 PxP N-K4 21 BxN PxB 22 Q-B3 R-K1 23 N-K6! and White's attack won; Saligo-

Boshoer, USSR Teams Corres Ch 1971.

b) 14...P-B3, aiming for the familiar positions discussed below, is a more likely reply. However, White need not play the old Q-Q2, which we shall see is rather ineffective. Instead, now Black has finally advanced his KBP, weakening the e6 square, White could try 15 N-Q2 intending once more the plan of advancing first the KBP and then the KNP, whilst he also has his pieces well-placed for blockading the QBP. We think that this suggestion offers real chances of resurrecting the Anderssen method against the Normal defence.

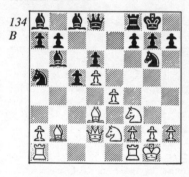

134
B

A great number of nineteenth-century games reached this position. White has a few quick threats against KN7, but they are fairly easily countered, after which it seems to take too long to bring up the 'big battalions'.

Black now tried:
C1: 14...B-Q2?!
C2: 14...B-N5
C3: 14...P-B3!

14...B-B2 and 14...R-N1 are likely to transpose to C3, as it is hard for Black to avoid ...P-KB3 in the long run.

14...P-B4? is met by 15 PxP BxP 16 BxB RxB 17 QR-B1 N-K4 18 NxN PxN 19 N-N3± — *Handbuch*.

C1:

14 ...   B—Q2?!

This move is not very constructive. It is better to clear the way for the QNP and then support its advance with the rook.

15 N—N3

Sovremenny Debyut gave the alternative line 15 QR-B1 P-QR3 16 N-N3 P-B3 17 N-B5 (Compare C32) 17...BxN 18 PxB N-K4 19 NxN QPxN 20 KR-Q1 K-R1 21 B-K4 B-R2 22 R-B3 P-QN4 23 P-Q6±.

15 ...   P—B3

Not 15...B-B2? 16 BxP! (Anderssen-Steinitz, seventh match game, 1866) when 16...KxB? fails to 17 N-R5+ K-R1 18 Q-R6 R-KN1 19 N-N5 forcing mate or the win of the black queen. This line shows the main reason for putting the queen on Q2. Black plays ...P-KB3 to avoid this combination and to rule out any P-K5 ideas.

16 K—R1   P—B5?

This move is badly mistimed. 16...B-B2 is correct, to keep control of d4 for at least one more move — compare C33.

17 B—K2   B—B2
18 N—Q4!   P—N4
19 P—B4   N—N2

20 N-K6 BxN 21 PxB N-B4 22 Q-Q5 Q-K2 (22...K-R1 saves a move.) 23 B-N4 K-R1 24 Q-R5 N-Q6 25 B-B5 Q-K1 26 B-Q4 B-N3? (26...B-Q1 is the last chance.) 27 P-K7 R-KN1 28 N-K2 Q-B2 29 R-B3 1-0 Anderssen-Neumann, Berlin 1864.

C2:

14 ...   B—N5

This move is also dubious, since the opening of the KN-file should profit White.

15 N—N3

15 K-R1 is also logical.

15 ...   BxN

15...P-B3 16 K-R1 N-K4!? led to atypical play in a game Taylor-Blackburne, Norwich 1870: 17 NxN BPxN 18 P-B3 B-Q2 19 P-B4 P-B5 20 B-K2 PxP 21 RxP RxR (21...Q-K2!) 22 QxR Q-KB1 23 Q-Q2± Black is in trouble on his K-side black squares: 23...Q-B7 24 Q-N5!B-Q5 25 R-KB1 Q-K6 26 Q-K7 and White won.

16 PxB   N—R5
17 Q—B4   N—N3
18 Q—B5   R—B1

19 B-B3 R-B2 20 K-R1 P-B3 21 R-KN1 R2-B2 22 B-B1! P-B5 23 B-R3 BxP 24 N-K2 N-K4? (He should take the exchange, although White can win it back with a subsequent B or N to K6.) 25 R-N2 B-K6 26 N-B4 BxN 27 QxB P-KN4? (Desperation. He should face the music with 27...K-R1.) 28 B-K6 and White soon won; Napier-Chigorin, Monte Carlo 1902.

C3:

14 ...   P—B3! *(135)*

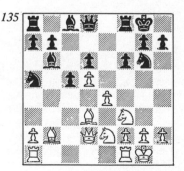

135

Now White does not have N-Q2, so it is not so easy for him to arrange the advance of his KBP. He generally made his choice between:

C31: 15 R-B1
C32: 15 B-B3
C33: 15 K-R1

C31:

15 R—B1   B—Q2

Others:

a) 15...R-N1 16 N-N3 B-B2 17 N-B5 P-QN4 and now nineteenth-century players invariably transposed to C33 by 18 K-R1.

b) 15...N-K4 16 K-R1 (16 BxN!?) 16...NxB 17 QxN Q-K1 18 N-R4 B-Q1 19 N-B5 BxN 20 PxB P-QN4∓ — *Handbuch*.

16 N—N3   P—QR3

Or:

a) 16...B-B2 17 N-B5 P-N4 18 P-N4 N-K4 19 NxN BPxN 20 P-B4 P-B5 21 B-N1 BxN (Neumann-Rosenthal, Paris 1867) 22 KPxB!±.

b) 16...R-B1 (The rook looks misplaced here.) 17 N-B5 Q-B2 18 P-N4 P-N4 19 K-R1 etc. and White won in de Riviere-Lowenthal, first match game, Paris 1867.

17 N—B5   B—N4!?

Presumably 17...B-B2, 18...P-N4 etc. is another plan, although not so consistent as the text.

18 KR—K1

Naturally 18 BxB PxB is what Black is after.

18 ...   B—B2
19 P—N4   BxB
20 QxB   P—N4

21 P-N5 (21 N-Q2 is better.) 21...N-QB5 22 B-R4 N5-K4 23 NxN BPxN 24 Q-KN3 Q-Q2 25 Q-N4 R-B2 26 R-K3 R1-KB1 27 R-KB3 N-B5∓ Rosenthal-Kolisch, Paris 1867. White has no hope of attack with his QB so firmly blocked.

C32:

15 B—B3

This looks even less constructive, and Black can just get on with his Q-side play. Freeborough and Ranken gave the possible continuation

15...B-B3 (15...N-K4 16 NxN BPxN 17 K-R1 is possibly±.) 16 N-N3 P-QR3 17 N-B5 P-N4! (17...BxN? 18 PxB N-K4 19 NxN Schallopp-Minckwitz, corres 1870-1) 18 QR-B1 N-N2? (18...BxN? was a Freeborough-Clarke game; but the text move is not strictly necessary.) 19 P-N4 BxN 20 NPxB N-K4 21 NxN QPxN=. The possession of Q3 as a square for his minor pieces gives Black much better defensive chances against pressure on the KN-file than in most lines of C33.

C33:

15 K—R1*(136)*

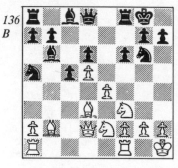

15 ...   B—B2

After White's last move, avoiding tricks on the a7-g1 diagonal, this piece has nothing more to do on N3 and so retired to let the NP advance. Other moves:

a) 15...N-K4? 16 NxN BPxN 17 P-B4

b) 15...R-N1 16 N-N3 B-B2 see below

c) 15...B-Q2 (Possibly too slow) 16 QR-B1 (16 B-B3!? — Lowenthal) 16...P-QR3 17 N-K1 (17 N-N3 was proposed by Freeborough and Ranken; 17 N-B4!? or maybe even 17 R-KN1 could be considered.) 17...B-N4 18 P-B4 P-B5 19 B-N1 P-B6!∓ Kolisch-L. Paulsen, Bristol 1861: reputedly the first game in which 10...N-K2 etc was played!

In reply to 15...B-B2:

C331: 16 N-N3
C332: 16 QR-B1

It is probably too late to try to hold up the advance of the QBP now. White might considered 16 N-K1, e.g. 16...R-N1 17 P-B4 (Freeborough and Ranken only gave 17 N-N3 P-N4 18 N-B2 P-N5 19 N-K3 N-K4!) 17...P-N4 (17...P-B4!?) 18 P-B5 followed by N-B4 — analysis.

C331:

16	N—N3	R—N1
17	N—B5	BxN

Most nineteenth century books tended to condemn this exchange at any stage. We shall follow the second Anderssen-Zukertort match game, Berlin 1868, which seems the best model for Black in the Anderssen variation.

18	PxB	N—K4
19	NxN	

Taking with the bishop seems no more effective.

19	...	QPxN∓

Compare our comment in C32 about Black's use of d6. The Anderssen-Zukertort game went on 20 QR-B1 Q-Q3 21 B-K4 P-QN4 22 Q-K2 P-N5 23 Q-R5 P-B5 24 R/B1-Q1 N-N2 25 P-B4 PxP 26 R-B3 N-B4 27 B-B2 N-Q2 28 R-R3 P-KR3 29 Q-N4 N-K4 30 QxBP N-Q6 31 Q-Q4 B-N3 32 RxN BxQ 33 RxB P-B6 34 B-B1 KR-K1 35 B-K3 R-K4 36 K-N1 R1-K1 37 K-B2 Q-B4 38 R-K4 Q-R4 39 RxR RxR 40 B-N3 P-B7 41 P-Q6+ K-B1 42 P-Q7 K-K2 43 R-N3 KxP 44 RxP+ R-K2 45 B-K6+ K-Q3 46 B-KB4+ Q-K4! 0-1.

C332:

16 QR—B1 *(137)*

After that game, Anderssen switc-

hed to the text move — but should it have really made much difference? The attack on the QBP prevents one plan, but Black has other ways of getting counterplay.

137
B

16	...	R—N1

Or 16...P-QR3 (Criticized by Anderssen) 17 N3-N1 P-N4 (17...N-K4!?) 18 P-B4 B-N3 19 N-N3 R-R2 20 N1-K2 R-QB2 21 P-B5 N-K4 22 N-B4 QN-B5 (22...NxB and 23...P-B5 is better.) 23 BxN NxB 24 RxN! (An inexpensive way to halt Black's **counterplay**) 24...PxR 25 B-B3 R-N2 26 P-KR4 Q-K1 27 N-K6 KR-B2 28 N-R5 B-Q1 29 Q-B4 BxN 30 QPxB R-B1 31 Q-B3 R-N4 32 R-Q1 Q-K2 33 Q-N3 R-N3 34 B-R5 R-N2 35 B-Q2 K-R1 36 N-B4 Q-QB2 37 N-N6+! PxN 38 PxP R-K1 39 B-B4 P-B6 40 Q-N4 K-N1 41 Q-R5 RxP 42 Q-R7+ K-B1 43 Q-R8+ K-K2 44 QxP+ K-K1 45 Q-R8+ K-Q2 46 P-N7 P-B7 47 R-QB1 R-K1 48 QxR+ KxQ 49 P-N8=Q+ K-Q2 50 P-R5 R-N8 51 P-R6 Q-R4 52 Q-N4+ K-B3 53 Q-K2 P-B4 54 QxBP RxR+ 55 QxR PxP. We are following a game Schallopp-Minckwitz; unfortunately White now spoilt his splendid play by 56 Q-R1 (56 Q-Q1 or 56 P-N4 would be more convincing.) 56...P-B5 57 P-N4 Q-R6 58 Q-KB1 Q-QB6 59 P-N5 P-Q4 60 K-R2? (60 P-R7 instead should win.) 60...P-K6 ½-½. This imperfect game

at least shows many of White's possibilities.

17 N—N3

The *Handbuch* rejected 17 N3-N1 on account of 17...N-K4 or 17...P-N4 in reply, but perhaps this idea is due for re-assessment? Schallopp's plan certainly seems no worse than Anderssen's.

17 ...   P—N4

Not 17...Q-K1? 18 N-Q4 as the bishop on c7 hangs; two Zukertort-Anderssen friendlies of 1865 vintage were won by White after the cumbersome 17...R-B2? 18 N-B5±. In the sixth Anderssen-Zukertort 1868 match game, Black wasted a tempo with the feeble move 17...P-N3?! after which the attack by 18 N-B5 BxB 19 PxB N-K4 20 NxN was more dangerous than in the earlier game, and White eventually won.

18 N—B5(138)

Wormald wrote: "This move has the sanction of Anderssen and the *Handbuch*, but it is questionable whether 18 N-K1, though less showy, is not really preferable."

138
B

Now:

C3321: 18...P-N5?
C3322: 18...P-B5!

Or:

a) Regrouping with 18...B-R3!? 19 R-KN1 N-N2 20 P-N4 B-R4 21 Q-K3 B-N3 "and Black has good prospects" — Alexander.

b) 18...BxN? 19 PxB N-K4 20 BxN BPxB (20...QPxB? 21 RxP — the point of White's sixteenth move!) 21 N-N5± — Wormald.

C3321:

18 ...   P—N5?

This move is insufficiently forcing. Anderssen won two famous games against it.

19 R—KN1

Else Black might play 19...P-B5, exploiting the skewer 20 BxQBP NxB 21 RxN B-R3.

19 ...—   B—N3

Or 19...BxN 20 PxB N-K4 21 BxN BPxB 22 N-N5 Q-Q2 23 N-K6 KR-B1 (Better 23...R-B3) 24 P-N4 P-N6 25 P-N5 PxP 26 P-N6! N-N6 (26...P-KR3 27 P-B6 N-N6 28 P-B7+ K-R1 29 QxKRP+) 27 PxP+ K-R1 28 Q-N5 B-Q1 29 NxB NxR (29...RxN 30 P-B6 R-N2 31 PxP+ QxP 32 QxR+) 30 **P-B6 ±± Anderssen-Steinitz, ninth match game 1866.**

20 P—N4!   N—K4

21 BxN   QPxB

Suetin wrote: "A serious error. Better 21...BPxB, to lessen the effect of P-N5". However, White could then play 22 N-N5, e.g. 22...P-KR3?! 23 N-K6 BxN 24 PxB N-B3 25 B-B4 K-R2 26 R-N3 or 26 P-N5 with a strong attack — analysis.

22 R—N3   R—B2

Trying to improve on an earlier friendly with 22...BxN and 23...R-N2.

23 P—N5!   BxN

24 PxB   QxP?

24...R-QB1 or 24...K-B1 had to be tried.

25 PxP! R-Q1 (25...RxP 26 B-B4!) 26 R1-KN1! (26 Q-R6? QxN+) 26... K-R1 (or 26...QxB 27 RxP+ RxR 28 RxR+ e.g. 28...K-R1 29 QxQ PxQ 30 NxP or 28...K-B1 29 R-N8+! K-B2 30 NxP+) 27 PxP+ K-N1 (27...RxP 28 Q-R6! RxR 29 Q-B6+ or 28...

R1-KN1 29 B-K4! QxB 30 QxP+!) 28
Q-R6! Q-Q3 29 QxP+! KxQ 30
P-B6+ K-N1 31 B-R7+! KxB 32
R-R3+ K-N1 33 R-R8 mate;
Anderssen-Zukertort, eighth West
German Congress, Barmen 1869.
This was one of the uncrowned World
Champion's most typical brilliancies,
and one of the finest sustained
attacks ever played with the Evans.

C3322:

18 ... P—B5!*(139)*

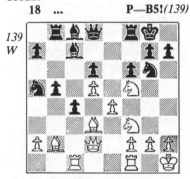

139
W

19 B—K2!
Relatively best, in view of 19 B-N1
P-N5 20 B-Q4 B-R3!:
a) 21 KR-K1 P-B6 22 Q-Q1 N-B5
a1) N3-R4 (23 BxRP N-N7 24 Q-N3
R-R1 25 B-Q4 B-B5 26 Q-B2 N-Q6
winning the exchange) 23...NxN 24
NxN B-N3 25 N-B5 B-B1 26 P-N4
BxN 27 NPxB N-Q7 28 B-K3e BxB 29
RxB NxB 30 RxN Q-B2 31 Q-B3
Q-B5 32 R-KN3 KR-B1 33 P-KR4
P-QR4 34 P-B3 Q-Q5 35 QR-KN1
R-N2 36 Q-N2 R1-B2 37 Q-QB2 Q-B5
38 P-R5 P-R3 39 R-N6 Q-B4! and

Black's Q-side pawns are stronger
than White's pressure on the KN-file
(40 RxRP QxR+). Black won in 57
moves in the game Maroczy-
Charousek, Budapest 1895 (match).
a2) No better here is 23-N-N1 B-N3
24 N-R3 R-B2 25 P-B4 BxB as in W.
Paulsen-Anderssen, Barmen 1869;
i.e. Anderssen refuted his own line the
day after the Zukertort game!
b) 21 R-N1 P-B6 22 Q-K3 or 22 Q-K1
N-QB5 also looks excellent for Black.
19 ... P—N5!?
Sokolsky's line 19...R-K1! 20 Q-B2
N-B5 is more convincing.
20 BxQBP!?
Zukertort analysed 20 B-Q4 P-B6
21 Q-K3 (21 Q-Q1!? B-N3 22 P-N4 or
21...P-N6 22 P-QR3 is unclear.)
21...B-N3 22 P-N4 N-K4∓. The text
move, giving up the exchange to
regain the initiative, seems stronger.
20 ... NxB
21 RxN B—R3
22 RxB QxR
23 R—B1 Q—Q2
24 N3—Q4
It is hard to find a good move for
Black:
a) 24...N-K4 25 N-K6 N-B5 26 Q-B4
KR-B1 27 ˜ BxP!± Heinrichsen-
Asharin, Riga 1893.
b) 24...N-K2 25 NxNP! KxN 26 R-B7!
Q-Q1 27 RxN!
c) 24...KR-B1 25 N-K6 RxR 26 QxR
R-QB1 and not now *Sovremenny
Debyut's* 27 Q-R6, because of the
reply 27...R-B7!, but rather 27 Q-R1!
— Botterill.

11 Unusual Defences

1	P—K4	P—K4
2	N—KB3	N—QB3
3	B—B4	B—B4
4	P—QN4*(140)*	

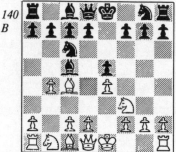

*140
B*

We shall now discuss:

A: 4...BxNP (Remaining Lines)
B: 4...B-K2
C: 4...P-Q4!?

4...B-N3 is the subject of Chapter 12.

Two other moves come into consideration:
a) 4...NxP when it is generally agreed that White cannot do better than 5 P-B3 N-B3, transposing to chapter 8.
b) 4...P-QN4 5 BxNP (5 B-Q5!?) 5...BxNP 6 P-B3 B-R4 7 0-0± — Pachman.

A:

    4 ... BxNP

Now:

A1: 5 P-B3 (Remaining Lines)
A2: 5 0-0?!

A1:

    5 P—B3*(141)*

*141
B*

So far, we have looked at 5...B-K2, 5...B-R4 and 5...B-B4. Some other moves have been played in this position and White should know about them, although we do not recommend them to Black. These are:

A11: 5...P-B4?!
A12: 5...P-QN4!?
A13: 5...B-B1
A14: 5...B-Q3

A11:

    5 ... P—B4?!

Black offers a piece in the hope of seizing the initiative. This idea was analysed by the German theorist Cordel towards the end of the last century, but it was soon shown to be unsound.

    6 PxB

There is no good reason to decline the offer. Black's idea worked in a game in which consulting amateurs played White against Blackburne (1894): 6 BxN PxP 7 Q-N3 (7 B-Q5!?) 7...Q-B3 8 N-N5 QxN 9 Q-B7+ K-Q1 10 PxB P-Q3 11 0-0 (11 Q-B8+ is better.) 11...B-R6 12 P-N3 N-Q5 13 N-B3 B-K3 14 Q-B8+ K-Q2 15 QxR RxB 16 QxNP N-B6+ 17 K-R1 Q-R4 18 P-KR4 Q-N5 19 Q-N5+ K-K2 20 N-Q5+ K-B2 0-1.

| 6 | ... | | PxP |
| 7 | P—N5 | | N—R4 |

7...PxN does not regain the piece, because of White's mate threat after 8 QxP.

8 NxP!?
This move was recommended by Keres in 1952. The older line ran 8 BxN!:

a) 8...PxN? 9 B-Q5 PxP (Quiet moves just leave Black a piece down.) 10 Q-R5+ K-K2 11 B-R3+ K-B3 12 Q-B7+ K-N4 13 B-K7+ etc.

b) 8...RxB 9 NxP Q-N4 10 P-Q4 QxP 11 Q-R5+ P-KN3 12 QxRP QxR+ (12...R-B1 13 QxNP+) 13 K-K2 QxB 14 QxR+ K-K2 15 Q-B7+ K-Q3 16 N-Q2! Q-B7 17 R-QB1! Q-N7 (17...QxR 18 N2-B4+) 18 Q-B6+ K-Q4 19 R-B5+ KxP 20 N-Q3 mate, following *Sovremenny Debyut*. The text line also recalls the 3 B-B4 PxP variation of the Latvian Counter-Gambit.

8	...		Q—N4
9	P—Q4		QxP
10	Q—R5+		P—KN3
11	B—B7+		K—B1

Or 11...K-K2 12 B-N5+ K-Q3? (12...N-B3? 13 Q-R4) 13 N-R3! P-B3 (13...PxQ allows mate in two.) 14 N5-B4+ K-B2 16 B-KB4+ P-Q3 17 BxQP+ K-Q2 18 Q-N7 QxR+ 19 K-K2 QxR 20 B-Q5+ K-Q1 21 B-QB7+ K-K1 22 Q-B7 mate. But see the next move.

12 B—R6+ NxB?
Not 12...K-K2 13 B-N5+? K-B1 when White, if he wants to win, would have to try 14 Q-R4 QxR+ 15 K-K2

threatening 16 Q-B4 and 17 BxN. It is not clear that this is good enough. Hence 13 Q-R4+! N-KB3 14 B-N5 QxR+ 15 K-K2 with a winning attack.

After the text move, White wins by 13 QxN+ K-K2 14 Q-N7 e.g. 14...QxR+ 15 K-K2 P-B3 16 QxR Q-QB8 17 N-Q2 QxR 18 NxKP — Unzicker.

A12:

| 5 | ... | | P—QN4!? |
| | | | *(142)* |

Another line stemming from Cordel.

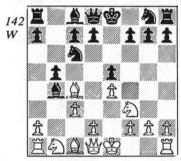

142
W

6 BxNP
6 B-Q5!? B-R4 7 0-0 can be met by 7...KN-K2 e.g. 8 NxP!? NxN! (8...NxB 9 NxN PxN 10 PxP PxP 11 B-R3!) 9 BxR P-QB3 and Black should obtain two pieces for the rook — analysis.

| 6 | ... | | B—Q3... |

After 6...B-B4 White clearly has a pleasant position if he continues with 0-0, P-Q4 etc. There is no need for him to adopt the hazardous line given by Cordel 7 BxN!? PxB 8 NxP!? Q-N4 9 P-Q4 QxP 10 Q-B3 since Black's two bishops might count for something in the ending.

7	0—0		B—N2
8	P—Q4		KN—K2
9	B—N5!?		

The manoeuvre 9 QN-Q2 followed by N-B4 looks quite promising.

9	...	P—B3
10	B—KR4	O—O
11	B—B4+	K—R1

White has more space, but his QB looks misplaced (it could have gone to K3). A game Seufert-Cordel, Berlin 1886, continued 12 P-Q5 N-R4 13 B-Q3 N-N3 14 QN-Q2 N-KB5 15 B-B2 B-R3 with good play for Black (drawn in 53).

A13:

5	...	B—B1

This retrograde move was mentioned in Lange's *Jahrbuch*, 1862, and subsequently adopted on one occasion by Steinitz. Black consolidates his K-side, but can hope for little active play. Zukertort wrote: "...retreating the bishop to B1, although safe for the bishop, puts the game in jeopardy."

6 P—Q4(143)

Not 6 Q-N3 Q-K2 7 P-Q4 N-R4.

6	...	PxP!?

Others:

a) 6...Q-K2 7 0-0 see Chigorin-Steinitz on page 24.

b) Lange also mentioned 6...Q-B3!?

c) 6...P-Q3 7 PxP PxP (7...NxP? 8 NxN PxN 9 BxP+) when:

c1) Unzicker recommends 8 BxP+ in the *Encyclopaedia of Chess Openings* but this looks unsound, e.g. 8...KxB 9 NxP+ K-K1! (9...K-K3 is not easy to refute, either.) 10 Q-R5+ P-N3 11 NxP N-B3. Compare D52 in Chapter 4.

c2) 8 Q-N3 looks correct, proceeding much as in Chigorin's line against the Lasker Defence, but with the important differences that Black is a tempo behind on his K-side development and that he does not threaten ...N-QR4.

7 0—0!?   N—R4

7...P-Q3 is safer, but White will have a strong centre and better development. Hence 7 PxP is simplest, to avoid the following complications:

8	BxP+!?	KxB
9	N—K5+	K—K2!

Here 9...K-K1 fails to 10 Q-R5+ P-KN3 11 NxNP N-B3 12 Q-K5+! and another difference from Unzicker's line is that 9...K-K3 may allow 10 Q-N3+ KxN 11 PxP+. Of course not 9...K-B3? 10 B-N5+! KxB 11 N-B7+ etc.

After the text move, the soundness of White's sacrifice is debatable. We follow a game Anderssen-Mayet, Breslau 1867: 10 PxP Q-K1 11 Q-R4 P-QN3? (11...N-QB3!, going for exchanges, is critical.) 12 N-QB3 P-B3 13 P-B4 (13 B-N5+ N-KB3 14 P-B4 P-Q3 15 P-Q5 — von Gottschall.) 13...P-Q3 14 B-R3 K-Q1 15 N-B3 B-Q2 16 QR-Q1 K-B2 17 P-Q5 P-B4 18 Q-B2 P-QN4? 19 P-K5 P-QR3 20 P-K6 B-B1 21 N-Q4 N-N2? (21...N-B5 — von Gottschall) 22 N-K4 with complications (1-0, 30).

A14:

5	...	B—Q3

An awkward move, interfering with Q-side development for the sake of strong-pointing the e5 square. This was known as the Stone-Ware Defence in the nineteenth century, after two amateur players from Boston, Mass.

6 P—Q4(144)

6 0-0 should not have independent significance. In the game Schiffers-Pillsbury, Hastings 1895, after

6...N-B3 White played 7 R-K1 but this was unnecessarily committal.

144
B

A141: 6...Q-K2
A142: 6...Q-B3
A143: 6...N-B3
    6...PxP 7 PxP N-R4 (7... B-N5+ see Chapter 8) 8 B-Q3 P-QB3 9 0-0 — *Handbuch.*
McDonnell used to play 6...P-KR3.

A141:
    6 ...   Q—K2
Introduced by Kieseritsky.
    7 0—0   N—B3
Others:
a) 7...P-QN3 8 R-K1 (8`N-N5 N-R3) 8...B-N2 9 QN-Q2 and 10 N-B1 — Schlechter.
b) 7...P-KR3 8 B-N3 P-KN4 9 PxP B-B4 10 N-R4 R-R2 11 B-K3 QxP 12 N-Q2± (A bizarre sequence!) Gudekas-Albin, corres 1900.
    8 N—N5!?
Or 8 QN-Q2 0-0 9 R-K1 (*Sovremenny Debuyt* gave 9 B-Q3 N-K1 10 N-B4 P-B3 11 N-K3 P-KN3 12 N-Q5±.) 9...N-QR4 10 B-Q3 P-B4 11 PxKP BxP 12 NxB QxN 13 Q-B2 P-Q4 14 N-B3 Q-R4 15 P-K5 N-Q2 16 B-B5! N-N3 17 P-K6! BxP 18 RxB! PxR 19 P-N4! RxB (19...Q-K1 20 BxRP+ K-R1 21 B-N2 Q-K2 22 N-N5 P-B5 23 B-B7! — Wills) 20 PxQ RxN 21 Q-K2±± Wills-Phillips, Essex v. Kent 1972.
    8 ...   0—0
    —

    9 P—B4
a) 9...PxBP 10 P-K5 BxP (10...NxP! 11 PxN BxP — Botterill) 11 PxB Q-B4+ (11...NxP!?) 12 K-R1 NxP 13 B-N3 P-KR3 14 N-R3 — *Handbuch.*
b) 9...P-KR3 10 BPxP QNxKP 11 PxN±± Felbecker-Grunke, corres 1972.
A142:
    6 ...   Q—B3
    7 0—0   P—KR3
Black is playing the Steinitz line from Chapter 7, except that the bishop is on Q3 rather than QR4.
    8 N—R3!
This seems preferable to 8 B-K3 KN-K2 9 QN-Q2 0-0 10 Q-B2 N-N3 11 K-R1 of Chigorin-Hanham, New York 1889, although White won that game.
    8 ...   BxN
Or 8...P-QR3 (To prevent N-QN5) 9 N-B2± — *Handbuch.*
    9 BxB   P—Q3
    10 PxP   PxP
Or 10...NxP 11 NxN QxN?! 12 Q-N3, or 12 P-B4 and P-K5.
    11 Q—N3   KN—K2
This position is rather like some from Chapter 3, but in White's favour as his opponent has no KB. A game Hanstein-Bilguer (*circa* 1840) went 12 B-Q5 R-QN1 13 QR-Q1±. Black's development is difficult, since castling would cost the exchange, while White threatens 14 QBxN NxB 15 BxP+ etc.

A143:
    6 ...   N—B3
    7 0—0 *(145)*
7 N-N5 comes into consideration again. A game Anderssen-Kieseritsky, London 1851, ran 7...0-0 8 P-B4 (Better than 8 NxBP?! of Bird-Pillsbury, Hastings 1895) 8...PxBP 9 P-K5 BxP 10 PxB NxP 11 B-N3 P-KR3 12 N-R3 P-KN4 13 0-0 P-Q3 14 N-B2 B-K3 15 N-Q2 Q-Q2 16

N/B2-K4 NxN 17 NxN P-KB4? (Until this error, the position was none too clear.) 18 N-B5! BxB (18...PxN 19 QxQ) 19 QxB+ Q-B2 20 NxP and **White eventually won.**

145
B

7 ...   0—0
If Black has to play 7...P-KR3, his position must be bad.

8 QN—Q2
A game Seidman-Mengarini, USA Ch 1951, varied with 8 N-N5!? B-K2 9 P-B4 P-Q3 10 N-Q2 PxQP 11 PxP P-Q4 (11...NxQP 12 B-N2) 12 PxP P-KR3? (12...NxP might be met by 13 NxBP!? RxN 14 Q-R5 B-K3 15 P-B5 B-QB1 16 P-B6.) 13 NxP RxN 14 PxN QxP+ 15 K-R1 QxR 16 Q-N3 and White won material. However, 12... N-QR4 was sound, and possibly Black's tenth move was not the best available.

8 ...   Q—K2
and the game has transposed to A141.

A2:
5 0—0?!*(146)*
Or 4 0-0 N-B3 (4...P-Q3 5 P-QN4!? compare Evans-McDonnell in chapter 1.) 5 P-QN4 BxNP transposing. Although the old move-order is still occasionally seen, it is certainly much less incisive than 4 P-QN4 BxNP 5 P-B3. The fact that Black has got his KN safely out to B3 makes a lot of difference. White has restricted his options by castling early.

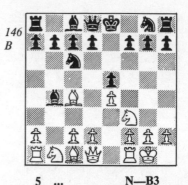

146
B

5 ...   N—B3
This is good, but perhaps not the only sound move. Others:
a) 5...P-Q3 6 P-Q4!? (6 P-B3 B-R5 7 P-Q4 B-N3 is the Lasker Defence.) 6...PxP (6...B-Q2 7 B-N2 — Keres) 7 P-B3 was a Tartakower line. According to grandmaster Evans, one adequate response is 7...PxP 8 Q-N3 Q-B3.
b) 5...B-K2 is a form of the line discussed in Chapter 2, with White playing rather tamely, e.g. 6 P-B3 N-B3 7 P-Q4 P-Q3 Podgorny-Filip, Prague 1949. If then 8 P-Q5, Black's best is 8...N-QN1 followed by ...QN-Q2-B4 — Persitz in *British Chess Magazine*, 1966: but see Vasquez-Blackburne, below.

6 P—Q4!?
6 P-B3 is inconsistent. Black's best reply is 6...B-K2! and after 7 P-Q4:
a) 7...P-Q3 see the previous note;
b) 7...PxP?! 8 PxP (not 8 P-K5 N-K5 9 PxP P-Q4! — but 9 R-K1 is feasible — Persitz) 8...NxP 9 P-Q5 N-R4 10 B-Q3 N-B4 11 B-R3 NxB 12 QxN 0-0 (12...P-Q3!) 13 P-Q6 PxP? 14 N-B3 P-QN3 15 N-Q5 N-N2 16 B-N2 N-B4 17 Q-K3 N-K3 18 N-Q4 B-B3 19 N-B6! PxN 20 NxB+ PxN 21 Q-R6 P-Q4 22 BxP Q-Q3 23 P-B4 R-K1 24 R-B3 1-0 Kolisch-Paulsen, second match game, 1861.
c) 7...0-0 8 P-Q5 (8 PxP!?) 8...N-N1 9 Q-K2 P-Q3 10 N-K1 QN-Q2 11 B-Q3

N-K1 12 P-KB4 and White managed to get some attack, although he finally lost; Vasquez-Blackburne, Havana 1891. This is just a reminder that White's play is not completely innocuous!

6 ... **PxP**

6...P-Q3 7 P-B3 B-R4 is considered in Chapter 7.

7 P—B3

Or 7 P-K5 P-Q4∓ — Unzicker.

7 ... **PxP**
8 P—K5 **P—Q4!∓**

Pinkus-Marshall, New York 1925.

B2:

4 ... **B—K2***(147)*

The more usual way to decline the Evans is by 4...B-N3, which we discuss in the next chapter. The main objection to the text move is that the queen is unable to defend KB2 for the time being.

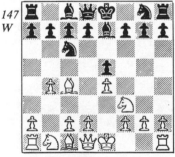

147
W

5 P—N5!?

5 P-B3 is quieter, but more likely to bring White an advantage. After 5...N-B3 6 Q-N3 0-0 White can build up quietly with 7 P-Q3± (Keres) or try 7 N-N5 Q-K1 8 P-Q3 P-KR3 9 N-B3± (Euwe), using a tempo to upset Black a little. In either case, White will soon expand on the Q-side.

5 ... **N—R4**
6 B—K2!

Not 6 NxP when Black has 6...NxB 7 NxN P-Q4! 8 PxP QxP (Wormald,

1875) e.g. 9 N-K3 Q-QN4 10 N-B3 Q-B3 11 QN-Q5 B-K3 12 NxB NxN 13 B-R3 N-N3 14 0-0 N-B5 15 P-Q4 0-0-0∓ Chigorin-Schiffers, Berlin 1897.

6 ... **P—Q4!?**
7 P—Q4! **QPxP**

If 7...KPxP perhaps 8 QxP B-B3 9 P-K5 B-K2 10 B-Q2 P-QN3 (10... P-QB3? 11 Q-R4!) 11 BxN and 12 Q-R4.

8 NxP **N—KB3**
9 0—0 **0—0**
10 P—QB4±

Sokolsky-Kirillov, Leningrad 1947. Black's QN is awkwardly placed.

C:

4 ... **P—Q4!?***(148)*

This spirited counter-gambit is designed to avoid the cramp which is so often Black's lot in the Evans. However, it does not seem to be as good as the more reliable defences that follow the acceptance of the gambit, as White is able to retain some positional advantage at no material cost.

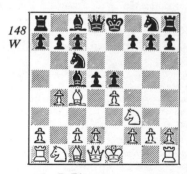

148
W

5 PxP!

Black's fourth move was first suggested in the *Chess Player's Chronicle* in 1845 and further analysed in the *American Magazine* (1847).

It was not long before the text was established as White's best reply. Inferior lines:

a) 5 B-N5 PxP (5...BxNP=) 6 PxB (6 NxP BxP+) 6...PxN 7 BxN+ PxB 8 QxP N-K2∓)

b) 5 BxP NxB 6 B-N3 (Or 6 N-B3 NxB 7 NxN P-QB3 8 N-B3 N-B3 9 0-0 B-KN5∓ — Wormald) 6...N-KB3 7 N-B3 0-0 8 0-0 B-N5 9 P-Q3 N-B3 10 N-K2 N-KR4!? 11 K-R1 K-R1 12 N-N5 (Kolisch-Anderssen, Paris 1860) 12...Q-K2= — Bachman.

5   ...   NxP
6 0—0!

As analysed by Chigorin, in *Shakhmatny Listok* (1877) and *Shakhmatny Vestnik* (1885). Others:

a) 6 NxP when:

a1) 6...B-Q5? 7 P-QB3 or 6...BxP+? 7 KxB Q-B3+ 8 Q-B3 QxN 9 R-K1±± ;

a2) 6...NxQP 7 B-N5+ P-QB3 8 NxQBP (Steinitz) is unclear.

a3) 6...Q-N4! was suggested by Cheney, a nineteenth century American amateur. Then if 7 0-0 B-R6 with complications after the exchange offer suggested by Staunton: 8 P-N3 BxR 9 P-Q4 Q-K2 10 KxB 0-0 11 P-B3 NxQP 12 Q-B3.

b) 6 B-R3 (Paulsen and Steinitz) when:

b1) Chigorin thought that Black might play 6...P-K5 with success. That is not completely convincing against 7 0-0! e.g. 7...PxN 8 P-B3 Q-R5 9 B-N5+ P-B3 10 PxP PxP 11 PxB B-Q3 12 P-N3 Q-R6 13 BxP+ — Bachmann, *Schachmeister Steinitz.*

b2) In that case, Black must try 6...Q-Q3 7 P-B3 NxQP 8 BxB QxB 9 Q-N3 KN-B3 10 NxP 0-0= — Freeborough and Ranken.

6   ...   N—KB3 *(149)*
Others:

a) 6...NxQP 7 R-K1 KN-K2 8 NxP 0-0 9 P-Q4 B-QN5 10 B-Q2 BxB 11 QxB B-B4 12 N-QB3 P-QB3 13 N-K4± Mindibayev-Maninym, USSR 1963

b) 6...N-K2 when:

b1) 7 NxP 0-0 (7...N5xQP may be better.) 8 P-Q4 B-Q3 9 N-QB3 B-KB4 10 B-N3 P-QR4 11 P-QR3 P-R5 12 NxRP N5xQP 13 P-QB4 RxN 14 PxN R-R4 15 Q-B3 B-N3 16 R-K1 B-N5 17 R-K2 N-B4 18 B-N2 Q-R1 19 P-N3 Q-R2 20 NxB RPxN 21 R-K5 BxP 22 P-Q6± Morphy-Salmon, blindfold simul, Birmingham 1858

b2) 7 P-B3 N5xQP 8 NxP 0-0 9 P-Q4 B-Q3 10 P-B4 P-QB3 11 B-Q3 N-B4 12 Q-R5 N-B3 13 Q-B3 B-K3 14 N-Q2 B-Q4 15 Q-R3± Solovtsov-Dannenberg, Russia 1887; White stands firm in the centre.

c) 6...B-N5 7 R-K1 P-KB3 8 P-B3 BxN (8...NxP 9 NxP! or 9 Q-N3) 9 Q-R4+! (9 QxB N-B7) 9...P-B3 10 PxN B-Q5 11 N-B3±± (Freeborough and Ranken) e.g. 11...BxN 12 PxKB BxQP 13 R-Q5 N-K2 (13...P-QN4 14. BxP!) 14 BxN P-QN4 (14...NxB 15 P-QB4 P-QN4 16 PxP) 15 BxP+ etc. — analysis.

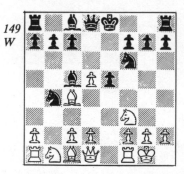

149
W

7 NxP   N5xQP
8 P—Q4
Now:
C1: 8...B-Q3
C2: 8...B-K2

C1:

8	...	B—Q3
9	B—KN5!	P—B3
10	N—Q2	0—0
11	Q—B3!±	

White now threatens to ruin Black's position by 12 B/B4xN or first 12 N-K4. Relatively best now would be 11...B-K2.

The game Schiffers-Pillsbury, Nuremberg 1896, continued 11... P-KR3 12 B-R4 B-K3?! 13 QR-N1! R-N1 14 N-K4 B-K2 15 NxN+ BxN 16 B-KN3 (Threatening 17 NxQBP) 16...Q-B1 17 B-Q3 N-K2 (17...P-KN3 18 NxNP or 17...N-B6 18 QR-K1 NxP 19 Q-K4 or 18...BxP 19 B-B5) 18 P-B3 R-R1 19 N-B4 (Romanovsky suggested 19 QR-K1 BxP 20 Q-K4 P-KN3 21 N-N4.) 19...B-Q4 20 Q-K2 P-QN4? (20...BxN) 21 N-Q6 Q-K3 22 Q-Q2 P-QR4 (22...P-R3 was better.) 23 KR-K1 Q-Q2 24 P-QR4! and White broke through to win on the QN-file.

C2:

8	...	B—K2

Chigorin thought this retreat was stronger; Black can try for ...P-QB4 without fear of B-KN5. Nonetheless he said that White gets the freer game.

This can be illustrated by Cafferty-Cubitt, Manchester 1971: 9 B-N3 0-0 10 P-QB4 N-N3 11 B-N2 P-B3 12 N-Q4 Q-B2 13 R-K1 B-QN5 14 R-K3 B-KB4 15 P-KR3 QN-Q2 16 P-B4 QR-K1? 17 N2-B3 NxN 18 BPxN P-KR3 19 Q-K2 N-Q2 20 R-KB1 Q-Q2 21 N-R4! QxN 22 RxB Q-Q2 23 Q-R5 N-B4 24 B-B2 (24 PxN? BxP skewering the rook) 24...N-K3 25 Q-Q1! (White has a lovely game with the two bishops, active rooks and strong pawns in the centre.) 25...R-K2 26 Q-Q3 KR-K1 27 R-N3 N-B1 28 B-B1 R-K3 29 R-R5 K-R1 30 R-N4 P-QB4 31 Q-KN3 N-N3 32 BxP! PxB 33 Q-K3 K-N1 34 QxP 1-0.

12 The Evans Gambit Declined

1	P—K4	P—K4
2	N—KB3	N—QB3
3	B—B4	B—B4
4	P—QN4	B—N3 *(150)*

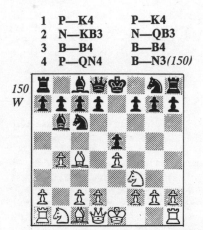

150
W

By declining the gambit, Black hopes to save a tempo or two in which to complete his development and then turn the game into positional channels. Although 4...B-N3 has been known almost as long as the Evans itself, it has only known one period of real popularity — between the two world wars when, among others, Rubinstein and Botvinnik tried the defence, and Tarrasch proclaimed it as the best reply to the gambit.

It was a long time before White's best plan was discovered. Captain Evans himself had thought White could simply play 5 P-N5 and 6 NxP but when this variation was thoroughly investigated later in the nineteenth century it was found that the resulting complications were in Black's favour. Other ideas had to be tried, including an adaptation of H.E. Bird's line against the Guioco Piano

(with P-QB3, P-Q3 followed by P-QN4, Q-N3, B-K3 or P-QR4), and soon the advance of the QRP, to embarrass Black's bishop and gain space, was hit upon. There remained the question of finding White's best move after 5 P-QR4 P-QR3. Tartakower practised 6 B-N2, while Ulvestad recommended 6 B-R3. However, White can continue to play in gambit style with 6 N-B3, intending to continue N-Q5, and it is this idea, developed by Soviet players, which causes Black more difficulties than any other against the Evans Gambit Declined.

From Diagram 147, we consider:

A: 5 P-N5

B: 5 P-QR4!

and, in brief:

a) 5 P-B3 P-Q3 6 0-0 (6 P-QR4 P-QR3 see B2) 6...B-N5 7 P-Q4!? PxP 8 BxP+? (Marshall-Short, Montreal 1894) 8...KxB 9 N-N5+? QxN‡‡.

b) 5 0-0 N-B3!? (5...P-Q3 is playable.) 6 P-N5 N-QR4 7 B-K2 NxP 8 B-N2 P-Q3 9 P-Q4 PxP 10 NxP 0-0 11 B-Q3 P-Q4 12 N-Q2 NxN 13 QxN N-B5 14 BxN PxB 15 QR-Q1 Q-B3 and White had insufficient attack for the pawn; Bakhmatov-Knyshenko, USSR Teams Ch 1956.

c) 5 B-N2 and now:

c1) Tartakower suggested 5...N-B3 e.g. 6 P-QR4 NxKP or 6 P-N5 N-QR4 7 NxP 0-0 with complications in either case.

c2) 5...P-Q3 was usually played, when:

c21) 6 P-Q4!? B-N5!? 7 B-N5 PxP 8
P-QR4 P-QR4 9 BxQP BxB 10 QxB
Q-B3 11 N-B3 PxP (Cordel-Hollan-
der) 12 N-Q5!± — Levenfish
c22) 6 P-QR4 P-QR4? (6...P-QR3 see
B4) 7 P-N5 N-N1 8 P-Q4 P-KB3 9 0-0
B-N5 10 Q-Q3 N-Q2 11 QN-Q2 Q-K2
12 B-Q5 R-N1 13 N-B4 B-K3 14 NxB
NxN 15 PxP BPxP 16 BxB QxB 17
N-N5± Schlechter-Wolf, 1910.

A:

5 P—N5*((151)*

This move, although recommended
by Captain Evans and Jaenisch, and
employed by Steinitz (in his early
years) and even Reti, is somewhat
dubious. For the subsequent capture
of Black's KP, albeit attractive, leads
directly to situations where White
must give up a piece for inadequate
compensation.

151
B

Black can reply:
A1: 5...N-Q5
A2: 5...N-R4!

A1:

5 ... N—Q5
6 NxN

Not 6 NxP? because of 6...Q-N4, e.g.
7 NxBP 8 R-B1 QxKP+ 9 B-K2 N-B6
mate.

6 ... BxN

‾
+

Or 6...PxN!? 7 0-0 P-Q3 8 P-Q3
N-B3 9 B-N5 P-KR3 10 B-R4 P-N4 11
B-N3 N-N5 12 N-Q2 Q-K2 13 P-QR4
(13 P-KR3!?) 13...P-KR4 14 P-R3
N-K4 (Better 14...P-R5 for if 15 P-B4
N-K6) 15 B-Q5 P-R5 16 P-KB4 PxP 17
BxKBP± Afonin-Safonov, Moscow
1959.

7 P—B3 B—N3
8 P—Q4 PxP

Or 8...Q-B3 9 0-0 P-Q3 (9...PxP 10
P-K5) 10 B-K3± Spielmann-Nyholm,
Baden 1914.

9 PxP P—Q3
10 0—0 N—K2
11 B—N5 0—0?!

White has good prospects, based on
his strong centre, e.g. 12 N-B3 P-QB3
(12...B-K3 13 N-Q5 BxN 14 BxB R-N1
— *Fernschach,* 1958) 13 P-Q5! P-QB4
14 P-K5! B-B2 15 N-K4 P-QN3 16
Q-R5 B-N2 17 N-B6+! PxN 18 BxP
1-0 Carls-Bannet, correspondence
game.

A2:

5 ... N—R4!
6 NxP*(152)*

Retreating with 6 B-K2 achieves
nothing:
a) 6...P-Q3 7 P-Q3 N-K2 8 QN-Q2 0-0
9 N-B1 N-N3 10 P-KR3 P-QR3 11 PxP
RxP 12 P-N4 (12 P-Q4 or 12 N-K3
should equalize — Levenfish.) 12...
N-R5 13 N-N3 NxN+∓ Zukertort-
Chigorin, Vienna 1882.
b) 6...P-Q4! seizes the initiative, e.g. 7
N-B3 (7 PxP P-K5 8 N-K5 B-Q5)
7...PxP 8 QNxP P-KB4 9 N-B3 P-K5
10 N-KN1 N-KB3 11 N-R3 Q-Q5 12
0-0 B-K3 13 Q-K1 N-B5 14 N-N5 B-N1
15 BxN BxB 16 P-Q3 B-R4 17 B-Q2
0-0-0! ∓ Spielmann-Burn, Karslbad
1911.

152
B

A number of moves were tried in this lively position. We shall look at:
A21: 6...B-Q5?
A22: 6...Q-B3
A23: 6...Q-N4
A24: 6...N-R3

A21:

	6 ...	B—Q5?
	7 NxBP!	Q—B3
	8 Q—K2	NxB
	9 NxR	

a) 9...BxR 10 QxN N-K2 11 P-QB3 P-Q4 12 PxP B-B4 13 0-0 e.g. 13... 0-0-0 14 P-Q6! RxP 15 B-R3 B-Q6 16 Q-KN4+ B-B4 (16...N-B4? 17 BxR BxR 18 KxB PxB 19 Q-QB4+ — Euler, 1864) 17 Q-B3 R-K3 18 BxN RxB 19 N-R3 and White comes out with two extra pawns.
b) 9...P-Q4 10 P-QB3 B-N3 11 0-0 N-K2 12 PxP N-Q3 13 P-Q4 B-KB4 14 B-B4 0-0-0 15 B-K5 Q-B1 16 P-QB4 B-R4 17 R-B1 K-N1 18 N-Q2 BxN 19 QxB and Black has to face a murderous attack; Florence-Bristol, corres 1913.

A22:

	6 ...	Q—B3
	7 BxP+	K—B1!

Not 7...K-Q1? 8 P-Q4 P-Q3 9 BxN RxB 10 B-N5 nor 7...K-K2 8 P-Q4 P-Q3 9 B-R3 N-R3 10 B-N3±.

	8 P—Q4	P—Q3
	9 BxN	

9 B-R3 is no good, e.g. 9...N-K2 10 P-KB4 PxN 11 QPxP QxB 12 Q-Q8+ Q-K1 13 BxN+ K-B2 14 QxQ RxQ 15 B-N4 B-Q2 16 P-QR4 P-QR3∓ — *Sovremenny Debyut.*

	9 ...	PxN

9...RxB? 10 N-KB3 and P-B3±.

	10 B—Q5	BxP

Not 10...P-B3? 11 B-R3+ K-K1 12 0-0 PxB 13 N-B3 BxP 14 NxP Q-B2 15 B-Q6!± — Euler and Neumann.

	11 P—KB4	BxR
	12 PxP	Q—N3
	13 0—0+	K—K1

14 B-B7+ QxB 15 RxQ KxR 16 Q-R5+ P-KN3 17 Q-B3+ K-K1 18 B-N5 BxP 19 Q-QR3 B-Q3 20 QxN K-B2 21 N-B3 R-K1∓ — *Sovremenny Debyut,* following Max Lange's analysis in the tournament book of Paris 1867. Black does indeed seem to be getting his pieces co-ordinated at last, but evidently the whole line needs more careful study before one would care to adopt it in practice.

A23:

	6 ...	Q—N4
	7 BxP+	

Or 7 NxBP QxNP 8 R-B1 QxKP+ 9 Q-K2 QxQ+ 10 KxQ NxB 11 NxR P-Q4∓ — *Deutsche Schachzeitung,* 1865.

	7 ...	K—K2

"7...K-B1 is also good" — Levenfish.

	8 BxN	QxN
	9 B—Q5	P—B3

"9...QxR is too risky, in view of 10 N-B3 P-Q3 11 0-0!" — Levenfish.

	10 P—Q4	BxP
	11 P—KB4	Q—B3
	12 P—B3	BxP+

13 NxB QxN+ 14 B-Q2 Q-Q5 (14... Q-QR6!?) 15 BxN Q-K6+ 16 Q-K2 QxQ+ 17 KxQ PxB 18 PxP P-QN3 19 B-B3 B-N2 and according to *Sovremenny Debyut,* the game is equal.

After 20 QR-Q1 White can keep his pawn for the time being, but 20... QR-QB1 21 B-N4+ K-B3 followed by ...KR-K1 or the penetration of the QR down the QB-file may give Black adequate counterplay, especially in view of the presence of opposite coloured bishops.

A24:

6 ...   N—R3

This move is generally recommended in preference to the queen sorties.

7   P—Q4   P—Q3
8   BxN*(153)*

153
B

Now:
A241: 8...PxB
A242: 8...PxN

A241

8   ...   PxB
9   BxP+

Others:

a) 9 NxP Q-B3 10 NxR NxB 11 P-QB3 B-K3 12 0-0 K-Q2∓ — *Sovremenny Debyut.*

b) 9 Q-R5 Q-B3 10 NxP 0-0! e.g. 11 NxRP+ K-N2 12 N-N4 BxN 13 QxB+ K-R1∓ — Max Lange.

9   ...   K—K2
10 N—B3   PxN

This is better than 10...P-B3, e.g. 11 Q-B3 BxP 12 PxP BxQN+ 13 QxB PxN 14 PxP BxP 15 B-Q5 BxB 16 R-Q1 N-B3 17 RxB Q-B2 18 P-B4!±

Shabelsky-Urusov, Russia 1894.

11 Q—B3   B—N5
12 QxB   KxB

According to an old analysis by Max Lange, Black stands better. Keres suggested 13 N-Q5, after which White's attack could still flare up. Unzicker, however, offers the continuation 13...R-KB1 14 PxP Q-N4 15 Q-Q7+ K-N3 16 N-K7+ K-N2 17 N-B5+ K-R1∓ and it is not easy to see any improvement upon this. Also taking variation A22 into account, it seems that 5 P-N5 must be consigned to the archives. Moreover, the next variation may also be good for Black!

A242:

8   ...   PxN
9   BxNP   R—KN1

Not 9...Q-N4? 10 BxR QxP (10... NxB 11 0-0 B-N5 12 Q-Q3) 11 R-B1 NxB 12 Q-K2 B-N5 13 P-KB3±± Steinitz-Dubois, eighth match game 1862.

10 BxBP+   KxB
11 BxP*(154)*

Wormald wrote: "Though White has gained four pawns for the piece he has sacrificed, most players, we imagine, would prefer Black's game." Tarrasch certainly did! It is true that Black's pieces have several obvious targets now, while White is behind on development. Nonetheless, White's connected passed pawns and the exposed state of Black's king ought to count for something; practical chances ought to be balanced.

See diagram next page

11 ...   Q—N4

Or 11...B-N5 12 Q-Q3 P-B4 13 N-B3 (13 P-QB3!?) 13...PxP 14 N-Q5 Q-K1 15 Q-KN3 NxB 16 Q-B4+ K-K3 17 P-KR3 B-QR4+ 18 P-QB3 BxP+ and Black soon won; Whittaker-Sir George Thomas, USA v. Great Britain

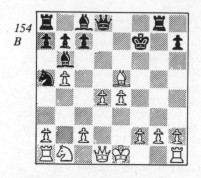

154
B

cable match 1930. White should have tried to maintain his pawn centre, play N-Q2 and castle.

12 N—B3

Possibly better is 12 N-Q2 (D.N. Pavlov, 1913), preventing Black's next move.

12 ... N—B5

13 Q—B3+

Not 13 B-N3 B-N5 14 Q-Q3 N-N7 15 Q-K3 QR-Q1! 16 QxQ RxQ 17 B-R4 BxP 18 N-K2 BxN 19 BxR? (19 KxB RxP 20 BxR RxBP+ is not much better.) 19...BxNP! 20 P-KB3 (20 BxR B-B6 mate) 20...R-KN1 21 P-KR4 P-KR3 0-1 Reti-Perlis, Vienna 1913.

13 ... K—K1

14 N—Q5 B—R4+

15 P—B3 NxB

16 PxN QxNP 17 Q-R5+ Q-N3 18 Q-R4 R-N2 19 K-Q2 Q-N4+ 20 QxQ RxQ 21 KR-KN1 and White managed to draw; Steinitz-Dubois, second match game 1862.

B:

5 P—QR4!

This is an altogether superior move, since after Black moves his QRP his KB is not so well protected. Then White's N-Q5 gains in force.

5 ... P—QR3(155)

Others are poor:

a) 5...NxP? 6 P-R5 B-B4 7 P-B3 N-B3 8 0-0 P-Q3 9 P-Q4 PxP 10 PxP B-QN5

11 P-Q5 NxP 12 Q-R4+ and wins — *Handbuch.*

b) 5...P-QR4? 6 P-N5 N-Q5 7 NxN (Unzicker gives 7 NxP? overlooking 7...Q-N4!) 7...BxN 8 P-B3 B-N3 9 0-0 (Or 9 P-Q4 with the more dynamic game — Sokolsky) 9...N-B3 10 B-R3 P-Q3 (10...NxP?! 11 Q-R5 Q-B3 12 P-Q4!) 11 P-Q4 B-N5 12 Q-Q3 Q-K2 13 N-Q2 0-0-0 14 P-B4!PxBP 15 RxP B-R4 16 K-R1 B-N3 17 QR-KB1 Q-Q2 18 Q-B3± Medina-Vilardebo, Spanish Ch 1945.

155
W

From the diagram:
B1: 6 0-0
B2: 6 P-B3
B3: 6 B-R3
B4: 6 B-N2
B5: 6 N-B3!

Also:

a) 6 P-Q4?! BxP 7 NxB NxN 8 0-0 P-Q3 9 P-B4 B-K3 10 BxB NxB 11 P-B5 N-N4 12 N-B3 P-R3 13 B-K3 N-B3∓ Zukertort-Englisch, Paris 1878

b) 6 P-R5 B-R2 7 0-0 N-B3 (7...P-Q3 is probably better; see B1.) 8 P-N5 PxP 9 BxNP NxP 10 Q-K2 N-Q3 11 BxN QPxB 12 QxP+ B-K3 13 QxP K-Q2± although Black got a draw in Meitner-Steinitz, Vienna 1873; this variation is a funny sort of Ruy Lopez!

B1:

6 0—0 P—Q3

7 P—R5

For 7 P-B3 compare B2. Black's

best reply may be 7...B-N5 followed by ...KN-K2.

	7 ...	**B—R2**
8	P—N5	PxP
9	BxNP	KN—K2

If 9...B-Q2 10 P-B3 and 11 P-Q4 — Levenfish. Now if 10 P-B3 B-N5. Not 9...B-N5 here, because of 10 P-R6!

10	P—Q4	PxP
11	NxP	B—Q2

Or 11...0-0 12 NxN!? PxN 13 B-Q3 N-N3∓ Marshall-Teichmann, Hamburg 1910.

12	NxN	NxN
13	B—N2	0—0
14	Q—Q5	B—B4
15	BxN	BxB

16 Q-B4 Q-R5 17 N-Q2 KR-K1 18 K-R1! (18...BxBP? 19 N-B3) with a sharp and balanced struggle; Vittek, Minckwitz & Chigorin v. Schwarz, Schwede & Schottlander, Berlin 1881.

B2:

6 P—B3

Bird's line, which usually gives rise to positions like those in the slow Guioco Piano line (1 P-K4 P-K4 2 N-KB3 N-QB3 3 B-B4 B-B4 4 P-B3 N-B3 5 P-Q3 P-Q3 6 P-QN4!?) which he also pioneered, around the middle of the last century. White is not really trying for any opening advantage, however, simply for little-known positions in which he may be at home.

	6 ...	**P—Q3**

Or 6...N-B3 7 P-Q3 P-Q3 8 Q-N3 0-0 9 B-KN5 Q-K2 10 QN-Q2 P-QR4 11 P-N5 N-Q1= Rojahn-Capablanca, Buenos Aires 1939.

7 Q—N3

Others:
a) 7 0-0 B-N5 8 P-Q3 Q-B3 9 B-K3 KN-K2 10 QN-Q2 N-N3 11 B-KN5? (11 P-R3 BxN 12 QxB QxQ 13 NxQ BxB 14 PxB P-B3= — Levenfish) 11...QxB 12 NxQ BxQ 13 BxBP+ K-K2 14 BxN B-K7 15 KR-K1 B-Q6

16 NxP P-Q4!∓ Chigorin-Zukertort, London 1883.
b) 7 P-R5 B-R2 8 P-N5 PxP 9 BxNP N-B3 10 P-R6 0-0 11 P-Q3 N-K2 12 PxP BxP 13 N-R3 P-Q4! 14 0-0 N-N3∓ Pollock-Lasker, Hastings 1895.
c) 7 P-Q3 N-B3 8 Q-N3 Q-K2 (Instead of Capablanca's 8...0-0) 9 B-KN5 P-R3 10 B-R4 N-Q1= Morphy-Boden, London 1858. Not 10 B-K3 (Steinitz) 10...BxB 11 PxB N-N5! 12 K-K2 P-B4! 13 QN-Q2 P-B5! 14 N-B1 P-QR4∓ Cafferty-Omelchenko, corres 1973-4.

	7 ...	**Q—K2**

The *Handbuch* suggested 7...Q-B3 followed by ...KN-K2.

8	P—R5	B—R2
9	P—N5	PxP
10	BxNP	N—B3
11	0—0	0—0

Not 11...NxP 12 Q-R4 — *Handbuch*.

12	BxN	NPxB
13	P—Q3	

Now, instead of 13...P-R3? (Lille-Paris, corres 1897-8), Levenfish suggested 13...B-R3 14 Q-B2 N-R4∓ in view of Black's excellent bishops.

B3:

6 B—R3

This move stems from analysis by Ulvestad in *Chess Charts*, 1940.

	6 ...	**P—Q3**

6...N-B3 7 P-N5 N-QR4 8 NxP P-Q4 'is all far from clear' — L. Evans. 7 N-B3 (reserving options) is also playable.

7 P—N5*(156)*

See diagram next page

	7 ...	**PxP**

Purdy suggested 7...N-R4 8 B-K2 B-K3 (i.e. without exchanging RPs) as a significant improvement upon the variation given in the next note. Instead of 8 B-K2, White's sacrificial

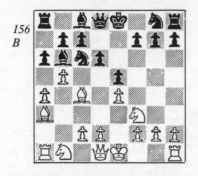

156
B

sound and gives chances. Careful play by Black will be necessary to equalize.

157
B

try 8 NxP is hopelessly unsound.

8 PxP   N—Q5

Now 8...N-R4 9 B-K2 B-K3 is met by 10 P-Q3 Q-Q2 11 N-B3 N-K2 12 0-0 0-0 13 B-N4 P-QB4 14 B-R3 P-KB3 15 Q-K1 P-Q4 16 N-QR4 (Not possible, of course, with the RP still there!) 16...QxP 17 NxBP BxN 18 P-Q4± — Ulvestad.

9 NxN   BxN
10 P—B3   B—N3!?

If 10...B-B4, not 11 P-Q4 PxP 12 PxP B-QN5+ (Ulvestad) but first 11 0-0.

11 0—0   Q—B3
12 K—R1   N—R3
13 P—B3   0—0
14 P—Q3   B—Q2
15 N—Q2   K—R1
16 Q—K2

a) 16...P-N4?! 17 R-R2 N-N1 18 P-Q4!± Purdy-Frantzen, ½-final 1 Corres World Ch 1947-50.

b) 16...Q-K2 17 N-N3 RxB! (17... P-KB4 18 R-R2) 18 RxR P-Q4 19 R1-R1 PxB 20 PxP B-K3 and one feels that Black should have the advantage, although he eventually lost; Muir-Frantzen, corres 1960.

B4:

6 B—N2*(157)*

None of the lines so far has given White anything to write home about, but this move of Tartakower's is

6 ...   P—Q3

6...N-B3 7 P-N5±; it is necessary to guard the KP now.

7 P—N5   PxP

7...N-R4 is dubious. Tartakower-Fahrni, Baden 1914, continued 8 B-K2 N-KB3 9 N-B3 B-N5 10 N-Q5! NxN (10...NxP 11 NxB PxN 12 NxP!) 11 PxN BxN 12 BxB P-KB4 13 0-0 0-0 14 P-Q3 PxP 15 PxP Q-K1 16 P-B4 P-K5 17 B-R5 Q-K2 18 K-R1 Q-N4 19 P-B4± since Black continues to suffer from the misplacement of his knight. Possibly 7...N-N1 could be played.

8 PxP   RxR
9 BxR

Now Black tried:
B41: 9...N-R4?
B42: 9...N-N1
B43: 9...N-Q5

B41:

9 ...   N—R4?
10 B—R2

Or 10 B-K2 N-KB3 11 N-B3 0-0 12 0-0 P-B3 13 P-Q4± Breyer-Nyholm, Baden 1914.

10 ...   B—N5
11 P—Q3   N—KB3
12 0—0   0—0

13 P-R3 B-Q2 (Pointless; Bogoljubow suggested 13...B-K3 in *Kagans Neuste Schachnachrichten*, 1922.) 14

N-B3 Q-K1 15 Q-N1 K-R1 16 N-QR4!
N-R4? (16...BxP fails to 17 NxB PxN
18 Q-N4, so 16...B-K3 is still best.) 17
NxB± Kostich-Yates, Rotterdam
1921.

B42:

    9   ...   N—N1
    10   P—Q4*(158)*

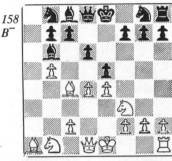

158
B⁻

    10   ...   P—KB3?!

10...PxP would be some improvement, e.g. 11 BxQP! BxB 12 QxB and
now:

1) 12...N-KB3 13 0-0 0-0 14 N-B3
QN-Q2 15 P-R3 R-K1 16 R-R1! P-R3
17 N-KR4 N-K4 18 R-R8 N3-Q2 19
N-B5! N-N3 20 RxB QxR (Tarta-
kower-Yates, Karlsbad 1929) and now
White should have played 21 B-N3!
followed by 22 P-B4± — *Sovremenny
Debyut.*
b) 12...Q-B3! 13 P-K5! PxP 14 NxP
B-K3 15 BxB QxB ∔6 0-0 N-KB3 17
R-K1 0-0 18 N-Q3 Q-B1± —
Tartakower.

    11   PxP   QPxP
    12   Q—K2!   N—KR3?

Not 12...B-R4+ 13 B-B3 BxB 14
NxB followed by N-Q5, but 12...N-K2
is superior — Tartakower.

    13   NxP!

13...PxN 14 Q-R5+ K-B1 15 QxP
BxP+? 16 K-K2! Q-Q2 17 R-Q1
Q-N5+ 18 KxB N-Q2 19 QxBP and
White won; - Tartakower-Prokofiev,
Paris 1934.

B43:

    9   ...   N—Q5*(159)*

159
W

Now:
B431: 10 NxN
B432: 10 BxN

B431:

    10   NxN   PxN
    11   P—QB3

11 P-Q3 is possible, e.g. 11...B-R4+
12 P-QB3 Q-B3 13 0-0 PxP 14 P-Q4
N-K2 15 NxP; Duhrssen-Schlage,
1927.

    11   ...   N—B3

Not 11...PxP?! 12 NxP P-QB3?
(12...N-B3 13 N-Q5 NxN) 13 Q-N3!
N-R3 14 PxP PxP 15 N-R4 1-0
Walkerling-Gross, corres 1928.

    12   0—0   0—0
    13   P—Q3   P—Q4!
    14   KPxP   NxP
    15   Q—B3   N—B3

Not 15...NxP 16 NxN PxN 17
BxQBP Q-Q3 18 Q-K4± — Tartakower.

    16   PxP

Or 16 P-R3 R-K1 when:
a) 17 N-Q2 PxP 18 BxP B-Q5 19
N-K4 BxB 20 NxB± Tartakower-
Rhodes, Southport 1950;
b) 17 PxP BxQP 18 N-B3± —
Tartakower.

    16   ...   BxP
    17   N—B3   N—N5
    18   N—Q5!   BxB
    19   RxB   N—K4

20 Q—N3
1) 20...R-K1 21 P-R3 P-QB3 22 PxP PxP 23 N-K3 (Tartakower-Rubinstein, The Hague 1921) 23...B-Q2 and if 24 R-R7 Q-N3 25 N-B5 P-N3 — Tartakower.
b) Levenfish recommended 20...NxB "seeking equality".

B432:

10	BxN	PxB
11	P—Q3	N—B3
12	0—0	0—0
13	QN—Q2*(160)*	

160
B

13 ...   P—B4?!
The critical line is 13...P-Q4! and if 14 PxP NxP with probably some advantage for Black — Levenfish.

14	PxPep	PxP
15	Q—R1	P—B4
16	R—N1	

a) 16...B-R4 17 P-R3 (17 R-N5 B-B2 18 Q-R7± Johner-Hromadka, Baden 1914) 17...N-R4 18 N-B1± Tartakower-Schlechter, Baden 1914
b) 16...N-R4 17 Q-R8 N-B5 18 B-Q5 B-R4 19 N-B1 N-K7+ 20 K-R1 B-QN5 21 R-R1 B-K3 22 Q-B6 N-B5 and Black drew the game by watchful defence; Ragozin-Panov, Leningrad v. Moscow 1939.

B5:

6 N—B3!
This move, found at the board by Kan in 1929 and subsequently analysed by Sokolsky and other Soviet players, is the best positional continuation since it develops the knight to its natural square, pressing on Q5, and preserves all White's major options. White will still be happy to offer a pawn or two if the occasion for an attack presents itself.

6 ...   N—B3
Others:
a) 6...NxP? 7 NxP Q-N4 8 Q-B3! (Kan) e.g. 8...N-KB3 9 NxBP Q-QB4 10 B-N3 NxP+ 11 BxN KxN 12 0-0 — Euwe
b) 6...P-Q3 7 N-Q5 and now:
b1) 7...N-B3 8 NxB PxN 9 P-Q3 NxP (9...B-N5 10 P-B3 0-0 11 B-KN5± Alexander-Broadbent, Nottingham 1946) 10 R-QN1 N-B3 (Or 10...P-QR4 11 P-B3 N-R3 12 Q-N3) 11 B-K3 N-Q2 12 N-N5 with a powerful attack — analysis.
b2) 7...B-R2 might be met by 8 P-Q3 P-R3 9 B-K3 (Euwe), 9 0-0 (Keres) or 8 P-N5 PxP 9 PxP N3-K2 10 P-N6!? — Blumenfeld.

7 N—Q5*(161)*
Other moves are too slow, e.g. 7 P-Q3 P-Q3 8 P-R5 B-R2 9 P-N5 N-Q5!? Mikenas-Alatortsev, 13 USSR Ch 1944.

161
B

Now:
B51: 7...0-0
B52: 7...NxP
B53: 7...NxN
7...B-R2 8 P-Q3 P-R3 9 B-K3±

— Sokolsky

7...P-Q3 8 NxB PxN 9 P-Q3 B-N5 (9...NxP 10 R-QN1) 10 P-B3± since Black has pawn weaknesses — Alexander.

B51:

7 ... 0—0

This move deserves more attention. It would be unwise for White to reply 8 B-N2 as his KP can safely be taken, but 8 NxB! PxN 9 P-Q3 is good (9...NxNP? loses the exchange after 10 B-R3 P-QR4 11 P-B3). Less convincing:

8 0—0 NxN
9 PxN N—K2?

9...P-K5 is critical: after 10 PxN PxN the game transposes to Sokolsky-Lilienthal in B5322, avoiding the Sokolsky-Goldenov line which favours White. However, White can play 10 N-K1!? setting the trip 10...NxP? 11 B-R3 followed by P-QB3 winning material; after 10...N-K4 or 10...N-K2 the game is unclear. This possibility deserves further investigation — analysis.

10 P—Q4 P—Q3

A wild pawn sacrifice.

11 PxP N—N3
12 B—N2 N—N3

13 P-K6 N-R5 14 B-K2 BxN 15 BxB PxP 16 B-K4 P-K4 17 B-B1 Q-B3 18 K-R1 N-B4 19 R-R3 Q-R5 20 Q-K1! P-N3 21 R-R3± Muratov-Budarin, USSR Spartakiad 1963.

B52:

7 ... NxP
8 0—0(*162*)

See diagram next column

8 ... N—B3!?

A little-known move, which leads to double-edged play. Other moves clearly favour White:

a) 8...0-0? 9 P-Q3 N-B3 (9...N-Q3 10

B-KN5 Q-K1 11 P-R5 B-R2 12 NxBP) 10 B-KN5 P-Q3 11 N-Q2!± e.g.:

a1) 11...B-N5? 12 BxN Q-B1 13 NxB PxN 14 P-KB3 B-K3 15 B-R4 NxP 16 B-K7 Q-B4+ 17 K-R1 KR-K1 18 N-K4 Q-B3 19 BxQP 1-0 Kan-**Botvinnik, sixth USSR Ch 1929**

a2) 11...B-K3 (11...B-KB4 12 P-QB3 intending Q-N3) 12 NxN+ PxN 13 B-R6 R-K1 14 BxB PxB 15 Q-N4+ K-B2 16 Q-N7 mate — Alexander.

b) 8...P-Q3 9 P-Q3 N-B3 10 B-KN5 e.g. 10...B-K3 11 P-B3 BxN? (11... P-R3 is relatively best.) 12 BxB P-R3 13 BxN PxB 14 P-R5 N-K2 (14...B-R2 15 P-N5 or first 15 Q-R4) 15 BxNP B-R2 16 BxR±± Crown-Sergeant, Nottingham 1946.

9 P—Q4!

This move in the true gambit style was recommended in Panov and Estrin's openings book. A game Agrinský-Hohlovkin, ½-final RSFSR Ch, Rostov 1961, went instead 9 P-Q3 (9 B-N2!?) 9...NxN 10 BxN and now:

a) 10...P-R3 11 P-Q4 0-0 12 PxP NxNP 13 B-N3 B-B4 14 P-B3 N-B3 15 Q-Q3 N-K2 16 N-R4 P-Q4 17 B-B2 P-B4 18 PxPep RxP 19 Q-R7+ K-B2 20 B-K3 Q-Q3 21 QR-K1 B-Q2 22 B-Q4 with an attack, although Black eventually won.

b)10...NxP!? is interesting. Play would be much as in the text, but with White's Q-pawn on a less useful square.

9 ...   NxN
Others:
a) 9...PxP? 10 R-K1+ K-B1 11 B-KN5±
b) 9...P-Q3 10 B-KN5 since 10... B-K3? fails to 11 NxB PxN 12 BxN and 13 P-Q5 forking two pieces.
c) 9...NxQP 10 NxP NxN 11 BxN 0-0 (11...N-K3? 12.BxN! BPxB 13 Q-R5+ or 12...QPxB 13 QxQ+ and 14 NxBP) 12 R-R3 intending R-KN3, with a strong attaek in prospect — analysis.
10 BxN   NxNP
Or:
a) 10...0-0 11 BxN QPxB 12 PxP B-N5 13 B-N2 Q-K2 (Or 13...QxQ 14 QRxQ BxN) 14 P-R3 QR-Q1 15 Q-K2 with about equal chances, is a line upon which it might be possible to improve.
b) 10...BxP? 11 NxB PxN (11...NxN 12 R-K1!±) 12 R-K1+ K-B1 (12...N-K2 13 QxP 0-0 14 B-N2) 13 Q-B3 Q-B3 (13...P-B3 14 Q-R5) 14 QxQ etc.
c) 10...NxQP 11 NxN (11 NxP 0-0 see note c to Black's 9th move.) 11...BxN 12 P-QB3 B-R2 (12...BxQBP 13 Q-B3) 13 Q-N4 P-KN3 (13...0-0? 14 B-KN5 Q-K1 15 B-B6±±)14 B-R6 with good attacking prospects — analysis.
11 BxBP+   KxB
12 NxP+ *(163)*

163
B

The analysis by Panov and Estrin

ends here, with the conclusion that White has a strong attack. Where should the king go?
12 ...   K—B1
Others:
a) 12...K-K2?? or 12...K-B3?? 13 B-N5+.
b) 12...K-K3? 13 Q-N4+.
c) 12...K-K1? 13 Q-R5+ P-N3 14 NxNP R-KN1 (14...PxN 15 QxR+ and 16 B-N5+) 15 N-K5+ (15 R-K1+ is also good for a win.) 15...K-K2 16 B-N5+ RxB 17 QxR+ K-K1 18 Q-N8+ followed by 19 N-N6+ and wins the queen.
d) 12...K-N1 is the other critical line, e.g.:
d1) 13 P-QB3?! N-Q4 14 Q-N3 P-B3 15 P-B5 BxP! 16 PxN BxN 17 PxP+ P-Q4 18 PxNP BxNP 19 QxB BxR∓∓.
d2) 13 Q-B3 Q-K2! 14 B-R3 (14 B-N5 Q-K3) 14...BxP (14...P-B4 15 BxN PxB 16 QR-K1! Q-B3 17 Q-QN3+ Q-K3 18 P-Q5) 15 BxN P-B4 16 BxP BxB 17 Q-Q5+ (17 QR-K1!?) 17...Q-K3 (17...K-B1 18 QR-K1 threatening N-N6+ or N-Q3) 18 QxB P-Q3 19 Q-B7 and the knight is saved, in view of the threat of 20 Q-Q8+ and QxR — analysis.
13 P—R5   B—R2
14 B—R3   P—B4
If 14...P-Q3 15 BxN BxP (15...P-B4 16 PxP in view of the pin on the Q-file) 16 QxB P-B4 17 Q-KB4+ or 17 BxP wins.
15 PxP   N—B3
Not 15...BxP 16 P-QB3.
16 N—B4±
Not now 16...NxP? as 17 P-B6+ wins, so White has a crippling bind in return for the piece. While Black struggles to develop his Q-side, White's QR comes strongly into play on the third rank, in conjunction with the queen and with the knight which can come quickly to the squares Q6 and KB5.

B53:

7	...	NxN
8	PxN*(164)*	

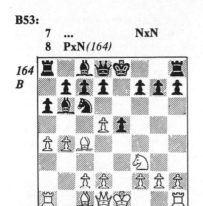

164 B

B531: 8...N-Q5
B532: 8...P-K5

8...NxP? loses the knight after 9 P-B3.

B531:

8	...	N—Q5
9	0—0!	

White could also try to win a pawn by 9 NxP 0-0 10 0-0 P-Q3:

a) 11 N-B3 B-N5 12 B-K2 NxB+ 13 QxN R-K1 14 Q-Q3 Q-B3= Bednarski-Minev, Warsaw 1961

b) 11 N-Q3!?, with an awkward but defensible game, is possible.

9	...	P—Q3

"9...NxN+ 10 QxN P-Q3 is better as Black can then hold up White's P-Q4" — Alexander, *Alekhine's Best Games of Chess 1938-45.* Or here 10...Q-B3 11 Q-QN3 P-Q3 12 P-R5 B-R2 13 P-N5 B-QB4 14 B-R3 0-0= Cafferty-Loose, Birmingham 1965.

10	NxN!	BxN
11	P—QB3	B—R2
12	P—Q4	Q—R5

Or 12...0-0 13 Q-R5 PxP 14 B-KN5 Q-Q2 15 B-Q3 P-R3 16 P-QB4 P-KB4 17 B-Q2 Q-B2 18 QxQ+ (White won) Bachmatov-Lazarev, USSR club game 1960.

13	B—Q3	0—0

If 13...PxP 14 R-K1+ and Black forfeits the right to castle.

14	PxP	PxP
15	Q—K2	R—K1
16	B—K3±	

We have been following the game Alekhine-Fuentes, Melilla 1945, which appears in most collections of Alekhine's games. This is the only recorded example of Alekhine playing the Evans in a serious contest.

B532:

8	...	P—K5
9	PxN	

Now:

B5321: 9...PxN
B5322: 9...0-0

B5321:

9	...	PxN
10	QxP	Q—K2+
11	K—Q1!	

Or 11 Q-K2 QPxP 12 QxQ+ KxQ 13 B-N2 B-K3 and White has nothing special, although he eventually won in Estrin-Ravinsky, ½-final Moscow Ch 1956.

11	...	QPxP
12	B—N2!+	

Not now 12...0-0? as 13 Q-KN3 P-N3 14 Q-QB3 forces mate.

This move, given by Alexander, is stronger than Panov's line 12 R-K1 B-K3.

B5322:

9	...	0—0*(165)*

165 W

10　B—N2!

Only this move gives White the advantage. Others:

a) 10 N-K5? and 10 N-N1? fail to 10...Q-B3∓.

b) 10 0-0 PxN 11 QxP QPxP 12 P-R5 B-R2 (12...Q-Q5? 13 Q-QN3 QxR 14 B-N2 and 15 Q-QB3) 13 P-QB3 B-K3= led to an early draw in Sokolsky-Lilienthal, 13th USSR Ch 1944.

10　...　　　　PxN
11　QxP　　　QPxP

He can do no better:

a) 11...R-K1+ 12 K-B1 with threats on KB7 and QN7.

b) 11...Q-K2+ 12 K-B1 QxP 13 B-N3! and White threatens 14 PxNP and 14 B-R3.

c) 11...NPxP 12 Q-KN3 P-N3 13 Q-QB3 etc.

12　Q—QB3

12 Q-KN3 is now met by 12...B-Q5.

12　...　　　　R—K1+
13　K—B1　　　Q—N4
14　P—R4　　　Q—R3
15　P—QR5　　　B—R2

16　P—R5　　　B—K3

16...B-KB4? 17 P-N4! QR-Q1 (17... BxNP 18 R-KN1) 18 P-N5! QxNP 19 R-KN1±.

17　R—R4±

Sokolsky-Goldenov, ½-final 14 USSR Ch 1945. White has some pressure, as 17...BxB would be met by 18 RxB followed by R-KN4, or 17...QR-Q1 by 18 B-Q3 (18 BxB PxB 19 R-N4 P-K4) envisaging R-K1-K4 etc.

CONCLUSION

In the Evans Gambit Declined, just as in the main lines of the gambit accepted, Black has chances of equalizing the game or of putting up a fair fight in positions too complicated for exhaustive analysis. Nevertheless, we have seen that White's winning chances are excellent in practice, while even against the theoretically-best defences there are interesting ideas, some very old and some very new, which make the Evans well worth playing.

Index of Complete Games

Bold indicates that the player named was White.

Index of Variations

The text move, 8...B-N3, brings about the *Normal Position.* This position can also arise via 5...B-B4 (see Chapter 8).

The discussion of the variations arising from the *Normal Position* commences on p.125, and takes in the whole of Chapters 9 and 10. The main sub-variations are as follows.

g) 9 P-KR3 see p.127-129.
h) **9 P-Q5** *Anderssen's Attack:* see Chapter 10 (p.143-151).

   9   ...   N—R4

a) 9...QN-K2 see p.130.
b) 9...KN-K2 see p.130-131.
c) 9...N-B3 see p.131.

d) **9...B-N5:**
d1) 10 Q-N3 see p.132.
d2) 10 Q-R4 *Fraser-Mortimer Attack:* see p.132-133.
d3) 10 B-QN5 see p.133-135.

   10   B—KN5

The Goring Attack. See p. 135-142.